AGE 11-14

Letts
EDUCATIONAL

NATIONAL
CURRICULUM

KEY STAGE THREE

C000087989

HISTORY

Peter Lane and Christopher Lane

First published 1992
Reprinted 1992

Editors
Andrew Thraves, Rachel Grant and Angela Royal

Designer
Keith Anderson

Text: © Peter Lane and Christopher Lane 1992

Illustrations: Ian Foulis Associates, Peter McClure

© BPP (Letts Educational) Ltd
Aldine House, Aldine Place
142–144 Uxbridge Road
London W12 8AW

All our rights reserved. No part of
this publication may be reproduced,
stored in a retrieval system, or
transmitted, in any form or by any
means, electronic, mechanical, photocopying,
recording or otherwise, without the prior
permission of BPP (Letts Educational) Ltd.

Printed and bound in Great Britain by
WM Print Limited, Walsall, West Midlands WS2 9NE

British Library Cataloguing in Publication Data
Lane, Peter, 1925-
   Key stage 3. History.
   I. Title II. Lane, Christopher
   941

ISBN 1 85758 110 5

Acknowledgements
Thanks go to David Bell and Robert Medley,
the advisers on this book.

The authors and publishers are grateful to the following for permission to reproduce illustrations and extracts (page numbers refer to this book unless stated):
Aerofilms Limited pp37, 170; The Ancient Art and Architecture Collection pp159, 162, 163, 164, 166; B T Batsford Ltd pp12, 13, 15, 22, 40, 51, 76; Blackwell Publishing p114; The Bodleian Library, Oxford pp12, 15, 28; The British Library pp13, 31, 34, 41, 46, 68, 158, 168; reproduced by courtesy of the Trustees of the British Museum pp8, 22, 66, 158, 168, 173; Cambridge University Collection of air photographs p155; City of Bristol Museum and Art Gallery p57; reproduced by kind permission of City of Bristol Record Office, owned by Bristol City Council, reference 04720(1) p21; Colchester and Essex Museum p148; Commissioner of Public Works in Ireland p29; Communist Party Library p96, 97; The Conway Library, Courtauld Institute of Art pp160, 162; The Corporation of London Records Office p10; Country Life p58; C M Dixon pp144, 145, 148, 150, 151, 153, 158; Dudley Library p99; From the collection of the Duke of Roxburghe p32; Edinburgh University Library p64; English Heritage pp31, 38, 164, 165, 166, 168, 169; Mary Evans Picture Library pp50, 58, 73, 82, 85, 101, 107, 108; The Fotomas Index pp20, 48, 69, 70; John Frost Picture Library p119; Photographie Giraudon pp24, 168; Sonia Halliday Photographs pp47, 144, 151, 154, 170, 171; Michael Holford Photographs pp8, 9, 40, 46, 147, 170; The Hulton Picture Company pp15, 17, 19, 40, 87, 94, 106, 114, 116, 128, 133, 138, 142, 146, 152, 167, 169; The Illustrated London News p93; Imperial War Museum, London pp109, 112, 114, 116, 118, 119, 122, 128, 129, 135, 137; *Paths of Glory*, 1917 by CRW Nevinson (1899–1946), Imperial War Museum, London/Bridgeman Art Library p110; A F Kersting pp25, 54, 160; Laing Art Gallery, Newcastle upon Tyne (Tyne and Wear Museums) p21; The Mansell Collection pp22, 26, 32, 33, 34, 35, 36, 58, 60, 61, 62, 65, 70, 74, 80, 82, 84, 86, 88, 91, 92, 93, 96, 97, 104, 117, 118, 125, 126, 145, 147, 150, 152, 154, 156, 170; The National Museum of Wales p30; By permission of the National Library of Wales pp156, 164; The National Museum of Labour History pp90; The National Portrait Gallery, London pp18, 48, 60, 61, 62, 63, 66; Novosti (London) 1992, *Panfilov Guardsmen's Exploit* (fragment) by V R Pamfilov p130; Reproduced from the 1:250 000 Ordnance Survey Salisbury Central map with the permission of the Controller of Her Majesty's Stationary Office © Crown copyright p45; Picturepoint p46; From the collection of Plymouth City Museum and Art Gallery p56; Popperfoto pp124, 139, 160; The Royal Commission on the Historical Monuments of England pp13, 18, 19, 24, 166, 168, 172; The Public Record Office, Richmond p10; Mick Sharp Photographer p154; Albeia Roman Fort, South Shields (Tyne and Wear Museums) p172; By courtesy of the Centre for the Study of Cartoons and Caricature, University of Kent at Canterbury: Low, David, *Evening Standard* 27th July 1945 p138; Low, David, *Evening Standard* 19th January 1933 p124; *Vicky: A Memorial Volume*, Allen Lane, The Penguin Press, 1967, p138: all copyright Solo Syndication & Literary Agency Ltd; Photograph: Statens Konstmuseer Nationalmuseum, Stockholm p72; Ian Thraves p168; The Master and Fellows of Trinity College Cambridge pp25, 48; University of Cardiff pp156, 164; University of Newcastle upon Tyne p37; The University of Reading, Institute of Agricultural History and Museum of English Rural Life pp80, 98; Courtesy of the Trustees of the V&A pp56, 64; Mr Harold Wingham p168; Jason Wood Photographs p160; Photos; Woodmansterne Ltd pp9, 18, 31, 42, 54.

CONTENTS

ABOUT THE NATIONAL CURRICULUM

As you complete the activities in this book and make progress through school, you will be following the National Curriculum. All students of your age across the country will be doing the same subjects.

The National Curriculum consists of 10 subjects which you must study at school. These are divided into core and foundation subjects.

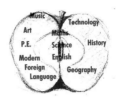

English, mathematics and science are the core subjects. They will help you study all the other subjects. The other subjects are the foundation subjects. Although it is not part of the National Curriculum, you will also study religious education at school.

KEY STAGES

You are now at Key Stage 3 (which goes from age 11 to age 14). It is one of the four Key Stages which you go through as you complete your education to age 16.
The four key stages are:

Key Stage 1 : ages 5–7   Key Stage 3 : ages 11–14
Key Stage 2 : ages 7–11   Key Stage 4 : ages 14–16

ATTAINMENT TARGETS

Each subject has its own objectives or goals. These are called Attainment Targets and explain what you are expected to be able to do. Each Attainment Target has 10 levels of attainment and you will progress through one level at a time. The average 14-year-old will achieve level 5 or 6 depending on the subject but you might do better than this in a particular subject.

TESTING AT AGE 14

When you are 14 and have completed Key Stage 3 you will be given a series of tests, not set by your teacher, but taken by all 14-year-olds across the country. These tests will measure the standard you have reached.

PROGRAMME OF STUDY

Each subject also has a Programme of Study. This describes the work you have to do to meet the Attainment Targets. This book provides practice in the work that makes up the Programmes of Study in history. By completing the activities in the book you will be much better prepared for the tests at age 14.

HISTORY IN THE NATIONAL CURRICULUM

At Key Stage 3 in history, you are expected to make progress in three Attainment Targets (AT). These are :

AT 1 : Knowledge and understanding of history
AT 2 : Interpretations of history
AT 3 : The use of historical sources

You will only be able to achieve the different levels of attainment within the attainment targets through studying the historical content of the Programmes of Study.

The content you will study is broken into **core study units** and **supplementary study units**. This book contains all of the core units and two of the supplementary units.

Core study units
All of the following:

1 The Roman Empire
2 Medieval realms: Britain 1066 – 1500
3 The making of the United Kingdom: Crowns, Parliaments and peoples 1500 – 1750
4 Expansion, trade and industry: Britain 1750 – 1900
5 The era of the Second World War

Supplementary study units
One from each of the three categories A, B and C:

A A unit which extends the study of the core British study units, for example:
   – Castles and cathedrals 1066 – 1500
   – Britain and the Great War 1914 – 1918
B A unit involving the study of an episode or turning point in European history before 1914. Examples could include:
   – The Crusades
   – The French Revolution and the Napoleonic era
C A unit involving the study of a past non-European society. Examples could include :
   – India from the Mughal Empire to the coming of the British
   – Black peoples of the Americas : 16th – early 20th centuries

So, in practice then, what will the relationship between the Attainment Targets and the Programmes of Study look like? Imagine you are doing a study on the Second World War. As you look at the countdown to war in the 1930s, you will be assessing the different causes of the War. In so doing, you could achieve a level in AT1 which says that you need to be able to recognise that causes and consequences can vary in importance. Another element of this Attainment Target is that you have to describe the different ideas and attitudes of people in an historical situation. So, you could describe how different sections of British society viewed Nazi Germany in the 1930s.

Or, think about a unit on Britain 1750 – 1900. How could you build up a picture of the effects of industrialisation? You could use diaries, memoirs, novels, public records and so on. Each source would give a different view. If you could demonstrate how different sources provide different interpretations of the past then you would achieve a level in Attainment Target 2.

What about Attainment Target 3? If you were studying the Roman Empire you might look at the work of writers such as Pliny or Juvenal. You would have to be aware of the circumstances in which they worked and how that would affect what they wrote. As an aspiring historian, you would be making judgements about the reliability and value of historical sources by understanding the circumstances in which they were produced. In so doing, you would achieve a level in Attainment Target 3.

So by the end of Key Stage 3, not only will you be familiar with many different periods in British, European and world history, you will have been learning how to think and act as an historian.

Good luck and enjoy National Curriculum history!

INTRODUCTION

HOW TO USE THIS BOOK

If you look at the contents page you will see that this book deals with:

(a) ALL the FIVE compulsory core units you have to study for Key Stage 3.

(b) TWO of the supplementary units which you are asked to study.

(c) Guidance on the subject of an Independent Study which you are recommended to undertake as part of the programme for Key Stage 3 ('The Project' on page 174).

You will find that the core and supplementary units have been broken down into a number of topics, each of which is covered on two pages, called a 'double-page spread'. Each double-page spread consists of FOUR sections:

(a) A short introductory text, describing the main events involved in the topic. This text will help you develop your ability to achieve Attainment Target 1: Knowledge and understanding.

(b) Two kinds of historical sources: written extracts and illustrations.

(c) Questions for you to answer after you have read the short introductory text and examined the sources. These questions are directed to the THREE Attainment Targets that make up the study of history at Key Stage 3: Knowledge and understanding, Interpretation, and Use of sources. You will find all the evidence you need to answer the questions in the text, extracts and illustrations on the double spread.

(d) Suggestions on how to work independently – questions asking you to do a little research, to paint or draw something, or to arrange a debate or discussion on a relevant issue.

You might find it useful to have either a folder or an exercise book in which to keep your answers to the various questions, and, to help with the fourth section, you will need pencils, felt-tip pens and drawing paper.

It is hoped that you will enjoy using the material offered in this book and thinking about the history involved. As you work your way through the book you will develop your knowledge of the past as well as your skills as an historian dealing with historical evidence.

Both of us would like to thank colleagues on various examining boards for their helpful advice over many years, as well as our many former pupils for their stimulating help. In particular Christopher Lane would like to thank the pupils and staff at St Anselm's School, Basildon for their support and understanding. Both of us appreciate the encouragement provided by our wives, Teresa and Catherine, who allowed us to have the freedom in which to work together on producing a book which we hope you, the reader, will enjoy.

Peter Lane
Christopher Lane

MEDIEVAL REALMS: BRITAIN 1066 – 1500

WE THREE KINGS OF ENGLAND ARE

Who was to succeed 'the saintly Edward' when he died on 6 January 1066?

Earl Harold of Wessex, Edward's brother-in-law, England's leading nobleman and Edward's choice, was crowned on 6 January after the Council *(picture 1)* had elected him as their King.

King Hardrada of Norway said that Harthacnut, King of England in 1052, promised the crown to his family. He was supported by the King of Scotland and Harold's brother, Tostig, the favourite of their sister, Queen Edith.

William, **Duke of Normandy** said Edward had promised *him* the crown *(extract B)* and that Harold had sworn to support him *(extract C and picture 2)*. Harold said that the oath had been made under pressure: he feared that he would be kept in prison or killed if he hadn't taken the oath. The Pope believed William, who took six months to prepare an invasion *(picture 3)*. On **27 September** he landed at **Pevensey** but rushed to **Hastings**, a better harbour from which to sail if he was defeated. He built a **motte-and-bailey castle** (page 36, picture 3) and waited for Harold, who had gone to Yorkshire to defeat **Hardrada** and **Tostig**.

The **Battle of Hastings** took place on **15 October 1066**, and the Normans were victorious *(extract D and picture 4)*. William took his time getting to **London** *(picture 6)* where he was crowned on **Christmas Day** and where he built a motte-and-bailey Tower of London *(picture 5)* as a refuge and stronghold.

The Bayeux Tapestry

(pictures 2–4) is a strip cartoon, approx. 71 metres (230 feet) long. It is sewn in wool on linen. Bishop Odo of Bayeux (William the Conqueror's brother) had it made for him by English needlewomen: it still hangs in Bayeux and is a valuable source for historians.

2 Harold promising the crown to Duke William

3 Preparing the invasion fleet

1 A Saxon King and his witan.

The Anglo-Saxon Chronicle

(extract A here but see also pages 10–11 and 14–15) is not one document but a series of records written in English between 900 and 1150. It is the oldest set of records in any European language, other than Latin. Some of the records were written at Winchester, others at Canterbury and Peterborough.

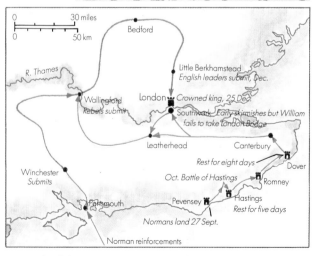

6 March of the Norman army, October–December 1066

4 To quell rumour of his death, William removes his helmet crying, 'Look at me well! I am still alive and by God's grace I shall yet prove victor'

The White Tower, Tower of London

Extract A Edward gives the Crown to Harold

And Earl Harold succeeded to the throne just as the King had granted it to him and as he had been chosen to the position.

(*Anglo-Saxon Chronicle*, c 11th century)

Extract B Edward promises the Crown to William

In 1063 Edward gave William, whom he loved like a son, and whom he had already named his heir in 1051, a more serious pledge. He sent Harold to William to confirm his promise by oath.

(**William of Poitiers writing in 1073 or 1076**)

Extract C William's account of Harold's visit: a speech made at Hastings, 1066

On the journey, Harold was in danger of being taken prisoner by Guy of Ponthieu. I rescued him by threat of war. Through his own hands he made himself my subject and gave me a firm pledge about the throne of England.

(**Quoted by William of Poitiers**)

Extract D A Norman account of the Battle of Hastings

The English were as brave as we were. With their battle-axes and with men hurling spears and stones, they repelled our attacks when we came to close quarters, and they killed many of our men shooting missiles from a distance. Indeed our men began to retreat; disobeying Harold's orders, the English footmen chased them from the field. It was only William's courage which saved us. Three times he had horses killed beneath him; each time he leapt to the ground and killed the footman who had killed his horse. Fighting on foot he split shields, helmets and coats of mail with his great sword. Seeing his men fleeing, he took off his helmet and cried; 'Look at me well! I am still alive and by God's grace I shall yet prove victor.' This inspired his tired men who gathered for a final charge in which Harold was killed. Seeing this, the English fled as quickly as they could, leaving the bloodstained battleground covered with the flower of youth and nobility of England.

(**William of Poitiers**)

THE YOUNG HISTORIAN AT WORK

Knowledge and understanding

1 From the text find out **(i)** one reason why William thought he should be King and **(ii)** one reason why Harold thought he should be King.

2 Using the text and *extract D*, give the reasons for William's victory over Harold.

Interpretation

1 Read *extract D*. Where does the writer give **(i)** an opinion and **(ii)** a statement of fact?

2 Having read the text and examined the various pieces of evidence, what do you think about the characters of William and Harold?

Use of sources

1 Look at *pictures 3, 4 and 5*. What do they tell you about the preparations which William made for his conquest of England?

2 Look at *picture 6*. How can this be used to help explain how William took control of England after the Battle of Hastings?

Project

1 Make a frieze or a tapestry (with some friends if possible) showing how William **(i)** claimed the throne; **(ii)** won battles and **(iii)** took control of England.

2 Write a play about The Battle for England, 1065 – 66. Perhaps you could find some friends to act with you and even to make costumes.

JUST WILLIAM

Some of Harold's followers were angry at William's success *(extract A)* and others refused to accept Norman rule. William had to cope with many rebellions *(picture 1)*. So how did he manage to **impose Norman rule on England**?

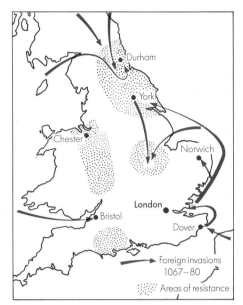

1 Revolts and invasions, 1067–80

1 He **promised** to follow 'saintly Edward's' laws and customs *(picture 2)*.

2 He acted as owner of all **the land**. He kept a quarter **for himself**, gave the **Church** a quarter, and rewarded Normans with most of the rest.

3 He, and his Norman barons, built **castles** from which they imposed their rule on the surrounding areas (pages 36–7).

4 Although his **barons** had sworn an oath of loyalty to him, William knew that, in Edward's England and his own Normandy, powerful landowners had challenged their overlord's power. They relied on the support of the knights to whom they had sub-let some of their land, and from whom they got an oath of loyalty. So, in **1086**, William made **every landowner swear an oath of loyalty** to him personally *(extracts B, C and D)*.

5 At **Christmas**, **1085**, William was at his Gloucester estate: he and other landowners went from one estate to another to 'live off the produce of their land'. It was at Gloucester that William decided to find out exactly what went on in his kingdom *(extract E)*. His **shire officers** worked so efficiently that by the time he came to **Salisbury in August 1086** they could give him the pages of sheepskin, sewn together to form a book, which contained all the details he had asked for. The book was so complete that it was soon called the **Domesday Book** because people compared it with what might happen on the Last Day of Judgement.

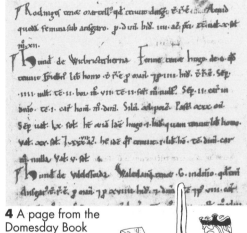

4 A page from the Domesday Book

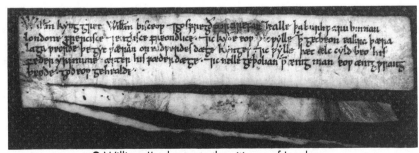

2 William I's charter to the citizens of London

3 A knight taking an oath to his King

Interpretations by later historians. Edward Freeman *(extract C)* was a famous historian who gave his own views (or interpretations) of past events. Such views are called **secondary sources**, although the historian will have studied many **primary sources** during his research. Other similar secondary sources will be found on page 13 (extract C), page 16 (extract A) and page 25 (extracts A and C).

Extract A An Angry Saxon Bishop on William's success

Such was the feebleness of the wretched people that after the first battle they never tried to rise up for their freedom. It was as though that when Harold fell so, too, fell the whole strength of the country.

(Quoted in *Social History of England*, A. Briggs, 1983)

Extract B The Oath of Salisbury, 1086

William came to Salisbury on 1st August. There came to him all the landowners of England, no matter whose vassal they might be. They all submitted to him and became his vassals, and swore oaths of allegiance to him, that they would be loyal to him against all other men.

(*Anglo-Saxon Chronicle*, c 10th century)

Extract C The significance of the Oath of Salisbury

On that day England became for ever a kingdom, one and indivisible, which since that day no man has dreamed of parting asunder.

(The historian Edward Freeman, 1868)

Extract D A baron's oath to the King

I become your man from this day forward, for life and limb and loyalty. I shall be true and faithful to you for the lands I hold from you.

Extract E The Domesday Book's origins

After this, the King met with his council to discuss this country - how it was occupied and with what sort of people. Then he sent his men over all England into every shire, and had them find out how many hundred hides there were in the shire, what land and cattle the King himself had in the country, what taxes were due in each year from the shire. He had a record made of how much land his archbishop had, and his bishops, abbots, earls... what or how much everybody had who occupied land in England, in land or cattle, and how much money it was worth. So very closely did he have it investigated that there was not a hide or virgate of land, not one ox or cow or pig which was left out of his record.

(*Anglo-Saxon Chronicle*)

Extract F Saxon-Norman continuity – the social classes before 1066

Laboratores (workers) are they who provide us with sustenance, ploughmen and farmers devoted to that alone.

Oratores (people who pray) are they who intercede for us to God and promote Christianity among people, a spiritual toil devoted to that alone for the benefit of us all.

Bellatores (fighters) are they who guard our boroughs and also our land, fighting with weapons against the oncoming army. (Aelfric, Abbot of Eynsham, medieval historian, c 1066)

THE YOUNG HISTORIAN AT WORK

Knowledge and understanding

1 Read the text and *extracts B and C*. **(a)** Why did William strengthen the feudal system in England? **(b)** How did this affect the English people?

2 In what ways do the text and *extracts B and F* show that the Normans **(i)** changed some aspects of life in England BUT **(ii)** left other aspects unchanged?

Interpretation

1 Do you think that *extract A* expresses **(i)** facts OR **(ii)** opinions OR **(iii)** both?

2 Read *extracts A and D*. Do these show differing views of William? Give reasons for your answer.

Use of sources

1 What do you learn from **(i)** the text; **(ii)** *extract B*; **(iii)** *pictures 1 and 3* about William's determination to control England?

2 Read *extract E*. **(a)** Make a list of the way in which William hoped to use the Domesday survey. **(b)** Make a list of the questions which you think the Domesday commissioners asked in a village.

Project

1 Write a diary of how William took control of England.

2 (a) Ask your local librarian where you might be able to see the pages in the Domesday Book concerning your area. **(b)** If you were making a Domesday survey today, what questions would you ask the people in your street?

TO THE MANOR BORN

William's barons rewarded their followers with grants of land. These were the **manors** where people produced almost everything they needed. *Picture 1* is a medieval plan of a manor. In the centre is the **manor house and the lord's private estate** (demesne) with some outbuildings – chapel, stables, kitchens, barns, perhaps a mill, and a forge *(picture 2)*. A wall gave the lord some privacy. To the north, three houses represent **villagers' homes**. Elsewhere you can see forests, animals to be hunted for food, and fields (pages 14–15). Villagers had to make various payments for their share of the **fields** *(extract A)*. The manor house was usually stone built, and built with an eye to defence. Inside, a **large hall** contained a grand table *(extract B)*, stools or chairs. The rest of the house was **poorly furnished**: rushes on stone floors, a few beds, some chests for clothes – and little else. The house was the centre of an **industrial estate** and, for two or three hundred years, the place where the lord acted as judge in the **manor court** *(extract D)* with the help of a jury of 12 men.

3 The barn at Godmersham —once the great hall of the manor

1 The village of Boarstall, Buckinghamshire, in the 15th century

Villagers' houses were small *(picture 4)*. The single room on the **ground floor** had a partition behind which **animals** were kept – a cow or two, a couple of pigs, chickens and so on. Some villagers made a bedroom from the loft which they reached by a ladder: others slept on the ground floor. They had **little furniture** – wooden dishes, a cooking pot and a few simple stools.

Both lord and villager **drank ale or wine**: water was usually unfit to drink. For the villager, the basic food was **black bread** which he had for breakfast at sunrise, for dinner at 10.00 am (with cheese or eggs) and for supper at 4.00 pm (with soup or stew). For most of the year they ate **salted meat**, mainly bacon from their pigs. Everyone **hunted** *(picture 5)* and **fished** to find extra food. Unlike the lord *(extract B)* villagers often had little to eat, and if there was a bad harvest, many died of starvation.

6 Entertainers and musicians

2 A 14th century blacksmith

5 A lady hunting

Ladies at the end of a stag kill

Extract A Manorial rolls

These give us details of how material estates were run. On one the villeins each had a virgate of land (about 14 acres), for which they had to plough, sow and till half an acre of the lord's demesne: they had also to give such services as the lord's bailiff would demand, pay a quarter of seed-wheat at Michaelmas, a peck of wheat, four bushels of oats and three hens on 12 November, and at Christmas a cock, two hens and two-penn'orth of bread. There were also cash payments – a halfpenny on 12 November and a penny whenever they brewed ale. Each villein had also to reap three days at harvest time, but for this he received ale and a loaf of bread, and as large a sheaf of corn as he could carry home on his sickle.

(Quoted in *Upper Class*, P. Lane, 1972)

Extract B Eating with the lord of the manor, c 1390

His bread, his ale were finest of the fine
And no one had a better stock of wine.
His house was never short of bake-meat pies,
Of fish and flesh, and these in such supplies
It positively snowed with meat and drink,
And all the dainties that a man could think.
According to the seasons of the year
Changes of dishes were ordered to appear.
He kept fat partridges in coops beyond,
Many a bream and pike were in his pond.
And in his hall a table stood arrayed
All ready all day long, with places laid.

(Geoffrey Chaucer, 1340 – 1400)

4 A villagers' home, Didbrook, built with timber, mud for the walls, and thatch

Extract C A man-made world

It was a hand-made world throughout, a world without power, a world in which all things were made one by one, a world dependent upon human muscular power and the muscular power of draught animals, a slow world. (E. Gill, quoted in *The Making of the English Landscape*, W.G. Hoskins, 1955)

Extract D At a manorial court, 1249

It was presented that Robert Carter's son by night invaded the house of Peter Burgess and in felony threw stones at his door so that the said Peter raised the hue. Therefore let the said Robert be committed to prison. Afterwards he made fine with 2s.

All the ploughmen of Great Ogbourne are convicted by the oath of 12 men... because by reason of their default (the land) of the lord was ill-ploughed whereby the lord is damaged to the amount of 9s... And, Walter Reaper is in mercy for concealing (not giving information as to) the said bad ploughing. Afterwards he made fine with the lord with one mark.

(*Select Pleas in Manorial Courts*, F.W. Maitland, 1889)

THE YOUNG HISTORIAN AT WORK

Knowledge and understanding

1 Make a list of the reasons why the manor was an important place for medieval people.

2 In what ways was life on the manor **(i)** different from BUT **(ii)** similar to life in your village or town today?

Interpretation

1 Does *extract D* contain BOTH statements of fact AND opinions? Give reasons for your answer.

2 Read *extract D*. How do you think that **(i)** Robert Carter; **(ii)** the ploughman and **(iii)** the lord felt after they had attended the manorial court?

Use of sources

1 Use the text, the illustrations and *extracts A and B* to help you write a description of the villagers' work, diet, clothing and entertainment.

2 Why would *pictures 3 and 4* (or visits to the places shown) be valuable to historians writing about medieval housing?

Project

1 Many surnames come from medieval occupations (e.g. Archer, Baker). Find FIVE such surnames which came from **(i)** beer making; **(ii)** furniture making; **(iii)** stone building; **(iv)** tool making; **(v)** the system of law.

2 As part of a frieze, draw or paint **(i)** the manor hall; **(ii)** a villager's house; **(iii)** catching rabbits.

DOWN ON THE FARM

In the Midlands and East Anglia manor farms consisted of **three huge, unhedged ('open') fields** (picture 1), **common land**, and the surrounding **forest**. Each field went through a **three-year cycle** ('rotation', picture 2). In year one it grew wheat or rye, in year two oats or barley, and in year three it was left unploughed ('fallow') to give the land a chance to recover.

Villagers were given portions of land for their own use. The **reeve** (picture 5) divided the land so that no one was luckier than another, and so no one man had all the good land, while another had all the stony land. Each field was **split into strips of about 200 metres by 20 metres** and each villager had a number of strips in different parts of each field: some had 50, others only five, depending on whether they were freemen or cottars.

The villagers' year was a **seasonal** one (picture 10): in the **spring** the reeve supervised the **preparation** of the soil (pictures 3, 4 and 9); **sowing** of seed was done by men carrying bags of seed which they threw out by hand. In the **summer** came **harvesting** (picture 5). Then, when the corn ears had been flailed from the straw, each villager took his **corn to be ground** (picture 8). Villagers resented paying the lord for the use of the mill (extract E).

Villagers **grazed their animals** on the large common, and used the **forest** as the source for firewood and wattles to build their hut walls; for food – nuts, berries and gamebirds; and as the place where pigs could forage.

Extract A The ploughman's view of life

I work very hard. At dawn I drive the oxen in the field and yoke them to the plough. However harsh the winter, I dare not stay at home, for fear of my lord. Every day I have to plough an acre or more. I have a boy who drives the oxen with a goad, and he is always hoarse from cold and shouting. I fill the ox-bins with hay and water, and I clear out the dung.

(Aelfric, Abbot of Eynsham, medieval historian, c 1066)

Extract B Diseases and hardship, 1131

In that year there was such a great animal plague as had never been before. It affected cattle and pigs; in a village that had 10 or 12 ploughs in action there was not one left. The man who had two or three hundred pigs was left with not one. Hens died, and meat, cheese and butter became scarce.

(Anglo-Saxon Chronicle)

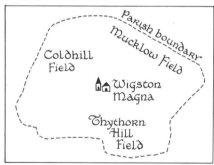

1 The three-field system, Wigston Magna, Leicestershire

Extract C Ploughman and shepherds

The art of the ploughman is in knowing how to make a straight furrow with the oxen. Ploughmen ought to encourage their oxen with melody and song. They must feed their animals, sleep with them at night, rub them down, make sure their food is not stolen. They should not be allowed to have a candle unless it is in a lantern. Shepherds should be intelligent, watchful and kind men who will not harry the sheep by their bad temper... should have a good barking dog and sleep with his sheep at night.

(Fleta, a Latin tract, 1289)

Extract D Dairymaids and swineherds

The dairymaid ought to be faithful and of good reputation, keep herself clean, know how to make cheese and salt cheese. The bailiff and reeve ought to inspect the dairy often.

The swineherd ought to be on manors where swine can be kept in the forest or woods or waste or in marshes without cost to the manor. During the winter there ought to be a pigsty where the swine can be kept day and night.

(Husbandry, Walter of Henley, c 1280)

Extract E The jolly (but wicked) miller

(a) There was a jolly miller once, lived on the river Dee;
He worked and sang from morn till night; no lark more blithe than he.

(Love in a Village, Isaac Bickerstaffe, 1762)

	S O N D	J F M A M J J A S O N D	J F M A M J J A S O N D	J F M A M J J A S O N D
Field 1			Fallow	
Field 2			Fallow	
Field 3		Fallow		

■ Ploughing ■ Sowing ■ Growing crops □ Harvesting

2 'Rotation' of the three-field system

(b) ...a master hand at stealing grain.
He felt it with his thumb and knew
Its quality and took three times his due.
(*The Canterbury Tales*, Geoffrey Chaucer, c 1390)

(c) 'What is the boldest thing in the world?'
'A miller's shirt, because it clasps a thief daily by the throat.'
(A medieval riddle)

3 A two-oxened plough

4 Horse-drawn harrow and plough

5 Reeve supervising peasants at harvest time

6 Shepherds keeping watch

7 Bee catching

THE YOUNG HISTORIAN AT WORK

Knowledge and understanding

1 Make a list of the various jobs that had to be done on the farm.

2 Read *extract B*. **(a)** Make a list of the possible reasons for food shortages, some of which are mentioned in this extract. **(b)** Why did manorial lords suffer less than the peasants during times of food shortages?

Interpretation

1 (a) Read *extracts A and C*. Make two lists to show **(i)** the differences and **(ii)** the similarities in these descriptions of the ploughman's work. **(b)** Why do these extracts give different views of ploughmen's work?

2 Read *extract E*. **(a)** Write down the statements of **(i)** fact AND **(ii)** opinion in this extract. **(b)** Why did different people have such different ideas about millers?

Use of sources

1 Use the text and the extracts. **(a)** Make a list of all the problems faced by medieval farmers. **(b)** Show why all the jobs done on the farm were important.

2 Look at *picture 10*. Work out which month the picture is describing.

Project

1 Write, and illustrate, one day from each month of the medieval farmworker's diary.

2 Find out the meaning of the following words: fallow; yoke; goad; furrow.

8 Carrying corn to the mill

9 Breaking up the soil

10 Harvesting – from a medieval calendar

THE BLACK DEATH AND SOCIAL CHANGE

By 1300 the **population** was three times what it had been in 1066. To produce more food, parts of forests were cleared and marshes were drained *(picture 1)*. Increased demand for cloth exports led to an **increased demand for wool**. Many landowners enclosed parts of the open fields behind hedges or stone walls, so that 'sheep could safely graze'. This helped speed up the process of **commutation**, by which peasants paid for their land with money instead of work-service *(extract A)*.

In 1348 England was attacked by a **plague** brought from abroad by black rats infected with plague-carrying fleas. People found large lumps under their armpits and their bodies covered with red and black spots (hence the **Black Death**).

It spread quickly *(extract B)*: one-third of the population died. Some places were left with no inhabitants *(extract C)*: everywhere there were too few people to do the farm work. Some thought the disease was caused by the smell from diseased people: they hoped to be saved by carrying flowers. Others prayed *(picture 2)*; many sold all they had *(extract D)* which pushed prices down. More land was turned into **sheep farms** which needed fewer workers. Some lords tried to attract workers by offering **high wages** *(extract E)* and peasants demanded the end of work-service *(extract A)*. Parliament passed laws to try to turn the clock back. In **1349** an Act ordered workers to return to their original manor. This Act and another in **1351** tried to force workers to accept lower wages *(extract F)*. But even landowners ignored these laws: workers had enjoyed their freedom and the better living standards resulting from higher wages and falling prices *(extract G)*.

1 The Somerset Levels: once marshy land drained between the 10th and 14th centuries

Extract A 'Commutation' – or money rents in place of work-service

In the 12th century many lords accepted money rents instead of work-service. Serfs still had to pay some work-service; they might even have to work on the lord's demesne for certain days if he chose to renew his claim. But reeves had learned that the demesne would be better cultivated by hired men, working the year round, than by the unwilling work of villeins taken from working on their own strips. (*Medieval English Wool Trade*, E. Power, 1941)

Extract B The coming of the Black Death, 1348

The plague penetrated the coasts from Southampton and came to Bristol; there almost the whole population died, very few kept their beds for more than three days, or even half a day. In the small parish of St Leonard in Leicester more than 380 died; in the parish of Holy Cross more than 400, and so in each parish a great number. (Henry Knighton, *Chronicle II*, Rolls Series, c 1363)

2 Praying for a plague victim

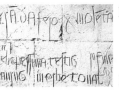

inscription telling
orror of the plague:
erable...wild...distracted'

Extract C Deserted monasteries, parishes and villages

After the pestilence many buildings, great and small, fell into ruins in every borough and village, for lack of people; many places became deserted, all having died who lived there.
(Henry Knighton, c 1363)

Extract D The immediate fall in prices after the Black Death

There were falling prices everywhere because of fear of death. Few people cared about money or anything. You could buy a horse, once worth 40 shillings, for six shillings; sheep and cattle wandered over fields and crops failed because there was no one to look after them.
(Henry Knighton, c 1363)

Extract E Rising wages, 1348

In the autumn no one could get a reaper for less than eight pence or a mower for less than 12 pence. So, many crops perished in the fields. But there was still such an abundance of corn that no one bothered. (Henry Knighton, c 1363)

Extract F The Statute of Labourers, 1349

Because many people have died in this plague, some workers will not serve unless they get excessive wages. We have decided that anyone not earning a living from a craft or fully employed on his own land shall be bound to work for any lord who asks him to work, and shall receive the wage that used to be paid in 1347. (Close Roll 23, Edward III, 1349)

Extract G Lords and labourers ignore Parliament and the law

The King sent laws that labourers should not take more than they had earned previously. But the workers would not listen. And if any lord wanted workers, he had to give them what they asked for. He had either to lose his crops, or satisfy the greed of the labourers.
(Henry Knighton, c 1363)

THE YOUNG HISTORIAN AT WORK

Knowledge and understanding

1 (a) Make a list of the reasons why the Black Death spread. **(b)** What effects did the Black Death have on **(i)** size of population; **(ii)** manors and monasteries; **(iii)** workers' wages?

2 Make a list of the reasons why sheep farming became more widespread **(i)** before and **(ii)** after 1348.

Interpretation

1 Read *extracts F and G*. **(a)** What do these extracts tell you about the attitudes towards the work and wages of labourers of **(i)** lords; **(ii)** workers; **(iii)** Parliament? **(b)** Why did lords and workers ignore Parliament's views?

2 Perhaps you know the children's poem:
Ring-a-ring of **roses**
Pockets full of **posies**
Tishoo, Tishoo
We **all fall down**.
(a) Show how the words in **bold type** were connected with the Black Death.
(b) Does the poem give a full explanation of the causes of the Black Death?
Give reasons for your answer.

Uses of sources

1 How does *picture 2* help us to understand the effects of the Black Death?
2 How are *extracts B, C and D* valuable in showing how tragic the Black Death was for some people?

Project

1 Write some pages from the diary of the only survivor of a village struck by the Black Death. You might describe the village **(i)** before; **(ii)** during and **(iii)** after the plague.

2 Here are some suggestions put forward at the time, to help people avoid the plague: avoid breathing the germs; sit next to fires; attack foreigners; keep the windows closed; clean the dirty streets; put toads and frogs on your skin. Which of these had any chance of success? Why?

FOR AND AGAINST THE CHURCH

The **manorial (or parish) church** was the second largest building in the village (page 12, picture 1) and **town churches** were also impressive buildings. And there were so many of them! In 1086, Norwich had 1000 houses, 20 churches and 40 chapels. The **Saxons** had built small, wooden churches: the early **Normans** replaced these with stone buildings. Between 1150 and 1250 their descendants built thousands of churches, many with spires rising above the town *(picture 1)*.

1 Parish church of St. Wilfred, Scrooby

2 Stories from the Bible shown on a wall painting

5 John Wycliff

The **Church** had an important part in **medieval life**. On Sundays and 100 Holy Days (**holidays**) the Church banned working; everyone went to Mass on those days, and learned about their **faith** from **wall paintings** *(picture 2)*, Biblical stories shown in **stained glass windows**, sermons and the **priest's advice**, although this often favoured the lord (page 42, extract A). Priests received some training before their ordination, and many ran **schools** for parish children.

The **priest's income** came from crops grown on **church land** (the **glebe**), from **fees** paid for baptisms, weddings and funerals, and from **tithes** or tenths: everyone had to give the priest one-tenth of what they produced or earned.

There were good and bad priests *(extracts A and B)*. During the 14th century many people criticised the Church. **Wycliff** *(picture 5)*, a priest-lecturer at Oxford, attacked the lives of worldly Bishops, greedy monks (page 50, extract B) and ignorant priests. He wanted a simpler Church and he got the name of Lollard, a European word for religious critic. Many craftsmen as well as Oxford lecturers supported him. In 1381, the year of the **Peasants' Revolt** (page 26) he was driven from Oxford because he attacked the Church's teaching on the Eucharist: his earlier attacks had been on Church discipline only. Wycliff died in 1384. Because some Lollards had been active in the Peasants' Revolt, Parliament passed an Act for the **burning of heretics** *(extract D and picture 6)*; Parliament saw a link between religious and social unrest (page 53, extracts C and D).

4 A carved font, Castle Frome

Extract A Geoffrey Chaucer's good priest

A holy-minded man whose good was known
There was, and poor, the parson of a town.
Yet he was rich in holy work and thought;
Truly he knew Christ's gospel and it preached
Within his parish, and all it reached.
He proved his goodness in adversity.
He'd hate to write out of the tithe or holy fee.

Indeed, he much liked beyond any doubt,
To give to poor parishioners all about,
From his own goods and gifts at Eastertide
For those with wants he'd put it all aside.
(*The Canterbury Tales*, c 1390)

3 A carving from Beverley Minster showing bear baiting

Extract B Langland's unworthy priest

I have been priest and parson for thirty winters past.
But I cannot solfa sing, nor read a Latin life of saints:
But I can find a hare in a field or in a furrow,
Better than construe the first Psalm or explain it to the parish
I can hold a friendly meeting. I can cast a shire's accounts,
But in mass-book or Pope's edict I cannot read a line.
(*Piers the Ploughman*, William Langland, c 1370)

6 Lollards burnt at the stake

Extract C Lollards against unworthy priests

At Leicester a priest called William of Swynderby preached against the clergy saying they were bad, and, as other Lollards said, people need not pay tithes to the impure or those too ignorant to teach and preach. Lollards said that tithes were a voluntary gift and that to pay evil clergy was to agree with their wickedness. The Bishop heard about this and banned William from preaching and excommunicated all who listened to him. So he put up a pulpit near the High Street chapel and more people came to hear him than had done so before he was excommunicated.
(*Chronicles*, Henry Knighton, c 1395)

Extract D The burning of heretics, 1401

Because of the heresies of the Lollards, Parliament decreed that no one should preach publicly without a Bishop's permit, and that no one shall preach doctrine contrary to the Catholic faith. If anyone is found guilty of any heretical teaching, and refuses to stop preaching, the sheriff of the county or mayor of the town shall have them burned in public as a warning to other heretics.
(Adapted from an Act for the burning of heretics, 1401)

THE YOUNG HISTORIAN AT WORK

Knowledge and understanding

1 Use the text and *extract A* to help you explain why the Church was important to medieval people.

2 Read the text, *extracts B, C and D*, and look at *picture 6*. Now make TWO lists to show **(i)** why some people attacked the Church; **(ii)** how such attackers were dealt with.

Interpretation

1 Read *extracts A and B*. **(a)** In what ways do they give differing views about medieval priests? **(b)** Why do you think there were these different views?

2 Read *extracts A and D*. Do you think that the evidence in these extracts and the text give you enough evidence to show that the Church's strengths were greater than its failings? Give reasons for your answer.

Use of sources

1 Look at *pictures 1–4*. How valuable are these pictures in showing the sort of faith that medieval people had?

2 Look at *picture 6*. How were reports of such scenes received by **(i)** a bishop; **(ii)** a Lollard; **(iii)** a nobleman? Explain your answer.

Project

1 Get hold of a map of the area where you live. Mark on it the different places of worship in the area. With some friends visit some of these places. You might do some drawing while there.

2 Write the speeches which might have been made by **(i)** a Lollard and **(ii)** a bishop during a debate about religion. Which side would you have been on? Why?

LET'S GO TO TOWN

1 Table of toll charges levied at Braydon Lane Gate, Carlisle

The Domesday book named over **100 small towns**: the **Danes** had built defensive **burghs**, from which we get **burgess** (citizen) and **borough**; Saxon defensive centres had names ending in **ham** or **ton**. Towns also grew as **ports**, convenient **river crossings** and **market centres**. During the 12th and 13th centuries over **140 new towns** were built. Some grew around **castles**, **cathedrals** and **monasteries** which employed craftsmen, some were built by **landowners** who got income from land rents and tolls (or taxes) on goods coming to **market** (picture 1) and from fines paid at the **local court**. The people, or burgesses, still paid the usual feudal work-service to their landowning lord.

The **small towns** (picture 2) had defensive walls (extract D and picture 3) with **gates** (picture 4) which were opened at dawn to admit 'foreigners' coming to market, and closed again at sunset when 'foreigners' had to leave.

In the towns were **craftsmen** who made things (pages 22–3) and **merchants** who sold things and who united in a **merchant guild** (or society) which was a social club, religious body and welfare society but, above all, an economic organisation. Its officers inspected the market (picture 5), checked weights and measures, and the quality of workmanship (pages 22–3).

The rich merchants tried to get their landowner to give them a charter freeing them from his control. Kings were always willing to sell such charters (extract B); the Church was less willing. A borough charter allowed the burgesses to elect a council and mayor (picture 6) to run the town free from feudal control.

2 Main English towns in the late 14th century

3 Defensive walls around Exeter

Extract A The Normans saw England as a wealthy country

England is a land which is fertile and rich because of the wealth which its merchants have increased by bringing in riches. Treasures have been gathered there which are remarkable for their number, quality and workmanship.

(Quoted in *Historical Atlas of Britain*, Falkus and Gillingham, 1981)

Extract B Henry III grants a charter to the Borough of Gloucester, 1227

By this charter we grant to our burgesses of Gloucester the whole borough, in return for an annual payment of £55. Their merchants' guild is exempt from appearing at any outside court, and from any tolls when entering any town throughout the land. They however have the right to charge tolls on any foreign merchants entering their borough. If a villein escapes from his lord and stays in Gloucester for a year and a day, then he shall become free, and his lord may not reclaim him.

(Charter Roll, Henry III, 1227)

Extract C Two monasteries fight over having a market, 1201

The King allowed the monks of Ely to set up a market at Lakenheath. We wrote asking them to stop it. They refused. We took them to court and the King decided against them. But the monks refused to accept the decision. So the Abbot of Bury St Edmunds ordered his bailiff to take a force of 600 men to pull down the market and arrest the wrongdoers. They did so. But the Bishop of Ely complained to the Justiciar and Parliament at this arrogance by the Abbot. This stirred many to indignation against the Abbot.

(Chronicles of Jocelin of Brakeland concerning the monastery of St Edmund)

Extract D An Italian's view of London, 1497

It is defended by handsome walls on the northern side. Within these is a strongly defended castle on the banks of the river where the King lives. There are also other great buildings, and especially a beautiful bridge which has on it many shops of stone and even a large church. The streets are so badly paved that they get wet whenever it rains, or when the water slops from the buckets being carried by animals. Then evil-smelling mud forms which lasts nearly the year round. So the people spread fresh rushes on the floors of their houses on which they clean their shoes when they come in.

(*Itinerarium Britanniae*, Andreas Franciscus, 1497)

4 Bargate, Southampton in the early 19th century

THE YOUNG HISTORIAN AT WORK

Knowledge and understanding

1 (a) Make a list of reasons why towns grew in the Middle Ages. **(b)** Make a list of the benefits of this growth to Kings; merchants; craftsmen; landowners.

2 In what ways did medieval towns **(i)** differ from and **(ii)** resemble the farming communities of the time?

Interpretation

1 (a) Read *extracts A and D*. How do they show **(i)** differences and **(ii)** similarities of opinions about English towns? **(b)** How do you explain why the author of *extract D* both praises AND criticises London?

2 Read *extract C*. **(a)** What does this tell you about differing opinions about the market? **(b)** Why do you think there were these differences?

Use of sources

1 How can you use *pictures 3–6* to discover what life was like for people in medieval towns?

2 Look at *picture 2*. **(a)** Find which ports are near **(i)** the sea; **(ii)** rivers. **(b)** In which part of the country are the largest towns? **(c)** How can the map be used to explain the growth of certain towns?

6 Swearing in the mayor of Bristol

5 A 15th century market-place

Project

1 Write to the publicity officer at the town hall of the following cities: Hull, Southampton, Exeter and York. Ask for a leaflet explaining how the city grew. Perhaps your own town hall can provide a history of your town.

2 Using *pictures 1 and 4*, write a page which might have appeared in the town's toll book for market day.

CRAFTS AND CRAFTSMEN

1 Blacksmiths working in the 12th century

Towns were centres for trade and industry. **Gold- and silver-smiths** made goods for use in manor house, castle, cathedral and abbey. **Blacksmiths** *(picture 1)* made tools, gates, armour and delicate clocks. There were **many other craftsmen** – weavers, tailors, makers of harness and saddles, jewellers, shoemakers and so on.

Most workmen lived in **small wooden houses** like the villeins' cottages (page 13, picture 4). Craftsmen had a **workroom and shop** facing the street *(picture 2)*. Men from the same craft lived near one another: names of medieval streets read like a list of occupations – Baker Street, Butchers' Row and so on.

2 Working in the workroom and shop

The noise from the workrooms and from the traders' shouting added to the confusion caused by cattle, horses and donkeys. Blood from slaughterhouses and butchers' shops, fish heads from fishmongers, coloured sludge from dyers and rubbish from other shops made **streets dangerous and dirty**.

Like the merchants, craftsmen had their **guilds**, one for each craft. Members paid a weekly fee to guild officers and in return had welfare benefits *(extract A)*. Guild officers made sure that members upheld the honour of the craft *(picture 3)*: they examined workshops and goods being made and sold; they laid down the hours when work was allowed, and the number of apprentices a man could have.

A boy became an **apprentice** to a master craftsmen who taught him the 'mysteries' of the craft. After about seven years as an unpaid apprentice, guild officers allowed him to become a **journeyman**, someone paid by the day (**le jour** in French). When he had enough money to buy his own tools, he could ask to be recognised as a **master**: in *picture 4* you can see an officer examining the work of a journeyman mason. He is making his **masterpiece** which, if good enough, will allow him to become a master mason.

4 Examining the work of an apprentice mason

3 A craftsman, who had been selling goods at unreasonable profit, on the pillory

Master craftsmen tried to keep down their **journeymen's wages**. They also pushed up the fees that new masters had to pay when promoted from being journeymen. Disputes between masters and workers were common *(extract C)*. However, all members worked together to produce their craft's mobile stage on which members acted out a Biblical story. These stories were called 'mystery plays'. In some towns, as many as 40 such carts took part in the entertainment, which lasted all day.

Extract A Rules of the Guild of Tanners of London, 1346

1 To each pay towards the cost of keeping a candle burning in the Church of All Hallows near London Wall.

2 To give seven pence a week from guild funds to members too old or ill to work.

3 To allow only apprentices to work in this trade.

4 Not to steal apprentices from one another.

5 To fine anyone breaking our rules, the first time two shillings, the second 40 shillings... the fourth time to banish him from the trade.

6 To permit the guild officers to confiscate bad work.

(Guildhall Letters)

Extract B Wage rates, 1425

To William Hykkedon, working for four days making an entry from the parlour to the Prior's hall, 16 pence; to John Coventry, with two servants, tiling the room for 4 days, 3 shillings and 4 pence.

(Account Roll, Maxted Priory, 1425)

Extract C Dispute between Master Saddlers and their journeymen, 1396

Masters say that serving-men, without their masters' agreement, have held meetings in various places. These inconvenience the masters, and worse might happen if the rulers of the city do not stop it. The men say that they have met for many years on 15 August, the Feast of the Assumption, to hear Mass. The masters argued that these meetings have only been going on for 13 years and that they were not held during the last few years. They claim that the men had been meeting to try to force up wages. Formerly a man worked for 40 shillings a year and his keep; now they ask for 100 shillings and keep. Decision by the City Council, 19 July, that the men have to be governed by their masters, that they do not form a brotherhood or hold meetings.

(Guildhall Letters)

THE YOUNG HISTORIAN AT WORK

Knowledge and understanding

1 Use the text to make TWO lists to show **(i)** changes that took place over a long period of time; **(ii)** changes that took place more rapidly.

2 Read *extract B* and then read page 17, extract E. Compare the wage rates given in these extracts. Why do you think wages had risen?

Interpretation

1 Read the text and *extract C*. Why was there a dispute between the Master Saddlers and their journeymen?

2 Why do you think the City Council agreed with the Master Saddlers?

Use of sources

1 Read *extract A*. What evidence is there that the guilds **(i)** were partly religious; **(ii)** were concerned for customers' welfare; **(iii)** protected good masters?

2 Look at *pictures 1–4*. How useful are these to us if we want to find out what working life was like in medieval England?

Project

1 Having read the text, write down FIVE surnames that remind you of medieval crafts (using different ones to those you chose in answer to Project question 1 on page 13).

2 Write some diary extracts made by a journeyman who was involved in **(i)** a miracle play; **(ii)** becoming a master; **(iii)** punishing someone who had broken the rules.

WOOL – ENGLAND'S WEALTH AND INDUSTRIAL FUTURE

For many centuries England's **main export was wool**, highly valued by clothmakers in Flanders, Germany and Italy. The main **sheep-rearing areas** were the Cotswolds, the Yorkshire Dales, East Anglia, the Mendips and the South West. Manorial lords, especially the great Abbeys, earned huge sums from their sale of wool, which encouraged many to enclose land for sheep-rearing (see page 16 and page 50, extract B).

After the sheep had been **sheared**, the wool was put into **packs** and taken to the nearest **market town** *(picture 1)*. Before export, it was gathered into **large sacks** which were stamped by one of the 400 members of the group called the **Merchants of the Staple**, appointed by Kings to supervise the export of wool and the collection of the **export tax**, which accounted for three-quarters of all the taxes collected by Edward III.

1 Taking the wool to market   **2** Spinning

Exporters did not pay for the wool in cash (gold). There developed a system by which merchants promised to pay in the future. This credit system had been used in Europe for many years. It was, and still is, the basis for almost all later industrial growth *(extract A)*. Edward III's advisers saw that European manufacturing countries got rich by using England's raw material. He invited **Flemish spinners** *(picture 2)* and weavers *(picture 3)* to teach their crafts to the English. They also taught the English how to make cloth *(picture 4)* and England became the world's leading cloth exporter. In time the export of wool was banned *(extract B)*.

Clothiers bought the wool and gave it to **villagers** to spin, weave and make cloth in their homes, in what became known as the **domestic system** (pages 82–3).

Clothiers made great profits, part of which they spent on great houses *(picture 5)* and part on paying for large churches, which can still be seen in the Cotswolds and East Anglia as a reminder of their former wealth *(picture 6)*.

6 Merchants had the money to pay craftsmen for ornate works

4 Clothmaking: carding the cloth

Extract A The Merchant Staplers develop a new system of payment

When the wool reached Calais, the foreign buyer paid a certain sum in cash and gave bills (promising to pay in the future). These bills were accepted as promises to pay by other traders. The trade custom of passing bills from one creditor to another is at least 500 years old. (*The Economic History of England*, E. Lipton, 1931)

Extract B Henry VII bans the export of English wool, 1489

For the increase of making of cloth within this land, the King, with the advice of Parliament, has decreed that no one from this first of March shall buy wool in any county of England unless it is for the making of yarn or cloth within this kingdom, and that no foreigner or agent acting for a foreigner be allowed to offer to buy English wool.
(**An Act to keep English wool for English clothiers, 1489**)

Extract C Capitalism and the breakdown of the guild system

The guild system was not favourable to the build up of capital. It was limited in outlook to the local borough and its structure was too tight. It gave way to a system which allowed for expansion and change. This we call merchant capitalism with its domestic industry. The merchant capitalist broke down old barriers. He defied the chartered town by giving out work to the country. (*Great Britain from Adam Smith to the Present Day*, C.R. Fay, 1950)

5 Banqueting room built for a rich wool merchant, 1470

3 The happy scene of women weaving contrasted with the tortures of hell: medieval manuscript

THE YOUNG HISTORIAN AT WORK

Knowledge and understanding

1 (a) Make a list of reasons for the growth in importance of the wool trade.
(b) How did this growth affect **(i)** manorial lords; **(ii)** merchants; **(iii)** clothiers?

2 (a) Do you think that the changes that Edward III brought to the wool trade come under the heading 'rapid change'? Why? **(b)** In what ways did Edward III's work have long-term effects on England?

Interpretation

1 Read *extract C*. List THREE ways in which merchant capitalists were different from guildsmen.
2 Read *extract B*. **(a)** How do you think wool merchants reacted to this law? Why?
(b) Which other groups agreed with this new law? Why?

Use of sources

1 Look at *picture 1*. Look again at the pictures on pages 20–1. Write the letter which might have been sent by a traveller who had faced the problems of **(i)** poor roads; **(ii)** slow pace; **(iii)** robbery; **(iv)** town walls and gates; **(v)** tolls; **(vi)** narrow streets.
2 How useful are *pictures 2–5* for helping us understand the lives of people involved in the medieval wool trade? Explain your answer.

Project

1 As part of your frieze, draw or paint **(i)** spinning *(picture 2)*; **(ii)** weaving *(picture 3)*.

2 (a) On an outline map of England mark the main sheep-rearing areas.
(b) Find the meanings of the following words or phrases that come from the cloth trade: spinning a yarn; following the thread of an argument; spinster; on tenterhooks; the web of life; a tease.

WE WON'T PAY THE POLL TAX, 1381

There were many causes for the **Peasants' Revolt, 1381**. Even **barons** were angry at the **recent defeats in France** after years of success: **merchants** resented the **loss of markets** in France where, in 1377, only Calais remained in English hands; **craftsmen** hated the restrictions imposed on them by the **craft guilds**. Most of those who rebelled were **peasants**. Some had become more **self-confident** because of their part in the **defeat of the French** (extract A). More had grown in **confidence** as their living standards improved after the Black Death (page 16) due, in part, to **landlords'** breaking of wages laws (extract B).

In 1381 Richard II's Parliament allowed the Chancellor, Archbishop Sudbury, to impose a **new tax**: everyone was to pay about five pence a head, whether rich or poor. Many people hid in the forests when tax collectors came: in **April 1381** Commissioners were sent with armed forces to force payment. **Hence the Revolt**.

---

30 May: Commissioners stoned at the manor of **Fobbing, Essex**.

2 June: Chief Justice sent to punish villagers: attacked by army of men from south Essex, led by **Farringdon**. They marched on to London.

4 June: Essex men camped out at **Mile End**.

2–4 June: Rioting in **Rochester, Kent**: castle attacked and prison opened.

7 June: **Wat Tyler** led Kentish rebels at **Maidstone** and marched on London.

12 June: Kentish men camped at **Blackheath**. Richard II went to meet them but retreated to the Tower (picture 1).

13 June: **Tyler and Lollard John Ball** spoke to the rebels (extract C).

14 June: Mob stormed into London, attacked **Savoy Palace**, home of Richard II's uncle, John of Gaunt. **The King** met Tyler at Mile End and announced the abolition of **villeinage**, the power of the **craft guilds** and **wage-fixing** by Parliament, and an **amnesty** for all rebels. Tyler demanded the punishment of the King's advisers: he rejected this. The Essex men **killed Archbishop Sudbury** (picture 2).

15 June: After a night's rioting in London, **Richard and Tyler met again**, at Smithfield (picture 3). **The King** was angry at Sudbury's death: **Tyler** demanded the right to remain as head of his 'army'. Richard refused; Tyler became rude and one of the King's men called Tyler 'a thief'. He drew his dagger and made to stab London's Mayor, who was saved by his coat of mail. He and another then **stabbed Tyler who fell in front of his men**. Richard bravely faced the rebels, asked them to accept him as **their leader**, reminded them of **his promises** and invited them **to go home**. They did so, and the Revolt was over.

The King then **punished** the rebels' leaders. **Tyler** was dragged from St Bartholomew's Hospital, beheaded and his head placed on London Bridge, where rebels had put Sudbury's head some days before. **Armed forces** were sent to arrest other leaders in Kent and Essex and to squash any local risings.

22 June: Richard told some Essex men: '**Villeins you are and shall remain**.'

2 July: Richard cancelled all his promises to Tyler and the rebels.

Extract A The success of the common soldiers against the French

They made all France afraid. And although they are not called 'Master' as gentlemen are, or 'Sir' as knights are, but only 'John' and 'Thomas' and so on, yet they have been found to have done great deeds at Crecy and Poitiers. (Quoted in *Illustrated History of England*, G.R. Trevelyan, 1926)

1 Richard II at Blackheath, approaching the rebels in his royal barge

2 The death of Sudbury

3 Richard and Tyler at Smithfield. Tyler (left) is being attacked while Richard rides over to the rebels

Extract B Fear of social unrest, 1380

It seems to me that laziness has put the lords to sleep and they do not guard against the folly of the common people, but allow that nettle to grow which is too violent in its nature. If God does not help us, the nettle will suddenly sting us.

(John Gowe (1330 - 1408) writing in 1380)

Extract C Equality for all, 1381

We are men formed in Christ's likeness, but we are kept like beasts. No lord should have lordship: it should be divided among all men, except for the King's own lordship.

(Wat Tyler at Blackheath, 13 June 1381)

When Adam delved and Eve span, Who was then the gentleman?

(John Ball, 13 June 1381)

THE YOUNG HISTORIAN AT WORK

Knowledge and understanding

1 Here are some causes of the Peasants' Revolt: the Black Death; the Statute of Labourers; John Ball's sermons; Poll Tax; French Wars; Wat Tyler's leadership. **(a)** Which of these were long-term causes? **(b)** Which were short-term causes? **(c)** Which cause or causes do you think were most important in leading to the Revolt? Explain your choice or choices. **(d)** Were there other causes not listed above?

2 What were the effects of the Revolt **(i)** in the short term and **(ii)** in the long term?

Interpretation

1 Read *extracts B and C*. **(a)** How do these extracts show different attitudes towards **(i)** lords and **(ii)** peasants? **(b)** Why did such differences of opinion exist?

2 Read *extract A*. Does this extract support the views expressed in **(i)** *extract B* OR **(ii)** *extract C*? Explain your answer.

Use of sources

1 Look at *pictures 1, 2 and 3*. **(a)** Are these primary or secondary sources? **(b)** How can we check the accuracy of these pictures? **(c)** Are the pictures useful to the historian? Explain your answer. **(d)** Do these pictures **(i)** support OR **(ii)** oppose statements made in the text? Explain your answer.

2 Read *extract C*. **(a)** What answer do you think **(i)** the peasants and **(ii)** the lords might have given to John Ball's question? **(b)** How would you use this extract to help explain why the manorial lords were frightened by the Peasants' Revolt?

Project

1 As part of your frieze, draw or paint Richard II **(i)** in Parliament; **(ii)** coming to the Tower; **(iii)** with Tyler.

2 With some friends produce a play in which **(i)** barons complain about defeats in France; **(ii)** some lords attack those who pay higher wages; **(iii)** some lords praise their soldiers; **(iv)** Richard asks for more taxes; **(v)** an MP explains why people hate the Poll Tax.

IRELAND – 'BRITAIN'S OTHER ISLAND'

Six 'Kings' ruled six Irish provinces, each of which had **many tribes** with their own 'Kings'. Traditionally a '**High King**' of Ireland claimed tribute from other 'Kings'. The last 'High King' was **Brian Boru**, King of Munster, who died in 1014 while defeating the Danes at **Clontarf**. His rival, the King of Leinster, aided the Danes who, after 1014, ruled Dublin, Waterford and Limerick. Four 'Kings' – of Leinster, Munster, Connaught and Ulster – fought for Boru's 'crown'.

In **1154**, **Henry II** persuaded **Pope Adrian IV** to give him authority to conquer Ireland. In **1166** he had his chance. **MacMurrough** (**Leinster**) had stolen the wife of O'Rourke of Breffney, a neighbour of **O'Connor** (**Connaught**). All 'Kings' condemned MacMurrough and banished him *(extract A)*. He asked for Henry II's help. He sent **de Clare** (**Strongbow**), Earl of Pembroke (page 30) to lead an army of chain-clad **knights**, supported by Welsh **archers** (page 31, extract C). The unarmoured Irish, with their Danish battle-axes *(picture 4)* were no match for them. The English took Wexford, Waterford and Dublin.

1 The marriage of an Irish 'King' to his country

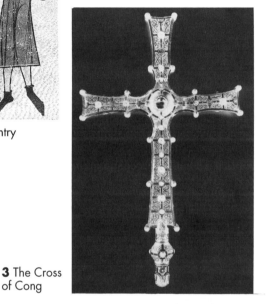

3 The Cross of Cong

2 Cross of the Scriptures, Clonmacnoise

4 Irishmen in combat

In **1175** Henry forced **O'Connor** to sign the **Treaty of Windsor**. This allowed him to act as Henry's deputy in Ireland, where English power was limited to the **area around Dublin** (page 64, extract A) where officials set up what they said was an Irish government *(picture 6)*. Their rule never extended to the far west and deep south where **Celtic tribal chiefs** ruled their people. Nor did they control the **ambitious barons**. Strongbow, for example, married the only child of the King of Leinster and so became 'King' himself; **Hugh de Lacy** married the daughter of O'Connor, the last 'High King' and gained influence in Connaught. After an Irish uprising (1177) other barons seized land. **De Courcy, Fitzstephens and Butlers** were among the gainers, building castles, abbeys, churches and Normanising Ireland. This became clear in the 14th century when **three great earldoms were created**: **Desmond** (Fitzgerald), **Ormond** (Butler) and **Kildare** (another Fitzgerald branch) and other **barons intermarried** with the native Irish, and **adopted** their language, dress and customs. The proclamation of Henry III as King had to be read in Gaelic to the Irish Parliament because only Ormond would have understood it in English.

Extract A One opinion of Diarmait MacMurrough

> O King of Heaven, dreadful is the deed that has been done in Ireland today. Diarmait, son of Donchad MacMurchada, King of Leinster and the Foreigners or Dublin Danes, has been banished over sea by the men of Ireland. Alas, alas, O Lord, what shall I do? (*The Book of Leinster*, c 1166)

Extract B Edward I, who 'united' the British Isles

Now are the islanders all joined together,
And Scotland reunited to the royalties
Of which King Edward is proclaimed lord.
Cornwall and Wales are in his power,
And Ireland the great at his will.
There is neither King nor prince of all the countries
Except King Edward who has thus united them:
Arthur never had the fiefs so fully.

(*Chronicle of Peter Langtoft*, 1297)

7 Ireland and its earldoms

Key:
Anglo-Irish Chiefs
Celtic Chiefs

O'Donnell
De Burgh
O'Neill
De Burgh (= Burke)
O'Connor
De Lacy
O'Kelly
Fitzgeralds, Earls of Kildare
O'Brien
De Clare
Butlers, Earls of Ormonde
Fitzgeralds, Earls of Desmond
McCarthy

5 Hugh de Lacy's castle, Carlingford

THE YOUNG HISTORIAN AT WORK

Knowledge and understanding

1 (a) Here are some reasons for Norman victories over the Irish: Irish divisions; Norman leadership; armaments; terrain. List these reasons in the order of their importance. Were there other reasons for Norman success?
(b) Why were the barons willing to help Henry attack Ireland?

2 (a) Was Henry's success **(i)** rapid OR **(ii)** gradual? Explain your answer.
(b) Why do you think he used Welsh-based barons for the invasion of Ireland?

6 The Irish 'government' sitting around the 'exchequer'

Interpretation

1 Find the meaning of the word 'assimilation'. Do you think that **(i)** the Irish assimilated the Normans OR that **(ii)** the Normans assimilated the Irish OR **(iii)** that the evidence supports the answer 'Yes' to both sub-questions? Explain.

2 Read the text and look at *picture 4*. Now read *extract B*. Do you agree that Edward had Ireland 'at his will'? Give reasons for your answer.

Use of sources

1 Look at *extract A*. **(a)** Why was MacMurrough called 'King of the foreigners'? **(b)** Which Irishmen had banished him? **(c)** Why had they done so? **(d)** To whom did he appeal? **(e)** How do you think modern Irish historians treat this document? Why?

2 Look at *pictures 2, 3 and 7*. **(a)** How do they help to explain the religious nature of Irish Kingship? **(b)** What is common to the names of Celtic chiefs shown in *picture 7*? **(c)** Why do you think the artist put the names of the Celtic chiefs in smaller print than that used for the names of the Normans?

Project

1 Look at *picture 5*. Give an account of the building of the castle as provided by **(i)** a Norman invader; **(ii)** a Celtic villager.

2 Draw the map of Ireland (*picture 7*), colouring the various regions in different colours.

EDWARD I AND THE CONQUEST OF WALES

1 A Welsh King: from a 13th century manuscript

William I created three powerful **Lords of the Marches** – at Chester, Shrewsbury and Hereford – to prevent any invasions from **Wales** where **Kings** *(picture 1)* ruled over a series of **provinces** such as Powys *(picture 2)*. It was these **lords** who invaded Wales and set up almost **independent lordships**. At first they built motte-and-bailey castles *(extract C)* but later replaced these with **fortresses** such as **Pembroke Castle** *(picture 3)* where de Clare (**Strongbow**) created an earldom in 1109 over which earls had sovereign rights until 1536.

During the **13th century** the Welsh fought back. **Llywelyn** 'the Great' of **Gwynedd** gained control of most of Wales from English Kings so that in **1216** all Wales accepted his **overlordship**. However, when he died, civil war broke out until his grandson, **Llywelyn Fawr,** regained control. In **1267 Henry III** acknowledged him as **Prince of Wales** *(extract E)*.

Edward I sought to control Wales. When Llywelyn refused to accept him as overlord, he invaded Wales (**1276 – 7**) and defeated the Welsh. When they rebelled, he led a **second invasion (1282 – 3)** during which Llewelyn was killed. To ensure his control over Wales, Edward built **eight great coastal castles**. His son, the future **Edward II**, was born in one (**Caernarfon**) in 1284: 1000 men worked on the building of another for many years (**Harlech**) while **Beaumaris** *(picture 4)* is described as 'a masterpiece of medieval fortification'.

In **1284** Edward issued the **Statute of Rhuddlan** which **divided Wales** into three northern counties (Anglesey, Caernarfon and Merioneth) and two southern ones (Cardigan and Carmarthen). The rest of Wales was ruled by Norman barons. The Statute put **English clergy** in charge of the Church, replaced Welsh **law** with English law and made **English** the official language – not spoken by the majority. In **1301** Edward made his eldest son '**Prince of Wales**' *(picture 5)* hoping that this Caernarfon-born Englishman would be accepted as true heir to Llywelyn. Later uprisings showed that the Welsh were not that easily fooled.

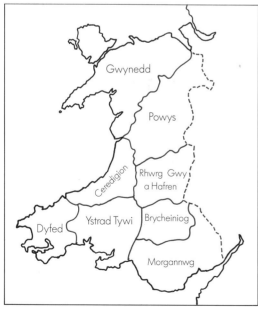

2 The provinces of Wales

Extract A A tricky coastline, 1188

We went along the seashore towards the River Neath and its quicksands. My packhorse, which had gone along the shore, sunk into the quicksands. It was got out only with great difficulty but the baggage was badly damaged. Although Prince Morgan, of that county, was our guide we were often in peril. We tried to rush through the quicksands, whereas we ought to have gone more slowly. The fords across the river change with every tide, so we did not try to cross by foot but took a boat.

(*Description of Wales*, Gerald of Wales, 1188)

Extract B Norman Marcher lords fighting in Wales, 1188

The Norman soldier is different from the Welsh. In Normandy the battle is on the level, here on rough ground. There they take prisoners, here they kill them. In their flat country their heavy armour is useful: here fighting in narrow passes and in woods, it is a handicap. Their troops march only with the greatest difficulty.

(Gerald of Wales)

3 Pembroke Castle

4 Beaumaris Castle

Edward I making his
...n Prince of Wales

Extract C Dangers from Welsh archers, 1188

Two Normans were crossing a bridge to get to safety in a tower built on a mound of earth. The Welsh chased them. Their arrows pierced the thick oaken door of the tower, William de Braose told me that one of his men was wounded by an arrow which passed through his thigh and its protective armour and through the saddle, killing the horse. Their bows are of elm, designed not to shoot a great distance but to inflict severe wounds in a close fight.
(Gerald of Wales)

Extract D Welshmen in battle, 1188

They are very fierce at the start. But if the enemy resist and they have to retreat, they become confused. They run away and do not try to fight back. Their only tactics are either to chase an enemy or to run away: they do not fight long battles or in hand-to-hand conflict. They harass enemies by ambushes and night attacks.
(Gerald of Wales)

Extract E Llewelyn ap Gruffydd, 'the Last' (1246 – 82)

And the King granted that the Prince should receive the homage of the barons of Wales, and that the barons should put themselves and their followers wholly under the Prince, and that there should be Princes of Wales from that time on, and that they should be so called.
(*Chronicles of the Princes*, 1267)

THE YOUNG HISTORIAN AT WORK

Knowledge and understanding

1 In what ways did the conquest of Wales **(i)** differ from and **(ii)** resemble the conquest of Ireland?

2 Make TWO lists showing which effects of the English invasions **(i)** took place immediately; **(ii)** took longer to come to fruition.

Interpretation

1 *Extracts A–D* were written by a monk, Gerald of Wales. Do you think he was biased towards the Normans OR towards the Welsh? Give reasons for your answer.

2 Do you see any inconsistency between the accounts given in *extracts B and D*? If you do, can you suggest how such differences might be explained?

Use of sources

1 Look at pages 40–1, pictures 1, 2 and 6 of Norman knights in their armour. Now read *extracts A and B* here. Why was this armour a handicap when they were fighting **(i)** along the coast *(extract A)* **(ii)** in the hills *(extract B)*?

2 Why are *extract B* and *pictures 3 and 4* valuable to historians writing about the conquest of Wales by the Normans?

Project

1 Using *extracts A–D*, give an account of a battle as seen by a Welsh warrior.

2 Mark on a map: Chester; Shrewsbury; Hereford; Caernarfon; Harlech; Beaumaris.

SCOTLAND FOR EVER – ALMOST

After 1066 relations between Scotland and England were uneasy. Scottish **Lowlanders** *(extract A)* **crossed the border** to steal cattle; **Scottish Kings** claimed to **rule northern England** until Malcolm IV's reign *(picture 1)* when they also agreed to do homage to the English Kings for land they owned (through marriages) in England. In **1174 William IV** was captured at Alnwick during an invasion of England and was forced to agree to do **homage to Henry II**. In **1189 Richard I** sold back that overlordship for money needed for a Crusade.

In **1287 Edward I** almost gained control of Scotland after Alexander III (page 35, picture 3) died in an accident. His successor was his six year old granddaughter, **Margaret, daughter of the King of Norway**. Edward agreed with him that she should **marry** the five year old '**Prince of Wales**' (page 31, picture 5). However **she died** in the Orkneys while on her way to Scotland: Edward's plan had failed.

The Scots then helped him. Thirteen nobles claimed the throne and, during a civil war, they agreed to have **Edward I as mediator**. He named **John Balliol** as King (**1292**) provided that he swore loyalty to him (page 10, picture 3). After Balliol's coronation at Scone, Edward ordered him to give money and men for Edward's French wars. Angry Scottish nobles made him refuse to do this, but instead to make a treaty with France, Edward's enemy.

1 King Malcolm IV (on the right) and his grandfather King David I, shown on a charter granted by Malcolm to Kelso Abbey in 1159

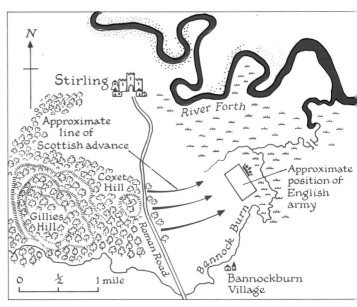

2 Statue of Sir William Wallace at Stirling

3 A plan of the Battle of Bannockburn

An angry **Edward invaded Scotland**, imprisoned Balliol, and removed the Coronation Stone from Scone to Westminster. Englishmen were put in charge of Scottish castles and government. **William Wallace** *(picture 2)* led a guerilla war against the invaders. In **1297** he defeated them at **Stirling** and drove them from Scotland.

In **1298** Edward came again: Wallace was defeated at **Falkirk** and became a hunted outlaw. Betrayed by a Scot, he was taken to London and **executed** *(extract B)*.

In **1306 Robert Bruce**, one of the claimants in 1287, had himself **crowned** at Scone and went to war against the English. Defeated at **Perth**, he fled to **Rathlin**, off the Irish coast. When Edward died (in **1307**) Bruce returned, won Scottish support and by **1314** had driven **the English from Scotland** save for Stirling and Bothwell. **Edward II** sent an army of **20 000** to defend Stirling. **Bruce** had only **7000** men, but foolish English tactics lost them the **Battle of Bannockburn** *(extract C and picture 3)*. After some more years of war the English signed the **Treaty of Northampton** (**1328**) by which Bruce was recognised as King of Scotland *(picture 4)*.

Extract A The Scottish countryside, 14th century

Scotia has areas of land bordering on the sea, pretty level and rich, with green meadows, and fertile and productive fields. In the uplands and the highlands, fields are less productive. There the country

is ugly, with moors and marshy fields. It is however full of pasturage for cattle, and has good grazing in the glens along the water-courses. This region has many wool-bearing sheep, horses, cattle and wild beasts; it is rich in milk and wood and is wealthy in fish from sea, river and lake.
(*Chronicles of the Peoples of Scotland*, John Fordun, 1381)

Extract B The execution of William Wallace, Smithfield, 1305

Wallace, a man without pity, a robber given to sacrilege, arson and murder, more hardened than Herod, madder than Nero, was condemned to a cruel but deserved death. He was drawn through London's streets at the tails of horses to an unusually high gallows. There he was hung by a halter. He was taken down while still alive: he was then mutilated, his bowels torn out and burned in fire, his head cut off, his body divided into four, and these quarters sent to four principal parts of Scotland.
(*Chronicle of Lanercost*, 1320)

Extract C The Battle of Bannockburn, 1314

When both sides were ready, the English archers were put in front of the line of knights. The Scottish archers fought with them but were soon put to flight. As the two armies drew closer, the Scots knelt to say the Lord's prayer before they advanced. They had two columns side by side in front of a third led by Robert Bruce. The great English horses charged the pikes of the Scots and there was the great noise of broken spears and fatally wounded horses. There was a stalemate: the English at the rear could not reach the Scots because the front line was in the way. So the rear fled, leaving many nobles, and great numbers of footmen dead. Then came another disaster. To get at the Scots the English had crossed a great ditch into which the tide flows. Now, when they wanted to re-cross it, many nobles and horses fell in. Some escaped only with great difficulty, while many never got out at all. Thus was Bannockburn spoken about by the English for many years. I got the account from a trustworthy person who was there.
(*Chronicle of Lanercost*, 1320)

5 Henry VII's daughter

THE YOUNG HISTORIAN AT WORK

Knowledge and understanding

1 (a) Next to each date listed below, write the major event in the story of English–Scottish affairs: 1174; 1287; 1292; 1298; 1306; 1307; 1314; 1328.
(b) Explain **(i)** the English victories; **(ii)** the Scottish victories.
(c) What was **(i)** similar and **(ii)** different about English attacks on Scotland compared to the attacks on Wales?

2 Look at *extract C and picture 3*. **(a)** Explain **(i)** why the English expected to win; **(ii)** why they lost. **(b)** Why did this Scottish victory have long-term effects on Anglo-Scottish relations?

Interpretation

1 Read *extract B*. **(a)** Does this contain **(i)** statements of fact OR **(ii)** opinions OR **(iii)** both? **(b)** How does the author show his anti-Scottish bias?
(c) How would a pro-Scottish writer describe Wallace's execution?

2 Does Edward deserve the title (evident in the text and extracts) of 'Hammer of the Scots'? Why?

Use of sources

1 How valuable are *pictures 2 and 4* in showing Scottish admiration for their leaders?

2 (a) Why is *extract A* valuable in explaining the reasons for English invasions of Scotland? **(b)** What other primary sources should we consult to get a fuller list of reasons for those invasions?

Project

1 Look at *extract C and picture 3*. Draw the map and write the diary which a Scottish soldier kept, in which he described the battle and the revenge for Wallace's death.

2 Find the words of the song 'Flower of Scotland'. What does that song say about the portion of Scottish history you have studied so far?

THE SLOW AND UNCERTAIN GROWTH OF PARLIAMENT

Early Norman Kings had a **Great Council** *(picture 1)* which they called when they needed advice. Other than this, they were almost dictators.

This power was challenged during **John's** reign (**1199 – 1216**). He had lost most of the English 'empire' in France, quarrelled with the Pope, angered people by stealing Church property and offended the barons by his high taxes. In **1215** the barons, led by the Archbishop of Canterbury, made him sign the **Magna Carta** *(picture 2)* which listed the rights which Kings had earlier given to freemen. It said nothing about ordinary people or Parliament: but it showed that Kings could be challenged. **Henry III** (**1216 – 72**) was only nine years old when he was crowned. His brother-in-law, **Simon de Montfort**, ruled on his behalf until Henry was 16. Then the King angered barons by high taxation and by having Frenchmen as advisers. In **1258** de Montfort led the barons who forced Henry to set up a permanent Council and to **call regular Parliaments**. De Montfort did not trust Henry *(extract A)* so he strengthened his position by calling for the **election of two knights to represent each county** and **two burgesses** from **each chartered borough**. This was the beginning of Parliament.

Edward I (**1272 – 1307**) accepted these ideas *(extract B)*. In **1295** he called what is known as '**the Model Parliament**', so giving Royal blessing to that body *(picture 3)*. Medieval Parliaments only **met** when Kings decided to call one, which was when they needed **money** to fight wars. **Edward's wars** led to several Parliaments and during the **Hundred Years' War** (1337 – 1435) Parliaments met more regularly.

Richard II (**1367 – 99**) tried to turn back the clock *(extract C)*: he abolished laws passed by previous Kings and Parliaments and bribed MPs to support him. He thought he was King by '**Divine Right**' *(extract D)*. In **1399** he was overthrown by barons who supported Henry Bolingbroke's rising.

During the **Wars of the Roses** Parliaments gained confidence: more MPs came from the 'new men' grown rich by trade, willing to challenge the Church (page 18) and Kings. **Henry VIII's Reformation** increased the power of Parliament (pages 50–1).

1 The King in Council

2 The Magna Carta

Extract A The nobles force Henry III to admit wrongdoing, 1258

The King acknowledged the truth of the accusations at last, and he humbled himself, admitting that he had been too often misled by evil advice. He promised and swore a solemn oath at the altar of St Edward that he would fully correct his old ways, and show kindness to his subjects. But because of his earlier crimes it was impossible to believe him. But the nobles had not yet learned how to tie a King down so that he would keep his promises. This was a very difficult matter: so Parliament was dismissed for the time being.

(*Greater Chronicle*, Matthew Paris, 1258)

Extract B Edward I agrees that he needs the consent of taxpayers, 1297

> And we have granted, for us and our heirs, that we will not take any taxes from our realm without the consent of all the realm.
>
> (*Confirmation of the Charters*, 1297)

Extract C Richard II wants to be free of Parliamentary control, 1397

> The Crown of England hath been so free at all times that it hath been in no earthly subjugation in anything touching the crown.
>
> (Statute of Praemunire, 1397)

Extract D The King as God's anointed and 'untouchable', 1399

> And shall the figure of God's majesty
> His captain, steward, deputy elect
> Anointed, crowned, planted many years
> Be judg'd by subject and inferior breath?
>
> (The Bishop of Carlisle in *Richard II*, William Shakespeare, 1595)

3 Edward I in Parliament. King Alexander of Scotland is to the left, Prince Llywelyn of Wales on the right

THE YOUNG HISTORIAN AT WORK

Knowledge and understanding

1 Here is a list of reasons for the growth of Parliament's powers:
John's quarrel with the barons; de Montfort's quarrel with Henry III; Edward I's wars; the Wars of the Roses; the growth of trade.
(a) Which do you think were the THREE most important reasons? Why?
(b) Why did wars help Parliament to grow while they limited the power of Kings?

2 Who was the ONE most important person involved in Parliament's growth? Why?

Interpretation

1 Read *extracts A, B, C and D*. **(a)** Do they show that Parliament was **(i)** weak; **(ii)** strong; **(iii)** a mixture of both? **(b)** Was the author of *extract A* biased toward the King OR towards the nobles? Explain your answer.

2 (a) Read *extracts B, C and D* again. Does Shakespeare *(extract D)* favour the views of **(i)** Edward I *(extract B)* or **(ii)** Richard II *(extract C)*?
(b) Why do you think that *extracts B and C* present different views about the relations between Kings and Parliament?

Use of sources

1 How valuable is *extract A* in showing how Henry III and Parliament got on with each other?

2 'We refuse to be bound by the King's laws until they have been passed by this Commons.' (Statement by the Commons to Edward III).
(a) What evidence does this offer about **(i)** the weak position of the King; **(ii)** the confidence of the Commons? **(b)** How useful is the statement to historians writing about the powers of Kings and Parliament?

Project

1 You have been elected MP for Exeter. Write a letter about **(i)** your journey to London; **(ii)** speeches you have heard; **(iii)** seeing the King; **(iv)** people you have met.

2 Make a series of drawings, based on what you have just read, showing important events in the growth of Parliament's powers.

CASTLES AND CATHEDRALS 1066 – 1500

GLOOMY CASTLES ON THE GROUND

1 Digging the ditch for William's first castle at Hastings

Picture 1 shows Saxons building William's first motte-and-bailey castle at Hastings as a place of retreat if he was attacked by the defeated Saxons. They first dug a large circular ditch, the earth from which was thrown into the middle to make a mound (or **motte**). On top they built a fort from timbers brought in William's invasion fleet.
This was done in four days. Then the Saxons dug another ditch to enclose a large area (a **bailey**) where, later, they put huts for castle servants, the blacksmith's forge, chapel, bakery and so on. Here, too, local people would gather if the village was attacked.

Around the castle and bailey, the Saxons put a wooden fence, another defence against attack. The **motte** was linked to the **bailey** by a wooden bridge: later this was replaced by a drawbridge which could be raised in an emergency. William gave his main followers large grants of land, which meant that Normans replaced Saxons as landowners. This made them unpopular with the people. So these **barons** also built castles as refuges: by 1070 about 400 had been built. Some have disappeared *(picture 2)*; others are mere ruins like Brough Castle *(picture 4)* which was built of stone. Once the Normans felt safe, they replaced their timber castles with stone ones. Wooden ones could more easily be set on fire by an enemy, and, in any case, wood got wet and eventually rotted.

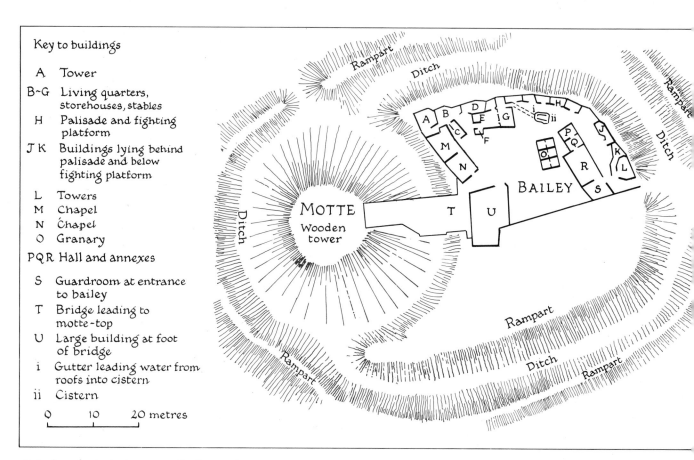

Key to buildings

A Tower

B~G Living quarters, storehouses, stables

H Palisade and fighting platform

J K Buildings lying behind palisade and below fighting platform

L Towers
M Chapel
N Chapel
O Granary

P Q R Hall and annexes

S Guardroom at entrance to bailey

T Bridge leading to motte-top

U Large building at foot of bridge

i Gutter leading water from roofs into cistern

ii Cistern

0   10   20 metres

3 A plan of a typical motte-and-bailey castle

Extract Making a motte

They made a mound of earth as wide and high as possible, and circled it with a very wide and deep ditch. Around the top edge of the mound, he put a strong wall of logs, and on the summit he put a tower. A bridge was the only entrance to the castle. It ran from the ditch to the mound, and was held up by two or three rows of logs.

(From a medieval account of the building of More Castle, Shropshire, c 1070)

2 Motte-and-bailey castle at Elsdon, Northumberland. The ditch is still visible, the wooden castle long gone

4 Brough Castle, Cumbria

THE YOUNG HISTORIAN AT WORK

Knowledge and understanding

1(a) Make a list of the reasons why the Normans built castles. **(b)** How were the lives of the local people affected **(i)** as castles were being built; **(ii)** in the longer term?

2 In what ways did castles **(i)** change; **(ii)** remain the same during the Norman period?

Interpretation

1 Does the *extract* express **(i)** opinions OR **(ii)** statements of fact? Give reasons for your answer.

2 Look at *pictures 2 and 3*. Which gives you a clearer idea of what life was like in the castle? Explain your answer.

Use of sources

1 Read the *extract* and look at *picture 1*. How can they be used to show how motte-and-bailey castles were built?

2 Look at *picture 4*. Do you think this is a valuable source for historians studying how castles had changed by 1175? Why?

Project

1 Make a model of a motte-and-bailey castle. You could use modelling clay or an egg container for the base, and a cut-out cardboard box for the tower.

2 Make a series of drawings or paintings to show the different stages in the building of a motte-and-bailey castle. Use the text, the *extract* and *pictures 1–4* as guides.

CASTLES AND BATTLES

1 12th century Norman keep at Castle Hedingham

Stone castles had to be put in the old bailey area: the motte of dug earth was not firm enough to support them.

The first stone castles were fairly simple *(picture 1)*. The stone tower was called a **keep**, since people's possessions were kept there during an attack. The walls might be well over three metres thick.

Later castles were much larger, and stone walls were also built around the castle area. These had several defensive towers: as builders became more skilled, and knights more concerned about safety, these towers became more rounded, and more difficult to attack. Walls and keeps were given crenellated battlements; men hid behind the higher parts and threw missiles through the gaps. Edward I's Welsh castles were even more developed, with their concentric walls and defensive towers (page 31, pictures 3 and 4).

Castles such as Hedingham had few rooms *(picture 2)* and its people lived uncomfortable lives: the damp air and winds came through the narrow slits or **wind eyes** making the stone building even colder.

Such castles were easy to defend, as long as food lasted and the well did not run dry. Attackers used various methods to try to break down walls. A wheeled belfry *(picture 3)* might be taken across a filled-in moat: men dug beneath the castle walls (**sapping**), filled the dug-out area with wood, set fire to this and hoped it would dry out the mortar holding the stones together. Part of the wall would then collapse. Other men tried to get over the wall by the belfry's **drawbridge**, while archers and others would fire at the defenders from the safety of the top of the belfry. However, defenders had an easier task *(picture 4)* as they fired from the shelter of the walls.

During the 14th century men learned to use gunpowder, which allowed the use of cannons and metal balls aimed at walls and defenders. Castles became less easy to defend, and many nobles gave up their castles and built more comfortable manor houses (pages 12–13, picture 3 and extract B).

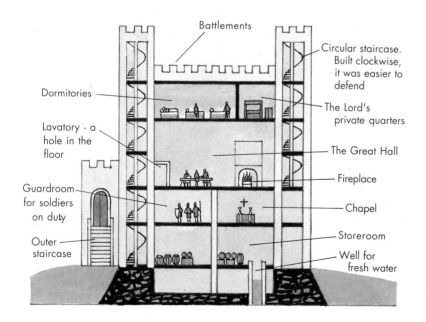

Battlements
Dormitories
Lavatory - a hole in the floor
Guardroom for soldiers on duty
Outer staircase

Circular staircase. Built clockwise, it was easier to defend
The Lord's private quarters
The Great Hall
Fireplace
Chapel
Storeroom
Well for fresh water

Winding mechanism for drawbridge
Raw hides
Filled-in moat

Extract A How King Stephen captured Exeter Castle, 1136

Its castle is on a high mound protected by towers of stone and strong walls. Inside, Baldwin had a strong garrison to man the walls and towers. They taunted the King and his men as they approached the walls. They made some unexpected sorties and fell upon the Royal army. At other times they shot arrows and threw missiles from above.

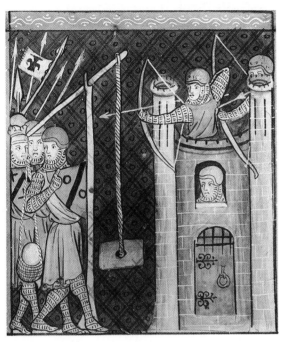

4 Defending the castle against attack

The King built lofty wooden towers from which he attacked the defenders, day and night. He got his slingers to annoy the enemy by hurling stones. He used miners to dig under the fortifications. He had all types of machines built, some of great height (to see what went on inside the castle), others level with the foot of the walls to batter them down. The besieged destroyed these machines: all the cleverness spent on their building was wasted – until the water supply ran out.

(Adapted from eyewitness account in a medieval chronicle)

Extract B An attack on Rochester Castle, 1215

As well as firing stones from catapults and slings, and arrows and bolts from handbows and crossbows, the knights and their men made many attacks. When some men tired, fresh ones took their place, and gave the defenders no rest. At last the King used miners. Many of the royal troops had been killed, and his siege machines were useless. Soon the miners undermined most of the wall. By now the defenders' food was running out; they even ate their horses.

(Adapted from an eyewitness account in a medieval chronicle)

THE YOUNG HISTORIAN AT WORK

Knowledge and understanding

1 Show how the castles described on these pages were **(i)** similar to and **(ii)** different from earlier motte-and-bailey castles (pages 36–7).

2 Here are some statements about castles. Use them to make TWO lists showing **(i)** why castles were built; **(ii)** why they were replaced by manor houses. Barons were not so important; fortresses against rebels; homes for the lords; England was peaceful; places for the King to stay when on his travels; the discomfort of the lord and his family; cannon attacks; a centre for the rule of the locality.

Interpretation

1 Is *extract B* giving **(i)** fact OR **(ii)** opinion? Explain your answer.

2 Look at *pictures 1 and 2*. In what ways do they give **(i)** similar and **(ii)** different impressions of why castles were built in medieval times?

Use of sources

1 Read *extracts A and B*, and look at *pictures 3 and 4*. How can these pieces of evidence be used to help describe how castles were attacked and defended?

2 How valuable would a visit to Castle Hedingham *(picture 1)* be for historians wishing to reconstruct life in a 12th century castle?

Project

1 Draw your own cross-section of the keep as shown in *picture 2*. Make a list of some of the things you would see in each room.

2 Find out the names of FOUR castles in your own or nearby county. Make a chart to show **(i)** when each was built; **(ii)** why the sites were chosen; **(iii)** what remains exist today. You may find your local Tourist Information Office a help.

'BARONS AND KNIGHTS LIVED TO FIGHT'

Medieval knights had to pay for the land they received from the King. They had to spend 40 days a year in the army, bringing their own horses, weapons and band of followers. *Picture 1* shows servants bringing the knight his armour. The trousers and long coat were made of iron rings linked together: this was **chain-mail**. The helmet had a piece covering the nose.

1 Servants with the knight's armour and his horse

2 Knights in a jousting tournament

Later on, as craftsmen became more skilled, armour changed. *Picture 2* shows two knights at a joust. The whole body was covered by a metal suit. Some suits weighed about 30 kg: knights' horses had to be powerful animals.

Knights' sons were prepared from an early age to become knights themselves. At seven years of age they were sent to live in another nobleman's castle. They had to be his personal servant, or **page**: they waited on him at table and helped him to dress. In return, the lord taught the page how to behave, wear armour, ride *(picture 3)* and use a sword and lance *(picture 4)*.

At the age of 15 the page became a **squire**. Now he had to follow his lord into battle, the hunting field *(picture 3)* and in the tournament *(extract and picture 2)*. He had to guard his lord from attack, look after his horse, carry his shield and help dress him in his armour *(pictures 1 and 5)*.

3 Hunting for fresh food

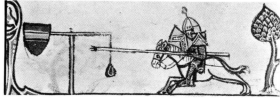

4 A knight practising with his sword and lance

When he was 21 years old the squire could become a knight if his lord or the king decided that he was fully prepared. The young man spent the night before his knighting in prayer (the **vigil**). He was supposed to think about his knightly duties – to be kind to women in particular and to everyone in general, to be brave and honest, to be loyal to his lord and King, and gentle with his inferiors. After the vigil, his baronial master, or perhaps the King, would take the young man to the other knights in the castle, palace, battlefield or tournament, and would tap him on the shoulders with a sword, present him with his **spurs** to wear behind his heels, and inform everyone that the young man was now to be called Sir, followed by his name.

A knight in the later Middle Ages

Gief une piere dun
benenree chlr denat

Extract A tournament at Smithfield, 1390

It was to take place on Monday. Sixty knights were going to tilt with blunt lances against all comers. The prize was a rich crown of gold. On Tuesday squires were going to tilt against others of their rank. Their prize was a war horse saddled and bridled.

On Sunday afternoon 60 decorated war horses, each ridden by a squire, processed out of London. Following them came 60 noble ladies riding highly decorated ponies, each leading a knight in armour. This procession moved through London to Smithfield where the Queen of England, her ladies, as well as the King were waiting. Servants led the ladies to the pavilions prepared for them. The knights waited until the squires had brought their war horses. When the tournament began many were unhorsed, and many more lost their helmets. The joust went on until night came. Then everyone went to the feast.

On Tuesday the squires tilted until nightfall, in the presence of the King, Queen and all the nobles. Supper was, again, at the Bishop's palace, and the dancing went on until daybreak. On Wednesday knights and squires all jousted together. The rest of the week was spent in feasting and dancing.

(*Chronicles*, Jean Froissart, c 1390)

5 Knighthood.
1 The squire of the knight holds his shield
2 The squire helps the knight to dress
3 The King ties the knight's sword, the squire puts on his spurs

---

THE YOUNG HISTORIAN AT WORK

Knowledge and understanding

1 (a) Make a list of the stages in the life of a young man on his way to becoming a knight, and note how, at each stage, his life changed.
(b) Which of the changes you have noted was **(i)** gradual and which **(ii)** sudden?

2 Look at *pictures 1 and 6*. **(a)** How does the armour of William's knights *(picture 1)* compare with the armour of a knight in the late Middle Ages *(picture 6)*?
(b) Explain why armour changed over the years. **(c)** What were **(i)** the advantages and **(ii)** the disadvantages of the two kinds of armour shown in these pictures?

Interpretation

1 Do you think that being a knight was all about fighting? Give evidence from the text, the *extract* and the pictures to **(i)** support and **(ii)** disprove that idea.

2 Do you think the *extract* is a factual account of a tournament? Give reasons for your answer.

Use of sources

1 How can we use the pictures in this section to help us understand **(a)** the duties of **(i)** squires and **(ii)** knights and **(b)** the customs of the time?

2 How valuable is the *extract* for historians writing about the life of knights and their place in English society?

Project

1 Make a piece of chain-mail. You could use milk bottle tops or painted pieces of cardboard, linked together with string.

2 Each knight had his own coat of arms on his shield and banner. Draw the coat of arms you would have if you were knighted. You should illustrate important events in your family history.

POLITICIAN-BISHOPS AND THEIR CATHEDRALS

Medieval kings wanted the Church to help **keep the country peaceful** *(extract A)*. William I brought men from France to become **bishops and abbots**. They were great **landowners and barons**: the Bishop of Durham guarded the northern border; the Bishop of Winchester *(extract B)* had more knights than any earl. The Archbishop of Canterbury *(extract E)* was 'the First citizen of the Kingdom'. Kings had to make sure that such men were **loyal** to them *(extracts B, D, and E)*. The country was divided into a number of **dioceses**, each with its bishop, with the Archbishop of Canterbury as the Primate (or chief bishop). Dioceses were divided into **deaneries** and, lower down, into **parishes**. Bishops set up **schools** in their dioceses: they **licensed teachers** and made sure that they taught what the Church, kings and lords wanted people to learn *(extract A)*. Each bishop had his seat (**cathedra**) in his own church (or **cathedral**).

The **first cathedrals**, built in the **11th century**, imitated the Roman style and are known as **Romanesque**. They had thick walls, massive columns, round arches and few windows *(picture 1)*. In the **13th century** builders learned how to use thinner columns and walls, with pointed arches: walls were supported on the outside by flying buttresses. This **Gothic style** allowed for more windows and ceilings *(picture 2)*. Later builders developed the **Decorated** style *(picture 3)* and the **Perpendicular** style.

Bishops ruled their dioceses and estates, and helped to run the country as government ministers or ambassadors. Some had too little time for Church work and **some of their priests became greedy and lazy**. Such behaviour was attacked by Chaucer in the **Canterbury Tales**, by rebels in the **Peasants' Revolt** (pages 26–7) and by the **Lollards** (pages 18–19).

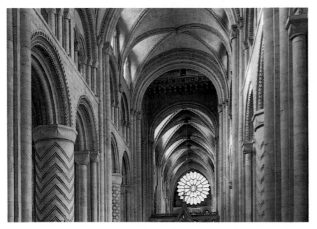

1 Durham Cathedral: The nave

2 Lincoln Cathedral: Angel Choir

3 Exeter Cathedral: showing decorated style

Extract A Religion and the control of the peasants

The priest should ask the peasants whether they have cheated by not paying their full tithes to the church; whether they have been obedient to their lord; whether they have done all the work they should for the lord; whether they have broken into a neighbour's land with plough or animal. They must be told that it is a sin to work hard only when their lord is present and to be idle when he is absent, and they must not grumble when he corrects them.

(From a handbook for the medieval clergy, c 1380)

Extract B Henry II names a new Bishop of Winchester, 1173

Greetings to my faithful monks of Winchester: I order you to hold a free election, but I forbid you to elect anyone except Richard, Archdeacon of Poitiers.

(Quoted in *Thomas Becket, Archbishop of Canterbury*, A. Duggun, 1952)

Extract C St Bernard opposes church decoration

What business have these useless monkeys, fierce lions, semi-human figures? Everywhere there is such a variety of shapes and forms that it is more pleasant to look at the marble than the books, and to spend the day like that and not on meditating on Divine Law.

(Quoted in *Civilisation*, K. Clark, 1969)

Extract D Politician-bishops

William Longchamp started as a clerk, became Chancellor in 1189 and Justiciar in 1190, the most powerful posts in the government. As Regent, he ruled when Richard I went to the Crusades. In 1190 he became Bishop of Ely and papal legate, which gave him control of the Church in England. He was overfond of power and used it to benefit his family. One monk wrote: 'The laity found him more than a king, the clergy more than Pope, and both found him a tyrant.'

(*Religion*, H. Bodey, 1973)

Extract E Electing a new Archbishop of Canterbury, 1313

The prior and chapter of Canterbury unanimously elected Thomas de Cobham, a learned noble. But, while the old Archbishop was dying, the Pope had said that he would name the successor. The King asked the Pope to transfer the Bishop of Worcester to Canterbury. So, Thomas was not chosen, even though the chapter named him: the King paid the Pope to name Worcester. So, instead of a learned man we had an illiterate one. That's what money does for the Church.

(*The Life of Edward II*, N. Denholm-Young, 1957)

THE YOUNG HISTORIAN AT WORK

Knowledge and understanding

1 Make lists of the ways in which, as time went on, cathedrals **(i)** changed in style; **(ii)** remained unchanged in purpose.

2 (a) Make TWO lists to show **(i)** the importance of the Church; **(ii)** why it became unpopular. **(b)** Why were English kings eager to gain control of the Church (*extracts B and E*)?

Interpretation

1 Read *extract D*. **(a)** Is this expressing **(i)** fact OR **(ii)** opinion OR **(iii)** both? Give reasons for your answer. **(b)** How would you check whether the opinions expressed are justified or not?

2 Read *extract C*. **(a)** What do you think the author of this extract would have said about the view of the art historian, Kenneth Clark, that church art and decorations were 'aids to prayer and devotion'? **(b)** How do you explain these differences of opinion about church decoration? Do you agree with Clark OR with St Bernard?

Use of sources

1 Read *extract A*. What light does this extract throw on **(i)** the power of the clergy; **(ii)** their relationships with peasants and lords?

2 Look at *pictures 1–3*. How valuable would historians find visits to these churches if they were trying to understand the religious faith of medieval people?

Project

1 As part of your frieze draw or paint **(i)** a stained glass window showing a religious person or story; **(ii)** a rounded arch and a pointed one; **(iii)** a steeple rising above the countryside (page 18, picture 1).

2 You are one of the team of craftsmen building and decorating a cathedral. Write the conversation between the men who **(i)** sculpted the statues; **(ii)** built the columns; **(iii)** carved the woodwork; **(iv)** made the ceilings; **(v)** erected the steeple.

MONASTERIES AND NUNNERIES

Anglo-Saxon monasteries followed the rule of **St Benedict**, 'the father of monasticism' *(extract A)*. In 910 Benedictines at Cluny in France started a stricter form of life; Cluniac monasteries were started in England after 1066, one at Lewes *(extract B)*. In **1098** other Benedictines started an even stricter monastery at **Citeaux** in France. Some of these **Cistercians** came to England and founded monasteries: their most famous houses were **Rievaulx** and **Fountains** in Yorkshire. By the time of the Black Death there were over **600** monasteries and the same number of nunneries in England, some with over **700** inhabitants.

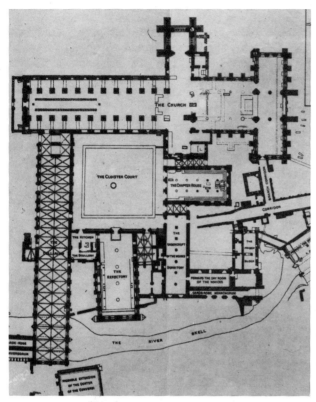

1 Ground plan of Fountains Abbey

2 A monk working on a manuscript

3 Taking monastic vows

Most were built to a similar **pattern**: Fountains *(picture 1)* lay in a sheltered **valley**, the stream providing **water** for **kitchens**, **lavatorium** (washing place) and for taking away sewage. The most important building was the **church**: many of these are our cathedrals (page 42, pictures 1–3). The **cloister** was the covered passageway, where the monks read, heard lectures and wrote *(picture 2)*. Each morning the monks met to read a chapter of their rule and, in the **chapter house**, reached decisions about work to be done. They slept in the **dormitory** which had a staircase to the church. Meals were taken in silence in the **frater**. Other buildings included the **abbot's private house** where he entertained important visitors and the **infirmary** where monks and neighbours were treated.

Some people joined a monastery when only seven years old. Most joined the **novitiate** (for newcomers) when they were older *(picture 3)*.

After a year, and provided he was 16 years old, a person could take vows of **poverty** (he would own nothing), **chastity** (or purity), **obedience** (to superiors) and **stability** (to stay in the same monastery for life).

In his simple **clothes** *(extracts A and C)* the monk **prayed** six times a day in the church: at 2.00 am (**Matins**), 7.00 am (**Prime**), 9.00 am (**Tierce,** or third prayer); 12.00 (**Sext**), 5.00 pm (**Vespers**, or evening prayer) and 7.00 pm (**Compline**, or final prayer).

In between there was **work** in the kitchen, farm or library, building *(picture 4)*, **choir practice** and so on. However, in time, many failed to live up to their ideals *(extracts D and E)*.

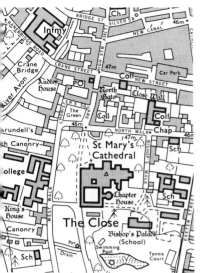

Salisbury today

Extract A From the Rule of St Benedict, AD 529

We are going to set up a home to serve God and we will never leave it. Eight times a day we will praise God. No one shall own anything – no book, pen, nothing. Monks shall be silent at all times, but especially after Compline. The normal clothes shall be a cloak and hood, a scapular for working time, shoes and stockings.

Extract B Founding a Cluniac house at Lewes, Sussex

My wife and I wish to fund some religious houses for our sins and souls. We give the monks a church built of stone, and as much land and beasts and goods as will keep 12 monks there.

(William de Warren, Earl of Surrey, 1077)

Extract C A novice on his hard but peaceful life, Rivaulx Abbey, 1239

Our food is scanty, our clothes rough; our drink is from the stream and our sleep often on our book. Under tired limbs there is only a mat; when sleep is sweetest we must rise at the bell's call. There is no room for self-will, idleness or misbehaviour. But everywhere is peace and serenity.

(Quoted in *Religion*, H. Bodey, 1973)

Extract D Dispute between merchants and the Abbot of Bury St Edmunds, 1304

Before the King's judges at the town of St Edmund, the merchants claim the right to form a guild and to make laws about their town. They agree the Abbot is lord of the town, but claim that they are free citizens who ought to be able to rule their town. The Abbot claimed that they had no such right and wanted to take away his control. The judges rule in the Abbot's favour, award him £200 in damages and send the leading merchants to jail.

(From a document in the British Museum)

4 Monks at work

Extract E Luxurious eating in a later monastery

He described with relish the number of well-cooked dishes and sauces he had eaten with the monks at Canterbury. He had no appetite left, he said, for the main course of vegetables, and he praised also the wine, mead and fruit juice that went with the meal.

(Quoted in *Food*, S. Ferguson, 1971)

THE YOUNG HISTORIAN AT WORK

Knowledge and understanding

1 Use the text, *extracts A–C and picture 5* to help you with this question.
(a) Make a list of ways in which monasteries changed the lives of **(i)** those who joined and **(ii)** people who lived outside the monasteries.
(b) Why did towns grow up around monasteries and cathedrals?

2 Why do you think so many people took up the monastic life?

Interpretation

1 In what ways does *extract E* give a different view of monastic life from that given in *extracts A and C*? Can you explain why there were these different views about monasteries?

2 Read *extract D*. **(a)** How does this help to explain why some townspeople joined the Peasants' Revolt? **(b)** Why do you think the judges supported the Abbot against the merchants?

Use of sources

1 In what ways are the pictures on these pages valuable to historians trying to understand medieval monastic life?

2 How do you think historians could test the reliability of **(i)** *extract E's* version of luxurious living; **(ii)** *picture 4* as a guide to monks' hard work?

Project

1 As part of your frieze, draw or paint **(i)** taking vows; **(ii)** book-writing; **(iii)** a procession of monks; **(iv)** monks' clothes.

2 (a) Why do you think fewer people become monks today than in medieval England? **(b)** Try to visit the site of a former monastery AND visit a monastery that is being lived in today. Your local librarian will help you with addresses if you need help.

A HOLY OR UNHOLY CHURCH?

1 Pilgrimage badge from Canterbury

Many people went on **pilgrimages** to places linked to their faith, such as **Canterbury** *(picture 2 and extracts A and B)*. Like modern 'fans' they collected badges *(picture 1)* from places they visited.

Becket's murder was the result of the continual rows between Kings and the Church *(extract C)*. **William I** allowed the Church to have its own **Courts of Justice** where people of '**the clerical order**' were tried if accused of crime. **Henry II**, trying to extend his power, wanted such 'clerics' to be sent to his Courts for sentencing. That is why he had his friend **Thomas Becket** made Archbishop of Canterbury: Becket was already

2 Pilgrims sharing a meal

3 Becket arguing with Henry II

Chancellor, or chief minister. Becket quarrelled with Henry over the Courts question *(picture 3)* and fled to France. When the Archbishop of York **crowned Henry's son** as 'king-to-be', Becket excommunicated him and his supporters, cutting them off from the Church's life, a serious matter in Catholic England. **Henry's anger** led him to call for **Becket's murder** *(extracts F and G and picture 4)*. The King had to bow before the storm of protest and accept **punishment** at Becket's cathedral *(picture 5)*. Shortly afterwards **two new orders** were founded. **Francis of Assisi** (1182 – 1226) founded an Order whose men were to lead poor lives *(extract H)*; **Dominic** (1170 – 1221) founded an Order to give the Church highly intelligent leaders. Both saw that the Church needed reform; so did others (see pages 50–1).

Extract A Becket's shrine

I saw the magnificent tomb of St Thomas at Canterbury – beyond belief... entirely covered with plates of pure gold covered with all sorts of valuable jewels.
(*The Italian Relation of England*, Camden Society, c 1500)

Extract B Chaucer's pilgrims

Then people long to go on pilgrimages
And palmers long to see the stranger strands
Of far off saints, hallowed in sundry lands,
And specially, from every shire's end
In England, down to Canterbury they wend.
(*The Canterbury Tales*, c 1390)

Extract C Kings versus Popes

The King of England, though he does not always behave as devoutly as we wish, has not destroyed the churches of God: he tries to govern in peace and justice; he has not done anything to hurt the Papacy; he is more worthy of honour and approval than other Kings.
(Pope Gregory, 1081)

4 The murder of Thomas Becket

Extract D Becket warns Henry II when he becomes Archbishop, 1162

If you were to ask of me anything which I could not bear quietly, the love you now bear me would turn to bitter hatred.
(Quoted in *Thomas Becket, Archbishop of Canterbury*, A. Duggan, 1952)

Extract E Becket gives in to Henry II – but not, quite, 1169

Thomas knelt before Henry and repeated the formula by which he accepted the King's power. Then he added the fatal clause, 'except for the honour of God and the rights of the Church and of my clerical order.'
(A. Duggan)

Extract F Henry's anger leads to murder

When news of the bishops' excommunication by Thomas reached Henry, he was at Sur-le-Roi near Bayeux. His anger burst through his reserve and he shouted words he was always after to regret. 'What sluggards and knaves have I fed in my house that they are faithless to their lord, and let him be tricked so infamously by one upstart clerk.'

(*Kings of Merry England*, P. Lindsay, 1935)

Extract G Becket's murder

In fury the knights called out, 'Where is Thomas Becket, traitor to the King?' He came down and in a clear voice said, 'I am here, no traitor to the King, but a priest. Why do you seek me?' 'Forgive the people you excommunicated,' they cried. 'I will not,' he answered. 'Then you shall die,' they cried. 'I am ready to die for my Lord, so long as the Church can have its freedom.'

(Edward Grim's eyewitness account, quoted in *Materials for the History of Becket*, 1875)

Extract H Francis of Assisi warns his followers against riches, 1226

Let all the brethren beware of accepting churches, houses or anything else provided for them unless they conform to Holy Poverty, to which we are vowed in our rule, always lodging as strangers and pilgrims.

(The Last Testament of Francis of Assisi)

5 Henry's penance at Canterbury

THE YOUNG HISTORIAN AT WORK

Knowledge and understanding

1 Here is a list of the causes of Becket's death. Make TWO lists to show which causes were (i) long term and which were (ii) short term: dispute over Church Courts; William I's grant to the Church of its own Courts; the Church's wish to be independent of the King; Henry's anger at the excommunication of his supporters; the wish of some knights to win the King's favour.

2 What were the consequences, for Henry II, of Becket's death?

Interpretation

1 'Religion was losing its hold over the people at this time.' Does the evidence from the text, pictures and extracts support this view? Give reasons for your answer.

2 What do you think was the opinion of Francis of Assisi (extract H) about (i) Becket's tomb (extract A) and (ii) the views of St Bernard (page 43, extract C)?

Use of sources

1 How valuable are *extracts C, D and E* for historians trying to explain the quarrel between the Church and Kings in the Middle Ages?

2 (a) How can we use *extracts D, E and F* to show what sort of people Becket and Henry were? (b) Can you now add ONE extra cause (of Becket's death) to the list given in Knowledge question 1 (above)?

Project

1 Draw a map showing a pilgrim's journey from London to Canterbury.

2 Use *extracts A and B*, and *pictures 1 and 2*, to help you write an account of the journey from London to Canterbury.

THE MAKING OF THE UNITED KINGDOM:
Crowns, Parliaments and peoples 1500 – 1750

THE TUDORS AND THEIR PARLIAMENTS

Henry VII (1485 – 1509) spent little money and rarely needed to call Parliament to ask for '**unusual taxes**'. **Henry VIII (1509 – 47)** had to call for money for his wars against France and Scotland (page 60): **he used Parliament** to pass the laws he needed to make his break with Rome legal (pages 50–1).
Most Parliaments did what monarchs wanted. **Henry VIII** got his Reformation; **Edward VI's** Parliaments passed **anti-Catholic** laws; **Mary** got her **Catholic** laws through. **Elizabeth I (1558 – 1603)** called many Parliaments. It was during this reign that **MPs first challenged** the Sovereign's rights, and so prepared the way for the more serious **disputes with the Stuarts** (pages 62 and 66).

1 Henry VIII opens Parliament, 1512

> **Secondary sources.** Read again page 10: *Interpretations by later historians:* examples of such interpretations used in that section were listed on page 10. You will find examples of such secondary sources in this section. Here (page 49) you will see two examples in extract F (which shows how later historians offer different views of the same subject) and in extract D (which shows how many secondary sources are based on a study of primary material). Other examples of secondary sources are found on page 53 (extract C), page 63 (extract C), page 64 (extract B – but note that this was written shortly after the event), page 68–9 (extract B) and page 77 (extract C).

2 Edward VI and his councillors allowed the Church more freedom. Henry VIII is shown ruling from his grave in an attempt to stop reform; the Pope is shown crushed by the English Prayer Book

3 The Queen presiding over Parliament

Extract A Elizabeth I scolds a restless Parliament, 1566 - 7

It does not become a subject to compel a sovereign. It is for me, the Anointed Queen, to provide for the succession and the country's future. I will never be forced to do anything to lessen my royal power, and the Sovereign's right to decide policy.

(Elizabeth I's message to the Commons, 1567)

Extract B Another clash, 1571

Her Majesty said that they would do well not to meddle with matters of state except those she put before them.

(The Lord Keeper to the Commons, April 1571)

Extract C A short but rebellious session, February-March, 1576

It is certain, Mr. Speaker, that no one is without fault. Not even our noble Queen. Since, then, Her Majesty has committed great faults, some of which are dangerous to herself and to the State, love forces me to utter them for the sake of Her safety.

(Peter Wentworth, MP, at the opening of the Commons, February 1576)

Extract D Parliamentary freedom and the religious question, 1593

Elizabeth I: Your privilege is the freedom to say 'yes or no' and to give reasons for your opinion. This is a liberal privilege, and not a licence to you to say what you like. You cannot claim, under the pretence of liberty, the right to encroach on the royal control of the Church, on the succession to the throne, and on policy in general. You, my Commons, are overbold when you use God's name as the excuse for criticising my Government. *Peter Wentworth, MP:* Sweet is the name of liberty. Parliament is a place where we may speak freely about all the griefs of the country. I will not refer Christian doctrine to the bishops. To do that would make the Bishops into 'Popes'.

(Adapted from quotations in *A History of England*, K. Feiling, 1974)

Extract E Parliament speaks out against Elizabeth's favourites, 1601

20 November. *Mr Martin:* The country groans under the burden of monopolies of starch, tin, fish, cloth, oil, vinegar... *Mr Hakewill of Lincoln's Inn called out:* Is not bread there? It will be before the next Parliament.

(Commons debate, 1601)

Extract F Which 'expert' is right?

1 Elizabeth dissolved Parliament on 2 January 1567. Henry VIII had never lost a head-on clash with Parliament. Elizabeth had.

(*Elizabeth I*, J. Ridley, 1987)

2 The declaration of 2 January 1567 marked a decisive moment in the relations between the Queen and Parliament. After this, there was never any question but that it was she who directed the ship of state, Parliament meeting to give her their counsel, advice and consent.

(*Freedom's Own Island*, A.S. Bryant, 1986)

THE YOUNG HISTORIAN AT WORK

Knowledge and understanding

1 (a) How does a study of the religious changes of the 16th century support the view that 'Tudor Parliaments usually did what monarchs wanted'?
(b) Under which Tudor monarch did Parliament become most independent?

2 Look back to page 34 to help you show that the causes of the growth of Parliament's power go back to the reigns of Edward I and III.

Interpretation

1 (a) Read *extracts A and B*. What are **(i)** the similarities AND **(ii)** the differences given in these extracts concerning the powers of Parliament and Queen? **(b)** What opinion do *extracts C and D* seem to give about Parliament's power?

2 Read *extract F*. Does the evidence in the other extracts support the views of **(i)** Ridley OR **(ii)** Bryant, concerning Elizabeth's control of Parliament?

Use of sources

1 Are *pictures 1 and 2* valuable to historians trying to discover how some people saw the power of monarchs over Parliament and Church? Why?

2 (a) How can we use *picture 3* to explain what the Elizabethan Parliament was like?
(b) How valuable is *extract E* for historians trying to find out whether MPs' criticism of Elizabeth was widespread?

Project

1 You are an Elizabethan MP. Write your diary of events in Parliament noting speeches made by MPs and by the Queen.

2 As part of your frieze, draw or paint ONE of the scenes shown on these pages.

HENRY VIII AND A NEW CHURCH – OR STILL THE OLD ONE?

In **1520 Martin Luther** attacked Catholic beliefs. **Henry VIII's** attack on Luther *(picture 1)* won him the Papal title of **Defender of the Faith**. Why then did he lead the Church in England away from allegiance to the Pope?

In **1509** he married **Catherine of Aragon**, widow of his elder brother, Arthur, who had died (1502). By **1527** he had a daughter, **Mary,** but not the son to whom he wanted to leave the Crown: he was also in love with **Anne Boleyn**. He sent his Archbishop, **Cardinal Wolsey**, to ask the Pope to let him **divorce** Catherine. When the Pope refused, Henry sacked Wolsey and appointed **Thomas Cranmer** as his Archbishop. Together they pushed the break with Rome through Parliament (1531 – 6). The **most important stages in that break** took place in:

1533: Parliament forbade appeals in Church matters being sent for Papal decision. Cranmer now dissolved Henry's marriage (**May**), married him to Boleyn (**June**) and baptised their child, Elizabeth (**September**). The Pope declared Henry and his supporters excommunicated – cut off from the Catholic life.

1534: Parliament named Henry **Supreme Head of the Church**. Most Church leaders in England accepted this. The few who didn't were executed *(extract D)*.

1535: A **Treasons Act** allowed Henry to punish any opponents.

1536: An Act allowed the **closure of smaller monasteries**. Henry put down the uprising known as the **Pilgrimage of Grace** *(picture 2)*.

Henry then **closed all monasteries** (**1537 – 9**) and took all their land. The sale of this land gave him an income of £100 000 a year for some years, double his usual income. The land was bought cheaply by MPs, courtiers and other influential people, who were then anxious to maintain the break with Rome. Henry continued to **burn Lutherans** *(picture 3)* and in **1539** pushed through an Act accepting Catholic teaching on the Mass, the Eucharist, the non-marriage of clergy and Confession. He died, as he thought, 'a good Catholic'.

1 By attacking the work of Martin Luther, Henry VIII earned the title 'Defender of the Faith'

Extract A Wealthy monasteries

In the diocese of Bath there are two convents, one for monks, named Glastonbury, and the other for women, named Santsbury. The abbot of the former has a yearly income of more than £25 000 and the abbess of the other above £10 000.

(Letter by Italian Ambassador to London, 1500)

Extract B Thomas More's attack on greedy monks, c 1520

Certain abbots do not content themselves with their usual yearly revenue from their lands. They now leave no ground for tilling; they enclose all pastures; they throw down houses as they make everything sheepland.

(Utopia, Thomas More, 1516)

2 Executing rebels who took part in the Pilgrimage of Grace

3 Burning Lutherans

Extract C Lords and Bishops ask the Pope to give Henry his divorce, 1530

If the Pope is unwilling, we are left to find a remedy elsewhere. Some remedies are extreme ones, but a sick man seeks relief in any way he can find.

(Letter signed by Bishops and Lords, sent to The Pope at Henry's request, 1530)

Extract D Thomas More refuses to accept Henry as Supreme Head of the Church

Sir Richard Rich: Master More, you are learned in the law. Pretend that an Act of Parliament said that I was King. Would you accept me as King?

Sir Thomas More: Yes.

Rich: Suppose an Act of Parliament said that I was Pope. Would you accept that?

More: Master Rich, Parliament may well meddle with the state of princes and make you King. As to your second question: suppose Parliament made a law that God was not God. Would you accept that?

Rich: No Parliament can make any such law.

More: No more can Parliament make the King Supreme Head of the Church.

(Interview during More's trial, 1535)

THE YOUNG HISTORIAN AT WORK

Knowledge and understanding

1 The 'break with Rome' had many causes. **(a)** Make a list of some of the long-term causes of hostility towards the Church (see pages 18, 46 and 53). **(b)** Do you think there would have been that 'break' if Henry VIII had not been King of England?

2 What were the effects of Henry VIII's religious policies on **(i)** the Church; **(ii)** his own wealth; **(iii)** many rich English families?

Interpretation

1 Do you agree that the evidence in these pages shows that 'Henry VIII was really a Catholic without the Pope'? Give reasons for your answer.

2 Read *extract D*. **(a)** What different interpretations are given in this extract about the power of Parliament over the Church? **(b)** Which interpretation was put into practice in England after this trial?

Use of sources

1 Read *extracts A and B*. **(a)** Which is the more valuable as evidence of what monks were like in Henry VIII's time? Why? **(b)** What other sources should historians check when writing about the monks in England?

2 (a) Use *pictures 2 and 3* to describe how Henry VIII dealt with both Catholic and Puritan opponents of his religious policies. **(b)** What sort of person do you think that these pictures show Henry to have been?

Project

1 You are the Pope's adviser in 1527. Here are some of the policies you could have suggested that he should follow regarding Henry VIII: **(i)** to declare his marriage to Catherine invalid; **(ii)** to persuade Catherine to leave Henry and so allow the Pope to give Henry permission to divorce her and then to marry Anne Boleyn; **(iii)** to refuse to allow Henry to divorce Catherine and to marry Anne Boleyn. **(a)** Give the arguments for and against each of these policies. **(b)** Arrange a debate amongst your friends about these policies.

2 Write the diary of **(i)** a Catholic OR **(ii)** a Puritan about the religious changes that Henry VIII brought about in England.

RELIGIOUS UNIFORMITY WILL BRING NATIONAL UNITY

Henry VIII's 1539 Act **outlawed** the teachings of **Lutherans and Calvinists** *(extract D)*. Before he died, Henry ordered that **his infant son** should be helped by a **Council** of equal numbers of Catholics and Reformers (page 48, picture 2). But extremists seized power, banning **the Mass** *(extract A)*, producing an **anti-Catholic Prayer Book** *(extract B)* and **plundering churches** *(pictures 1 and 2)*.

When **Mary** became Queen (**1553**) she tried to **restore** 'the old faith' but greedy MPs and courtiers refused to allow the restoration of the monasteries. Like her father, she **persecuted religious opponents**: because of her unpopular marriage to Philip of Spain, this offended many people who saw it as Spanish policy. Most **politicians**, like the Cecils, and Princess Elizabeth, saved their lives and wealth by **accepting Mary's religious changes**.

When **Elizabeth** became Queen (**1558**) she tried to find a middle way (a **via media**). Many Catholics accepted this *(extract C)*: others wanted a full return to Rome. It was easy to show that these were **pro-Spanish traitors** who deserved to be punished *(picture 3)*. On the other hand, her policy failed to satisfy the **Protestant extremists** *(extract D)* who had their supporters in the Commons (page 49, extract D). They would trouble her Stuart successors (pages 62–3).

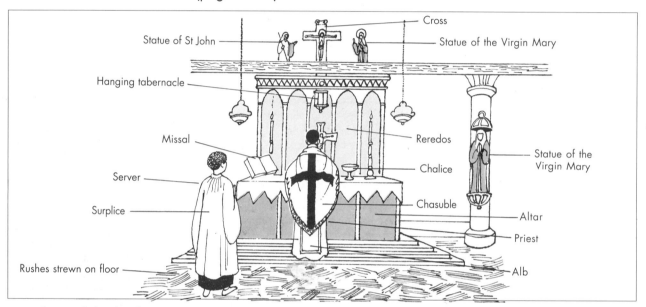

1 Inside a Catholic church

2 Inside an Anglican church

Extract A Edward VI forbids Mary Tudor to have Mass said, 1547

My duty most humbly remembered unto your Majesty... I trusted that you would have allowed me your poor sister to have the traditional Mass, which the King, your father and mine with all his predecessors had; wherein I was brought up from my youth to which my conscience binds me as also the promise made to the Emperor by your Majesty's Council which agreed that in so doing I would not offend the Laws. And when I last had an audience with you and told you that I would prefer that you should take my life rather than forbid me the Mass, your Majesty made me a very gentle answer...

(Letter from Princess Mary, 1547)

Extract B Mary Tudor refuses to use Cranmer's Book of Common Prayer, 1549

You hope that I will not refuse God's word. I cannot tell what you mean by God's word. But what is called God's word now was not God's word in my father's day. You would not have dared call that (book) God's word in my father's day.

(Princess Mary to Nicholas Ridley, Bishop of London, 1549)

Extract C Elizabeth I looks for a religious middle way, 1558

'To unite the people of the realm in one uniform order' everyone was obliged to attend their parish church on Sunday; non-attendance was to be punished by a modest fine and, if persisted in, by imprisonment. In Elizabeth's Act of Uniformity and in the Thirty-Nine Articles which laid down guidelines for the Anglican Church, there was no abuse of Pope or Rome while the words of the Cranmer's Communion Service left people free to accept or reject the Catholic teaching about the Real Presence of Christ in the Eucharist. Elizabeth's own attitude towards this beautiful but unprovable teaching was shown in some lines which she is said to have written:

3 Torturing religious opponents

'Twas Christ the word that spake it, He took the bread and brake it;
And what the word did make it, That I believe and take it.'

(*Freedom's Own Island*, A.S. Bryant, 1986)

Extract D Critics of the Elizabethan Church, 1598

There is a sect in England called Puritans. These, following Calvin's teachings, reject all ancient ceremonies, they do not allow any organs or altars in their places of worship. They oppose any differences in rank among churchmen, such as bishops, deans etc. They were first named Puritans by the Jesuit Sandys. They do not live separately but mix with those of the Church of England in the colleges.

(*Travels in England*, P. Hentzner, 1598)

THE YOUNG HISTORIAN AT WORK

Knowledge and understanding

1 Show how, after Henry VIII's death, religious laws and practices became **(i)** sometimes more Protestant than they had been; **(ii)** sometimes more Catholic.

2 (a) Why was Mary Tudor unpopular? **(b)** Why were Catholics generally under suspicion after 1553? **(c)** How did Elizabeth behave towards Catholicism **(i)** before 1558; **(ii)** in her religious policy (extract C)?

Interpretation

1 Read *extracts A and B*. **(a)** Where, in these extracts, are there **(i)** statements of fact; **(ii)** opinions? **(b)** Why, do you think, did Edward VI and Mary Tudor have different interpretations about religious matters?

2 Read *extracts C and D*. **(a)** How popular do you think Elizabeth's religious policy was with **(i)** Puritans; **(ii)** devout Catholics; **(iii)** people who didn't care very much about religion?

Use of sources

1 Look at *pictures 1 and 2*. **(a)** How can we use these pictures to show **(i)** similarities AND **(ii)** differences between the Church in Henry VIII's time and in Elizabeth's time? **(b)** Do you think these drawings are completely reliable guides to what happened to the Church in Tudor times? Why?

2 Use *picture 3* to show what happened to both Catholic and Puritan opponents of English monarchs if they were caught by government spies.

Project

1 Discuss with your friends the following questions. **(a)** Is religion as important in this country today as it was in Tudor times? **(b)** Are there any causes for which it is worth becoming a martyr today?

2 Using television, newspapers and your library, find out about people in today's world who are persecuted for their religious beliefs.

THE COUNTRYSIDE – CHANGED YET UNCHANGING, 1500 – 1750

During this period most people lived in small villages, and worked on the land. Their lives were very similar to those of their ancestors (pages 14–15). Of course there were **some changes**. **Books** were published to tell farmers about **new crops** such as the turnip, potato and clover, some of which enriched the soil, or gave winter food for animals, and provided a better diet for the people. The books also told farmers about **improved tools** (e.g. better spades and scythes) and how to improve the soil by **marling** (adding lime and clay to light soil), and **manuring**.

Most of these improvements depended on the work of **reforming landowners**. Many were the politicians who had gained from the sale of the monastic lands (page 50). They bought land to show that they were members of the 'upper class' and because they hoped to make money from it *(extract A)*. They **enclosed** much of their land so that they could run flocks of **sheep** *(extracts A and C)*: arable farmers were pushed off the land, and many villages became deserted (page 17, extract C).

1 Hatfield House, Hertfordshire

These new landowners also built great **country houses**. Hatfield *(picture 1)* and Longleat *(picture 2)* were typical. The famous **Bess of Hardwick** *(extract B)* supervised the building of four such huge houses, the most famous being Hardwick Hall. These owners paid for **huge windows** which made their homes much lighter than the gloomy castles, and for many **fires** (and **chimneys** – a feature of these houses). They bought **furniture** designed by great craftsmen, had their **portraits** painted by English or foreign artists, and bought expensive **clothes**, **gold plate** and other things which showed **their wealth**. However, enclosures meant that many people were driven off the land. In the past such poor people would have been looked after by the monasteries, the guilds or the local church. Now the Government had to pass a series of **Poor Laws** which, by **1601**, had created a system by which every parish was responsible for its poor: church leaders had to collect a **Poor Rate**, build a **workhouse**, and provide **work and a dole** for the poor. But what if someone left his parish to look for work? Such a one, if unemployed or sick, might become a burden to another parish. So the law allowed '**wandering beggars**' to be **branded** with a 'V' for vagrant, to be **whipped** from parishes other than their own *(picture 3)* and forced back to that parish. In **1662** an **Act of Settlement** forbade people to leave their parishes. If this Act had remained in force we would never have had the late growth of industrial towns (page 78).

2 Longleat House, Wiltshire

Extract A New and improving landlords

These owners of old monastic lands now improve their soil by liming, marling, draining, hedging and enclosing. Their hearts, hands, eyes and all their powers concur in one thing – to force the earth to yield her utmost.

(John Norden, mapmaker, on the squires of the West Country, c 1580)

Extract B A female 'improver': Bess of Hardwick, (1518 – 1608) Countess of Shrewsbury

She was proud, furious, selfish and unfeeling, a builder, a buyer and seller of estates, a money-lender, a farmer and a merchant of coals, lead and timber. She kept close accounts and was a terror to her servants.

(*Country Life*, K. Butcher, 1970)

3 Whipping a vagrant back to his home parish

Extract C Bishop Latimer's protest against the new landowners, 1549

My father was a yeoman. He had no land of his own, but rented a farm for three or four pounds a year at the most. Here he tilled as much land as employed six men. He had land for 100 sheep, and my mother milked 30 cows. He put me to school, otherwise I would not be preaching before your Majesty now. He married off my sisters, giving them five pounds each. He gave hospitality to poor neighbours, and alms to other poor. And all this from that farm. Today the tenant has to pay 16 pounds a year, or more; he is unable to do anything for his children or the poor. All the raising of rents and rearing of sheep and cattle bring profit only to the landowner.

Extract D A wealthy country

In England there are more things to produce riches and manufacture than in any two countries in the world. There is great wool, the most and best tin and lead and flesh to feed the workers and corn enough for the life of man, and the safest and best harbours.

(*England's Improvement*, Andrew Youranton, 1677)

THE YOUNG HISTORIAN AT WORK

Knowledge and understanding
1 (a) Make a list of the changes made in English farming in this period.
(b) What were the most important consequences of those changes for **(i)** poor people; **(ii)** the appearances of fields; **(iii)** some landowners' homes?

2 Look back at pages 14–15. **(a)** What do you think were **(i)** the similarities and **(ii)** the differences between farms of the 11th century and farms of the 16th and 17th centuries? **(b)** Which people played the most important part in bringing about the changes you can find?

Interpretation
1 Read *extracts A and C*. **(a)** Do these extracts give **(i)** similar OR **(ii)** different interpretations about the new landowners? Give reasons for your answer. **(b)** Why do you think there were differences of interpretation about the activities of new landowners?

2 Read *extract B*. Does this contain **(i)** statements of fact OR **(ii)** opinions? Give reasons for your answer.

Use of sources
1 How can *extract D* be used to explain why England was becoming a rich country in this period?

2 Why are *pictures 1, 2 and 3* useful to historians writing about **(i)** the pleasant and **(ii)** the harsh aspects of life in Elizabethan England?

Project
1 Collect illustrations from magazines, tourist brochures (from tourist agents), and newspapers, to make a collage on 'country homes'.

2 Arrange a debate among your friends on whether the changes in the countryside were beneficial or harmful.

OVERSEAS TRADE AND COLONIES

1 An English gentleman —the sort who commanded ships around the world

Turkish conquests in Asia Minor and the Balkans closed the old Mediterranean **routes to the Far East**. Europeans had to look for new routes: the **Portuguese** found a new way via the **Cape of Good Hope**; the **Spaniards** sailed west; both countries founded **empires in South and Central America**. England played little part in this exploration.

After 1551 there was a drop in European demand for English cloth; merchants had to look for **new markets**. Adventurous sailors such as Humphrey Gilbert, Francis Drake *(picture 3)*, Martin Frobisher and others *(picture 1)* faced great dangers as they sailed their small ships, knowing that Spanish and Portuguese fleets might attack them.

Even when trading with Europe, men had formed the Company of Merchant Staplers and the Company of Merchant Adventurers (pages 24–5). Elizabethans formed such Companies to trade with the wider world. Each Company had its **Royal charter** *(picture 2)*, giving its members the **monopoly of trade** in a certain area. Merchants formed '**joint stock ventures**' and received a share of profits: a man who put in £100 received twice the profit of the man who put in £50.

The Muscovy Company (**1553**) traded with **Russia** *(extract A)*.

The Eastland Company (**1578**) traded in **the Baltic**.

The Levant Company (**1581**) traded in the **eastern Mediterranean**.

The East India Company (**1600**) traded in the **Far East** *(extract C)*.

Some people thought England did well from this trade *(extract B)*. Spain and Portugal resented England's growth; Spain resented any English intrusion into her **slave trade with Spanish America**.

During the 17th century England fought wars against France and Holland over foreign trade and England's search for colonies. England's **first colonies** were small ventures on the eastern seaboard of America. Private investors got **Royal charters** giving a Company their right to take over a certain area: so the Virginia, Massachusetts and other Companies were formed.

Merchants from Bristol and Liverpool also developed the profitable **triangle of trade** *(picture 4)* based on the slave trade. The **Treaty of Utrecht** (**1713**) ended a long period of wars with France and Spain and gave England a monopoly of that cruel trade *(extract D)*.

By 1750 **trade with colonies** in North America, the West Indies and Asia gave some merchants large **profits** which would be used to **finance** the first stages of the **industrial revolution** (pages 82–3).

2 The charter of the Hudson's Bay Company, May 1670

3 The Drake Cup, presented in 1582

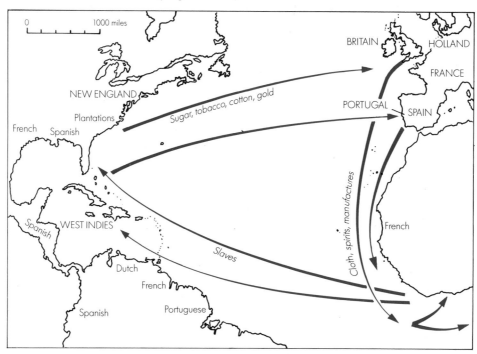

4 The 'triangle of trade'

Extract A The Muscovy Company's exports from Russia, 1560

5th May 1560. The goods we want you to prepare for our ships to carry are wax, tallow, oils, flax, cables and ropes, and furs, mainly sables. We look for a trade worth £3000.

(Directors of the Muscovy Company to their agent in Russia, Anthony Jenkinson, 1560)

Extract B England, the most successful trading nation, 1589

The English in searching every quarter of the globe have excelled all the nations. For which of our people, before this reign, had ever seen the Caspian Sea? dealt with the Emperor of Persia? or Constantinople? Who, before her Majesty won for her merchants great privileges, ever found English agents in Syria, Aleppo, Babylon, Basra, and which is more, at Goa? What English ships before this anchored in the River Plate? went through the straits of Magellan? travelled the coast of Chile? went to the Philippines in spite of the enemy? When before did our merchants trade with the princes of the Moluccas and bring home the goods of China?

(Richard Hakluyt, 1589)

5 Broad Street quay, Bristol, in the 18th century

Extract C Jehangir Khan, ruler of India, to King James I, 1614

The letter of friendship which you sent, and the presents, I have received from your ambassador, Sir Thomas Roe. I have given command to all my dominions to receive all the merchants of the English nation, that wherever they choose to live, they should be treated well; that they be free to sail or buy as they wish; and at whichever port they arrive, neither Portugal nor any other shall dare to attack them.

Extract D The Treaty of Utrecht, 1713, and the Assiento

This peace was beneficial to Great Britain: several advantages were gained – Hudson's Bay, the island of St Christopher's, all Novia Scotia, Minorca, Gibraltar and all that **Assiento trade** which allows us alone the privilege of sending ships to trade with Spanish America and of taking there 4800 slaves a year.

(Somers Tracts, 1715)

THE YOUNG HISTORIAN AT WORK

Knowledge and understanding

1 (a) Make a list of the difficulties facing English merchants seeking new foreign markets.
(b) Which individuals or groups were responsible for developing English trade with **(i)** Russia; **(ii)** the Baltic; **(iii)** the eastern Mediterranean; **(iv)** India; **(v)** South America?

2 Make TWO lists to show **(i)** the short-term and **(ii)** the long-term effects of the setting up of merchant companies.

Interpretation

1 Does *extract B* give a valid interpretation of the extent of English trade at that time? Explain your answer.

2 Read *extracts A and C*. **(a)** Why do these extracts give different pictures of English trade during this period? **(b)** Are there any similarities in the information contained in these extracts?

Use of sources

1 Is *extract D* a valuable source for historians trying to discover the effects of the Treaty of Utrecht? Give reasons for your answer.

2 How can the pictures shown on these pages be used to help us learn about **(i)** merchants' wealth; **(ii)** what Elizabeth thought of Francis Drake; **(iii)** the nature of British trade with Africa and the West Indies; **(iv)** the appearance of trading ports?

Project

1 Find out more about the voyages of Francis Drake.

2 Using *picture 5*, write an eyewitness description of a day in the port of Bristol (describing the sounds, smells, ships, goods being traded, where ships are going to, and the companies organising the trade).

TOWNS – AND TRADE, WEALTH AND HEALTH

Most people lived in villages (page 54) but some **towns grew** in this period (1500 – 1750). **London** *(picture 1)* spread on both sides of the Thames; Norwich, the second largest town, grew with the cloth trade; **Exeter** (page 20, picture 3) was the centre of the West Country cloth trade as was **Bristol** (page 57, picture 5), which also gained from the growth of colonial trade and slavery. **Liverpool** *(extract A)* developed rapidly; **Leicester** *(extract D)* was a typical small town – in 1700 its population was 3000. **Older towns** showed their **medieval origins**: **walls and gates** (pages 20–1, pictures 3 and 4), **market crosses** and **lack of water supply** *(extracts C and D)*. In old and newer towns, wealthy men showed off their wealth in larger and **more comfortable houses** *(picture 2)*, with the **furniture** made by great craftsmen, and in their **fashionable clothes**.

However, all towns and even new houses were all too often **very dirty**. In 1660 the country suffered another **Black Death**, **or plague**, with London suffering more than the rest *(extract E)*. Even so, **businessmen** continued to meet in their coffee houses *(picture 3 and extract F)*, another outward **sign** of the **industrial growth** which formed the **basis for the later industrial revolution**.

2 St Peter's Hospital, Bristol: a typical town house from c1600

Extract A Liverpool: a wonder of the age, 1698, 1724 and 1833

Mostly new houses of brick and stone after the London fashion. It was a few fishermen's houses, and now is a large fine town with very handsome streets, persons well-dressed, it is London in miniature.

(Celia Fiennes, 1698)

It is still visibly growing in wealth, people, business and buildings. It has an increasing trade, not only rivalling but outstripping Bristol in trade to the American colonies. They send ships to Norway, Hamburg, the Baltic, Flanders... like Londoners they are universal merchants.

(Daniel Defoe, 1724)

A small town 60 years ago, the slave trade to the Spanish colonies was the basis of its commercial greatness. A beautiful town.

(Alexis de Tocqueville, 1833)

3 Meeting in the coffee house

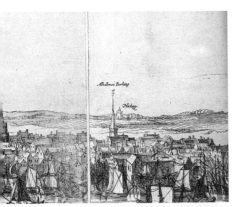

1 London in 1600

Extract B Upwardly Mobile Merchants, 1726

Trade in England makes gentlemen; for tradesmen's children, or their grandchildren, come to be as good gentlemen, MPs, judges, and noblemen as those of ancient families. As they grow wealthy they get coats of arms which they put on their coaches, furniture and new houses.

(Daniel Defoe, 1726)

Extract C London's water supply, 1599

Spring water is enclosed in stone cisterns in different parts of the town. It is let off into iron-bound buckets which men carry to houses and sell.

(*Travels in England*, Thomas Platter, 1599)

Extract D Leicester's water supply, 1690

They have a water house and a mill to turn the water into pipes to serve the town as it is in London. It comes on only once a day, so they save the water in deep cisterns; there are wells in some streets to draw water by handwheel for the use of the towns.

(*Journeys*, Celia Fiennes, 1685 – 1698)

Extract E The diarist Samuel Pepys on the plague, 1665

30 April:	great fear of the sickness in the City: houses already shut up.
7 June:	saw houses in Drury Lane with red crosses on the doors.
10 June:	the plague is come into the City.
21 June:	I found almost all the town leaving, coaches full of people.
13 July:	about 700 dead of the plague this week.
27 July:	the weekly list of deaths, about 1700 of the plague.
10 Aug:	about 3000 died of the plague this week. Wrote my Will.
31 Aug:	every day sadder. Number of dead this week near 10 000.

Extract F Coffee Houses as business centres, c 1700

You have all manner of news there: you have a good fire which you may sit by as long as you please: you have a dish of coffee: you meet your friends for the transaction of business, and all for a penny if you don't want to spend more.

(*Memoirs*, Maximilian Misson, 1719)

THE YOUNG HISTORIAN AT WORK

Knowledge and understanding

1 (a) Make a list of the reasons for the growth of towns in England (see page 20).
(b) What reasons are common to the growth of many towns? **(c)** How was the growth of some towns linked to the activities of individuals and companies that you read about on pages 56–57?

2 (a) In what ways was the growth of towns **(i)** beneficial to some groups but **(ii)** harmful to others? **(b)** What was the ONE most important long-term effect of the growth of towns in England?

Interpretation

1 Read *extracts A and E*. **(a)** Show that these offer different interpretations of life in towns in the 17th century. **(b)** Do you agree that there are valid reasons for these differences of interpretation, given the place, author and time of the writing of each extract? Explain your answer.

2 Read *extracts C and D*. **(a)** What are **(i)** the similarities and **(ii)** the differences between the pictures of town life given in these extracts?
(b) How do you explain these similarities and differences?

Use of sources

1 (a) How can *extracts B and F* be used to reconstruct what life was like for merchants in 18th century towns? **(b)** Do you think that these primary sources are totally reliable? Give reasons for your answer.

2 Look at *pictures 1 and 3*, and read *extract E*. These show different aspects of London life in the 17th century. Comment on the differing values of each of these sources for historians trying to understand life in 17th century London.

Project

1 Using *picture 3* and *extract E*, write an eye-witness account of a visit to a coffee house.

2 You are a craftsman who helped to build a town house *(picture 2)*. Describe your work to an apprentice who wishes to learn your trade.

SCOTLAND, 1500 – 1603

In 1503 Henry VIII's sister, **Margaret**, married **James IV of Scotland** (page 33, picture 5). But in **1512** Scotland sided with France and went to **war against England**, James being killed in the disaster of **Flodden** (1513). **James V (1513 – 42)** confirmed the alliance with France by marrying **Mary of Guise** (*picture 1*). In **1542** he led Scotland into **war against England**: he died two weeks after the defeat at Solway Moss. His daughter, **Mary**, **now became Queen of Scots**. In 1547, during an English invasion of Scotland, she fled to France and her mother, Mary of Guise, went to rule on her behalf.

1 Mary of Guise

2 Mary, Queen of Scots

She was opposed by **Protestant Reformers** and by **nobles** hoping for a share in Church lands. In 1559 **Knox** (*picture 3*) became the Protestants' leader: **Elizabeth I** helped them in the fight against 'French Mary Guise' who was forced to sign the **Treaty of Edinburgh** (1560): the French had to leave and a Parliament was called. That **Reformation Parliament** (1560) abolished the Catholic religion and Papal power in Scotland, and outlined plans for a Scottish Church. **Mary**, **Queen of Scots** came from France (1561), the widow of the late King Francis II of France. Her private practice of her Catholicism **angered Knox** (*picture 3*): her **two marriages** lost her the support of most Scots. The first was to her cousin, **Henry Darnley**, who grew jealous of her secretary, Rizzio. He planned Rizzio's death (1566) only to be murdered himself in 1568. Mary then married the **Earl of Bothwell**, her lover and the person suspected of arranging Darnley's death. Her Catholicism and her marriage to Bothwell led Scottish nobles to rise against her. She was **defeated**, but escaped from prison to flee to England. Elizabeth I condemned the Scottish rebels (*extract A*) but kept Mary under house arrest. She was the centre for **Catholic plots** against Elizabeth, especially after the Pope had excommunicated 'good Queen Bess' in **1570**. **Parliament** clashed with Elizabeth over her moderate treatment of Mary, but it was in Elizabeth's own interests **to keep Mary alive**: the Armada attacked England only after her death. Mary's son, **James VI**, ruled Scotland in his own right after 1587. He was involved in the argument about what sort of Church Scotland should have. Was it to be:

(a) Presbyterian, governed by delegates elected by local churches? OR

(b) Episcopalian, governed by bishops?

Knox's supporters wanted the more democratic form: James managed to keep some powers for the bishops, but not as much as English bishops had in their Church. When Elizabeth died (**1603**), **Cecil** sent for James and brought this great-great-grandson of Henry VII to the throne as **James I of England**, **Wales and Ireland**. One of his first meetings was with various religious leaders in **1604** (*extract C*). That meeting contained the seeds of future problems for later Stuart monarchs.

Extract A Elizabeth I and the Divine Right of the Queen of Scots

> They had no authority by the law of God or man to dethrone their Queen, and to act as superiors over their Sovereign, no matter what they think of her.
>
> (**Quoted in** *Freedom's Own Island*, A.S. Bryant, 1986)

Extract B A French warning about the Queen of Scots, 1586

If you proceed to the extreme with the Queen of Scots, those connected with her in blood and friendship will take the same course (against you). If you show your goodness to her, all princes will watch over your preservation. Our King promises to hinder in every way all attempts made against you, as a sincere friend and brother. You will be more secure if she lives than if you kill her, as you know better than any other person.

(French envoy to Elizabeth I, December 1586)

3 John Knox at the court of Mary

4 James I of England

Extract C James and the English Puritans, 1604

Dr Reynolds, for the extremists, referred to the synod, where a bishop, with his presbytery, determined all points. At this His Majesty stirred, thinking they proposed a Scottish presbytery. He said: 'I will tell you a tale. After Edward VI's religion was overthrown by Mary here in England, we in Scotland felt the effect of it. Master Knox wrote to the Queen telling her that she was Supreme Head of the Church and asked her to suppress the Popish bishops who oppose reform. By her authority the Popish bishops were suppressed. Then Knox and his followers felt strong enough to undertake the Reformation themselves. They made small account of the Queen's power as they made this further Reformation.' Then he said; 'My lords bishops, these men think they cannot win against you except by appealing to my supremacy. But, if once you were out and they were in, I know what would become of my supremacy. As I have said before; "No bishop, no King". I will make these men conform themselves, or I will harry them out of my kingdom.'

(An account of the Hampton Court Conference, 14 January 1604, by William Barlow, later Bishop of Rochester, and then of Lincoln)

THE YOUNG HISTORIAN AT WORK

Knowledge and understanding

1 Here is a list of reasons why Mary Queen of Scots was a threat to Elizabeth I: Marriage of James V to Mary of Guise; marriage of James IV to Margaret Tudor; Protestant opposition to the Catholicism of Mary of Guise; Mary Queen of Scots' marriages; the Pope's excommunication of Elizabeth I; plots against Elizabeth by Mary and her supporters while she was in prison. Make TWO lists to show **(i)** the long-term reasons and **(ii)** the short-term reasons why the Queen of Scots was a threat to Elizabeth.

2 What were the effects of the conflict between Mary Queen of Scots and Elizabeth on **(i)** Mary herself; **(ii)** the Spanish; **(iii)** James VI?

Interpretation

1 Read *extract B*. Do you think that Elizabeth **(i)** had no choice but to allow the execution of the Queen of Scots OR **(ii)** do you agree with the opinions given in the extract? Give reasons for your answer.

2 Is *extract A* **(i)** a statement of fact; **(ii)** opinion; **(iii)** a mixture of both fact and opinion? Give reasons for your answer.

Use of sources

1 How can we use *extract C* to help us understand **(i)** James I's attitude towards the Puritans; **(ii)** the attitudes of many Scottish religious leaders towards the Catholics; **(iii)** the attitude of the author of the extract?

2 Look at the pictures on these pages. Are they valuable for historians who want to know more about the characters of **(i)** Mary of Guise; **(ii)** Mary Queen of Scots; **(iii)** John Knox? Give reasons for your answer.

Project

1 Write the letter which a Catholic might have sent supporting Mary's claim to the English throne.

2 Draw or paint the posters which might have appeared to tell people about **(i)** the death of Elizabeth I; **(ii)** the coronation of James VI as James I of England.

CROWN AND PARLIAMENT, 1603 – 42

Plain Copy of Record of Meeting

	s	d
John Hampden, Esquier	31	6
Thomas Lee, Esquier	41	3
Mrs Wentall	5	6
Thomas East	23	6
Peter Aldridge	19	3
Richard Blackwell	16	9
Widow Brompton	10	0
The Occupiers of Hessell's Grove } Matthew Aldridge	24	9
Thomas Lane	10	9
Thomas Hellows	11	0
Nicholas Statharn	22	0
Jeffrey Goodchild	16	6
Widow Goodchild	19	3
Griffith Reynolds	5	6
Thomas Well	13	9
Micheal Neele	11	5
M Smith	5	6
Thomas Statham	5	10
William Yeoman	6	0
John Giles	10	6
Widow Temple	16	6
Thomas Rutland	16	6
Robert Atkins	12	0
Henrie Short	5	6
Rowland Reynolds	11	0
ffrancis Clarke	7	6
Thomas ffisher	2	9
Steven Lasie John Jennings }	12	4½
Robert Stratton	16	6

Kimball Magna Januarie the 9th, 1635

We returne our warrant of their names herein written, for refusing to pay such portions of money as are herewithin assessed by the Assessours for the raysing of the sume of £21 11s 5½d

PETER ALDRIDGE THOMAS LANE } Assessours.

JOHN GOODCHILD THOMAS RUTLAND } Constables.

2 A list of those residents of Great Kimble, Buckinghamshire refusing to pay Ship Money. Hampden's name is at the top of the list

In this period, **two Kings quarrelled with Parliament**. The issues involved were:

1 Royal claims to Right (extract A). **Elizabeth I** had also made this claim (page 49, extracts A–D). But in **1601** she had the wisdom to **give way to Parliament's anger**.

2 Religion. **James I's** defence of the **bishops** (page 61, extract C) angered the Puritans. More people were alarmed by **Charles I's Catholic marriage** and the 'Romish' policies of **Archbishop Laud** (extract C).

3 Wars and taxation.

1625: **MPs refused** Charles the money to fight his unsuccessful war against **Spain**. He then forced the **collection of illegal taxes** and made many enemies.

1627: An attack on **France** was badly organised, led to 4000 deaths and the disgrace of Charles' favourite, **Buckingham** (extract B).

1628: Charles called a Parliament to get money for his war. **Pym** (picture 3) and **Hampden** (picture 2) attacked his war policy and illegal taxation. **Coke** (picture 1) drew up the **Petition of Rights**, listing Charles' errors. Because he needed money, Charles accepted the petition.

1629: MPs voted Charles the taxes he asked for, but for only one year, because he rejected their criticism of Laud (extract C). He, in turn, rejected their offer of a year's taxes as limiting his freedom, and he dissolved Parliament.

4 Ship money. This was an old tax once paid by coastal towns for coastal defences. Charles imposed it **throughout the country**. Many wouldn't pay (picture 2).

5 Scotland. The Scots were angry at **(a)** Charles's cancellation of the grants of Church land made since 1540; **(b) Laud's** attempts to bring the Scottish Church into line with the Anglican Church. The introduction of a **new Prayer Book** led to rioting, the formation of a **National Committee**, and the signing of a National Covenant for the defence of 'the true religion'. In November 1638 a Scottish General Assembly **deposed all bishops** and **banned the new Prayer Book**. Charles invaded Scotland and began **'The Bishops' Wars'**. He was forced to make peace and to call an English Parliament. He brought his friend, **Wentworth**, from Ireland (page 65, extract D) to lead a new attack on Scotland. But Parliament refused him the money he needed for this. Instead, it criticised his policies and his choice of advisers. He dismissed Parliament, but was forced to recall it when a **Scottish army invaded England** and occupied Newcastle.

1 Edward Coke: led the opposition to Charles I

4 Charles I attempting to arrest his leading opponents—but they had fled

3 John Pym

6 Wentworth. The new Parliament included many **Puritans**. Wentworth wanted Charles to arrest Parliament's leaders. He hesitated and the Commons persuaded the House of Lords to try Wentworth (Lord Stafford). When he was found guilty of misconduct, Charles weakly accepted the decision and **signed his adviser's death warrant on 9 May**.

7 Ireland. A fresh Irish rebellion forced Charles to ask for money for a new army. Instead Parliament drew up a list of grievances (page 65, extract E).

8 'The birds had flown'. In January 1642 Charles went to arrest the five leading anti-royal MPs *(picture 4)*. They escaped. Charles then left London – to which he would return as a prisoner awaiting trial (page 66–7).

Extract A James I's idea of Divine Right, 1610

The state of monarchy is the supremest thing on earth. Kings are God's lieutenants. They exercise a manner of divine power on earth. To dispute what God may do is blasphemy: so it is sedition for subjects to dispute what a King may do.

(James I to the Commons, 1610)

Extract B Parliament versus Buckingham and Charles I, 1626

Eliot moved that, as we intended to supply his Majesty with money, we should also give him advice. He asked for a declaration to the King of the danger in which the kingdom stood by the decay of religion, the insufficiency of his generals, the weakness of his councils, the deaths of his men, the decay of trade, the loss of shipping, the many and powerful enemies, the few and poor friends abroad. *Coke* protested that the cause of these miseries was Buckingham which led to acclamation by the House.

(Thomas Alured, 1626)

Extract C The High Anglicanism of the active Archbishop Laud

Laud departed from the Reformation and drew near to Rome. His theology was far from that of the Calvinists. His love for ceremonies, for holy days and sacred places, his dislike of the marriage of clergy, the zeal with which he asserted the claims of the clergy, made him hated by Puritans.

(*History of England*, T.B. Macaulay, 1849)

THE YOUNG HISTORIAN AT WORK

Knowledge and understanding

1 There were many causes of the conflict between Parliament and the Crown. Having read the text and the extracts, make three columns and put as many causes as you can under three headings: **(i)** causes going back before 1629; **(ii)** causes which grew between 1629 and 1640 **(iii)** causes which emerged after 1640.

2 (a) Using the lists you have drawn up, mark the causes EITHER **(i)** Political OR **(ii)** Economic OR **(iii)** Social, and explain your answers. **(b)** Show that the quarrel between Crown and Parliament grew more bitter at some times than at others.

Interpretation

1 Read *extracts A and B*. How do these extracts give different interpretations of the powers of King and Parliament?

2 Do you think that historians would be right to blame EITHER the King OR Parliament for the quarrel that led to the Civil War? Explain your answer.

Use of sources

1 How valuable is *extract C* for historians trying to discover more about Laud's policies? Note the date of the extract and the fact that Macaulay was biased in favour of the Parliamentary argument.

2 (a) How useful is *picture 2* as providing evidence of opposition to the King in 1629? **(b)** Does the fact that this source concerns only one place put a limit on its value as evidence? Give reasons for your answer.

Project

1 Look at *pictures 1, 3 and 4*. You are a journalist in the House of Commons. Write a report of the speeches by **(i)** Coke; **(ii)** Pym; **(iii)** Charles, on the occasions noted here.

2 Produce a short play about the Ship Money crisis.

IRELAND – CONTINUALLY RESTLESS

With Anglo-Irish nobles controlling some areas and Celtic chiefs even more, royal power in Ireland was limited to the Dublin Pale *(extract A)*. The Irish supported Simnel *(extract B)* and Warbeck in their attempts to take the throne. **Henry VIII** closed the monasteries and schools as part of his Reformation. A Catholic rising ended in 1537 with the **execution of five Earls at Tyburn**. Henry tried to bribe Celtic chiefs with titles: **O'Neil became Earl of Tyrone**. But nationalism and Catholicism were stronger than such worldly considerations. **Mary I** planted English settlers in **King's County** (Leix) and **Queen's County** (Offaly), failing to see that, to the Irish, these were merely 'colonisers'.

Elizabeth I feared that Spain would use Ireland as a base for attacks on England. She planted areas of Ireland: Raleigh and other favourites became major landowning 'colonisers'. In **1595**, Hugh **O'Neil (Earl of Tyrone)** had Spanish help in his rebellion. After his defeat of the English at **Yellow Ford (1597)** Elizabeth sent **Essex to Ireland** as Lord Lieutenant *(picture 2)*. He failed to beat Tyrone, whose army *(picture 1 and extract C)* used the terrain wisely and forced Essex to sign a **truce**. An angry Elizabeth recalled Essex whose foolish ambition led him to challenge Elizabeth, who had him **executed**.

James I signed a truce with **Tyrone and Tyrconnel** who were made **viceroys** to rule on his behalf. However, they led **another rising** (**1607**); when this failed they fled and James gave their **Ulster estates** to English and Scottish settlers.

Charles I sent his favourite, **Thomas Wentworth**, to rule Ireland. His ruthless and 'thorough' rule *(extract D)* united Ulster Puritans and Irish Catholics. It was the **Catholics who rose in 1641** *(picture 3)* when Charles was involved in his Scottish Wars (page 62). Parliament refused him the money he needed for this, but issued its **Grand Remonstrance** *(extract E)* taking the country to the brink of civil war.

Extract A England controls only the Pale, 1574
Continued revolts against the English planted here forced them into certain shires in Leinster open to receive help from England, a Pale from which they dared not peep.
(Walter Devereux, 1st Earl of Essex and Earl Marshall of Ireland)

1 Marching through Ireland

Extract B The Irish use Lambert Simnel, 1487
...Simnel went to Ireland. There he called a meeting of Irish nobles whom he understood were opposed to Henry VII. He told them he was the son of the Duke of Clarence. This story was believed by the nobles who named him King Edward VI.
(*History of England*, Polydore Vergil, 1534)

Extract C An English view of the Irish soldiers, 1603
Their cavalry do not use saddles, stirrups, boots or spurs, so they can nimbly jump off their horses. They carry heavy spears and swords. They have no armour except a helmet. They use hit and run attacks... fly off, knowing we dare not follow them into the bog. Their real strength are their foot soldiers.
(*The Glory of England*, Thomas Gainsford, 1618)

3 The massacre of Protestants by Catholics

Extract D Wentworth and 'Thorough' in Church Matters, 1633

You fear the Church is bound by Common Law. No such considerations shall direct me until I see my master's power set above Coke and his Year Books, and I am not assured that the same resolution governs your lordship. Let us then, in the name of God, go cheerfully and boldly. And thus you have my Thorough and Thorough.

(*Illustrated History of England*, G.M. Trevelyan, 1926)

Extract E The Grand Remonstrance, November 1641

183. Our intention is to reduce that power which the bishops have taken.

184. It is far from our purpose to leave people to take up what form of worship they please, for we believe there should be conformity to the law.

185. We desire a general synod of the most learned divines of this country with some from abroad, to consider all things necessary for the Church, the results of their consultation to receive the authority of Parliament.

197. That His Majesty be petitioned to employ such ministers as Parliament has confidence in, without which we cannot give him supplies for his own estate nor assistance for the Protestant party abroad.

(*History of the Great Rebellion*, Earl of Clarendon, c 1670)

THE YOUNG HISTORIAN AT WORK

Knowledge and understanding

1 (a) Name THREE English leaders who did most to conquer Ireland. Explain your choices. **(b)** Why did the English want to conquer Ireland? **(c)** Write down the effects in **(i)** the short term and **(ii)** the long term of English attempts to conquer Ireland.

2 Why did the English find it difficult to conquer Ireland?

Interpretation

1 Read *extract E*. Now read page 49, extracts A–E. **(a)** Compare the interpretations of the powers of King, Parliament and Church as given in *extract E* with the interpretations given on page 49. **(b)** What is the significance of these differences of interpretation?

2 Read *extracts A, B and C*. Do these give complete explanations of why the English found it difficult to defeat the Irish? Explain your answer.

Use of sources

1 Is *extract D* a useful source for historians writing about the policies of Charles I and Wentworth towards the Churches? Why?

2 How useful are *pictures 1–3* for explaining **(i)** how the Irish fought; **(ii)** the character of Essex; **(iii)** relationships between Irish Catholics and Irish Protestants?

Project

1 Write a Protestant account of the events shown in *picture 3*.

2 Write a speech made by an Irish patriot lamenting over defeats and praising Irish victories.

THE CIVIL WARS

The first war began when Charles left London after failing to arrest the five leading MPs (pages 62–3). He **went to the north** hoping to find more supporters as he moved further away from London. In **August 1642** he raised his standard at **Nottingham**

1 Pikeman and musketeer of the New Model Army

and asked his people to follow him. **Parliament** began to raise an **army in London**. The Civil Wars did not involve most ordinary people unless they joined one of the armies. Most people in the **south** and **east** of England **supported Parliament**; the **north** and the **west** (except for Plymouth) **supported the King**. Most of **his supporters** were **noblemen** and **their followers**; they were good horsemen (and were called **Cavaliers**). They were trained in using weapons so that they **won most of the early battles**. Parliament's support came from **townspeople**, **small farmers** and **merchants**. They were called **Roundheads**. Few of them had horses, so they fought on foot and, at the start, were at a disadvantage. However, as they gained control of more of the country, they could pay and equip troops while Parliament's **control of the navy** made it difficult for the King to get supplies from France. **Oliver Cromwell** was Parliament's best general. After early defeats by the Cavaliers, Cromwell trained a '**New Model Army**' (picture 1): he insisted on discipline, training and the preaching of the idea that God supported their Puritan faith. Cromwell's troops won important victories at **Marston Moor** and **Naseby** which persuaded **the Scots** to side with Parliament in 1643. In **1646** the Scots captured the King and sold him to Parliament.

In **1647** while the King was a prisoner, Cromwell offered him the Heads of Proposals to end the war. Parliament was to have control of the army for 10 years, before handing it back to the King, who would allow people freedom of worship. Charles rejected this reasonable offer, escaped from prison and made a deal with the Scots who wanted to have a weak King rather than a strong Cromwell in power in England. Cromwell defeated the Scots at Preston (**1648**), and the King was re-arrested.

In **December 1648** Cromwell cleared the Commons of all MPs sympathetic to Charles

2 Charles I on trial

3 The execution of the King

and demanded that he be put on trial in **January 1649**. He was accused of many crimes *(extract A and picture 2)* but refused to defend himself in front of what he saw as an 'illegal court' *(extract B)*. He was found guilty and executed *(extract C and picture 3)*. England now became a Republic led by Cromwell (pages 68–9).

Extract A The accusations against Charles I, 1649

Charles Stuart, King of England, who was entrusted to govern according to the laws of the land, had a wicked design to create an unlimited and tyrannical power, to rule according to his will, and to overthrow the rights and liberties of the people. He traitorously waged war against Parliament and the people. He renewed the war in 1648. He is thus responsible for all the treasons, murders, rapings, burnings, damage and desolation caused during those wars. He is therefore, a tyrant, a traitor, and a murderer, and an enemy to the Commonwealth of England.

(Quoted in *British Monarchy*, J. Cannon and R. Griffiths, 1988)

Extract B Charles denies the court's right to try him, January 1649

I wish to know by what power I am called hither. I would know by what lawful authority. Remember I am your King, your lawful King, and what sins you bring upon your heads, and the judgement of God on this land, think well on it. I say, think well on it, before you go from one sin to a greater one. I have a trust given me by God, by old and lawful descent. I will not betray it to answer to a new and unlawful authority.

(Charles I to his judges)

Extract C An eyewitness at Charles I's execution

I stood amongst the crowd in the street before Whitehall-gate where the scaffold was erected and saw what was done, but was not so near as to hear anything. The blow I saw given, and can truly say with a sad heart: at the instant whereof, I remember well, there was such a groan by the thousands, as I never heard before and desire I may never hear again. There was one troop of soldiers sent immediately marching to scatter and disperse the people, so that I had difficulty to escape home without hurt.

(*Diaries*, Philip Henry, edited in 1882)

THE YOUNG HISTORIAN AT WORK

Knowledge and understanding

1 Here are some of the factors that brought Charles I to the scaffold:
Cromwell's generalship; Cromwell's ruthlessness as a politician; Charles' stupidity; the strength of Parliament's army; the navy; support for the army.
(a) Place these factors in order of importance, and explain your answer. **(b)** How far did **(i)** changes in the countryside (pages 54–5); **(ii)** the development of a strong merchant class (pages 56–7); and **(iii)** the growth of towns (pages 58–9) provide long-term reasons for Parliament's success?
2 The short-term reasons for Charles' death are explained in these pages. Look back at pages 62–3 and list the long-term reasons for his death.

Interpretation

1 Read *extracts A and B*. **(a)** Were the charges made in *extract A* an accurate description of Charles' failings as King? Explain your answer. **(b)** How does *extract B* offer a different interpretation of the power of the King from that given in *extract A*? **(c)** What interpretation of royal power is suggested by the engraving of the trial *(picture 2)*?

2 Read *extract C* and look at *picture 3*. Do they agree or disagree in their interpretation of the events of the execution? Explain your answer.

Use of sources

1 How valuable is *picture 1* for historians writing about Cromwell's army as regards **(i)** weapons; **(ii)** clothing; **(iii)** methods of fighting?

2 Look at *extract C* and *picture 3* again. Compare the strengths and weaknesses of each of these sources as evidence for historians writing about the execution.

Project

1 You are an eyewitness of the death of Charles I and sympathetic to the King. Write the conversation you might have had with a Puritan about this event.

2 Arrange a re-trial of Charles I with some friends, with people representing the prosecution, defence, jury, judges and with presentations of evidence for and against the King.

CROMWELL'S RULE

1 Cromwell's allocation of land, 1650

England now had to find answers to two questions:

1 Who had the lawful right to rule? Some wanted **the King's son**, **Prince Charles**, to be crowned as Charles II. Others thought that **Parliament** should rule. But in **1646** Cromwell had dismissed all MPs who had supported the King. The remaining MPs in '**the Rump Parliament**' hardly had the right to rule.
2 Who had the power to govern? Clearly **only the army had** – but it had no right to govern. This was a confused situation.

Cromwell was made **President of the Council of State** set up to govern while answers were sought to the two questions. First he crushed the Irish rebels led by the Earl of Ormonde, by **cruelty** (extract A) and by a harsh land settlement (picture 1). He then returned to attack the **Scottish rebels** (picture 2 and extract C) and by **1653** had imposed his rule on Scotland. He then turned to England:
(a) He used the **army** to dismiss the Rump Parliament (picture 3).
(b) He allowed the **independent Churches** to elect a Parliament which spent its time arguing about the form of a future government. So the army wrote **An Instrument of Government**. This named **Cromwell** as **Lord Protector for life** and called for **fresh elections**. A group of extremists thought that everyone had the right to vote: these '**Levellers**' were crushed by the army.

(c) The **new Parliament** criticised Cromwell's decision to allow people (except Catholics) to worship as they wished. So he **dismissed** Parliament and imposed **taxes** without its consent. He sacked **judges** who ruled against him in the courts and named **five Major-Generals** to govern the country. They imposed a **Puritan-like** system of rule. In **1656**, because of a **war with Spain**, Cromwell called a Parliament to discuss taxation. Although only 'special' people were allowed to be candidates in the election, some MPs criticised his rule. Once again he dismissed Parliament and used the army to help him collect taxes.

2 Cartoon showing the Scottish rebels

Extract A Cromwell on the massacre at Drogheda, September 1649

The enemy were about 3000 strong in the town. They made a stout resistance. Nearly 1000 of our men entered, but the enemy forced them out. God gave a new courage to our men: they entered again and beat the enemy from their defences. They had made three fortifications to left and right of where we entered, out of which they were forced to leave. We refused them quarter. I believe we put to the sword the whole number of defendants. I do not think 30 of them escaped. Those that did are in safe custody waiting to be sent to the Barbadoes. I am persuaded this is the righteous judgement of God upon these barbarous wretches who dipped their hands in innocent blood.
(Letter, 16 September 1649)

Extract B Cromwell's Irish land settlement

This, by far the worst part of Cromwell's work within the British islands, outlived him largely in the form he gave it. It completed the transfer of the soil from Irish to British owners, which had begun under the Tudors and pushed forward under the Stuarts. The object was three-fold: to pay off in Irish land the soldiers who had fought and the capitalists who had provided the money for the conquest; secondly to render the English hold upon Ireland secure against a rebellion like that of 1641; and lastly, to stamp out Catholicism. The first two objects were attained.

(Illustrated History of England, **G.R. Trevelyan, 1926)**

Extract C Cromwell on the Battle of Dunbar, 3 September 1650

The enemy's numbers were great – about 6000 horse and 16 000 foot at least: ours, about 7500 foot and 3500 horse. We resolved to put our business into this position: that six regiments of horse and a half of foot should march in the van... Colonel Monk to command the foot. The horse beat back all opposition, charging through the enemy's horse and foot; who were made by the Lord of Hosts as stubble to their swords. It became a total rout – about 3000 slain.

(Letter to Speaker of Parliament, 4 September 1650)

3 Cromwell dismissing the Rump Parliament

THE YOUNG HISTORIAN AT WORK

Knowledge and understanding

1 (a) When did Cromwell show the most ruthlessness in his dealing with EACH of **(i)** the Irish; **(ii)** the Scots; **(iii)** Parliament? **(b)** What were **(i)** similar but **(ii)** different about the ways in which Parliament was treated by Charles I and Cromwell?

2 Look again at pages 66–7. Then study these pages. What do you learn about the effects of the Civil War **(i)** in the short term; **(ii)** in the long term?

Interpretation

1 Read *extract A*. **(a)** Does Cromwell's letter contain statements of **(i)** fact OR **(ii)** opinion OR **(iii)** a mixture of both? Explain your answer.
(b) How do you think that the Catholic Irish interpretation of the events at Drogheda differs from that given by Cromwell?

2 Read *extract B*. **(a)** How does the author interpret the aims of, and the success of, Cromwell's Irish policies? **(b)** Do you agree with Trevelyan's interpretation of Cromwell's policy and success? Why? **(c)** How do you think the Irish interpreted Cromwell's policies?

Use of sources

1 Read *extract C*. **(a)** How valuable is this account to historians examining Cromwell's military methods in Scotland? **(b)** Do you think that this source is likely to be reliable as a record of **(i)** what happened at Dunbar, and **(ii)** Cromwell's conquest of Scotland? Why?

2 (a) Do you think that *picture 1* is a reliable guide to the effect of Cromwell's land policy in Ireland? **(b)** What other sorts of primary sources would help us write a full account of the impact of Cromwell on Ireland?

Project

1 Look at *picture 3*. You are present at Cromwell's dismissal of the Rump Parliament. Write the speeches made by **(i)** Cromwell and **(ii)** MPs who were being thrown out of the Commons by Cromwell and the army.

2 Draw a cartoon, like that in *picture 2*, to celebrate Cromwell's invasion of Scotland.

CROWN AND PARLIAMENT, 1660 – 88

In **May 1660**, English politicians invited the exiled Charles II to return as King. By the **Treaty of Breda**, **he was allowed (i)** to decide when elections were to be held and when Parliament was to meet; **(ii)** to choose his ministers. He, in turn, **had to agree (i)** to pardon his enemies; **(ii)** to allow freedom of worship; **(iii)** not to restore land to former Royalists. **Charles broke his promises** (extract A). The **1662** 'Cavalier' Parliament let him **execute** those who had signed his father's death warrant (picture 1) and to **dig up and burn** the bodies of Cromwell, Ireton and Bradshaw. His chief minister, **Clarendon**, pushed through the **anti-Puritan Act of Uniformity** (extract B). The **Clarendon Code** banned Puritans from places on local councils, the universities, and the army and navy. People who attended non-Anglican churches were fined or imprisoned.

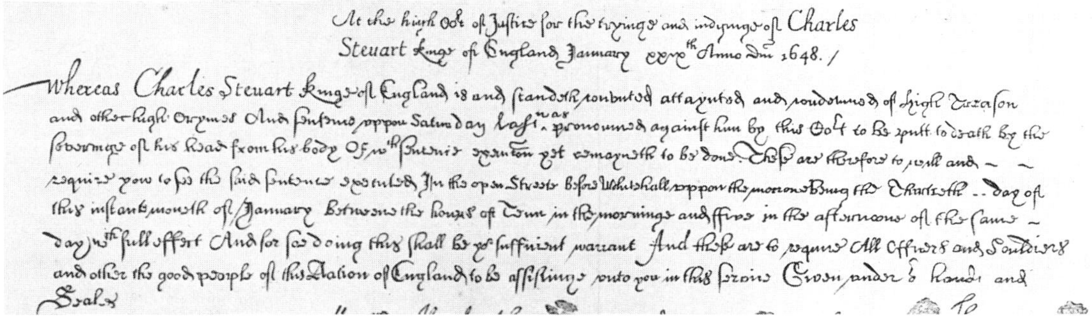

[handwritten 17th-century document]

1 The death warrant of Charles I

By the **Declaration of Indulgence** (**1672**) Charles abolished all anti-Catholic laws. In the **Treaty of Dover**, Louis XIV of France gave him £170 000 a year as a reward for his Catholic policies, and to help pay for England's part in the war against the Protestant Dutch. However, in **1673**, Parliament refused to give Charles the taxes he needed to pay for that war until he withdrew his Act of Indulgence and accepted Parliament's anti-Catholic Test Act (extract C). The **Earl of Shaftesbury** led the anti-Royalists, and **London merchants** gave the money to bring out the **London mob** in anti-Catholic riots. Shaftesbury's followers were nicknamed '**Whigs**' and they called the Royalist Catholics '**Tories**'. The Commons approved Shaftesbury's **Exclusion Bill** (extract D) but it was rejected in the Lords. In **1683** Shaftesbury's plan to murder the King at **Rye House** was foiled and the plotters executed. Shaftesbury lost popularity and **James II's** accession to the throne was welcomed by Tories and many Whigs. Once Monmouth's rebellion had failed, James seemed safe and Parliament gave him the money to maintain a **full-time army**, something they had refused Charles II. However, James tried to **govern without Parliament** and adopted a set of **Catholic policies**: **(i)** he appointed Catholics to important posts in **government and army**; **(ii)** he **abolished anti-Catholic laws** and got the courts to agree to this (extract E); **(iii)** he issued a **Declaration of Indulgence in 1685**; **(iv)** in 1688 he arrested **seven bishops** who refused to have the Declaration read in their churches. The courts freed them (picture 2), a sign that his Catholic policies were illegal and unpopular.

2 The seven bishops are released

Fears that his **new-born son** would ensure a **Catholic succession** led Tory and Whig politicians to unite in inviting **William of Orange** to take the throne. He was James' nephew and married to his daughter, **Mary**. James II's navy, led by Catholics, was kept in London by unfavourable winds: James' chief general, **Churchill**, left him to side with William. James fled the country and **William and Mary were crowned** as joint monarchs.

Extract A Charles II a clever deceiver, says a bishop of Salisbury

He charmed all who came near him, till they found how little they could depend on fair promises. He seemed to have no sense of religion but disguised his Popery to the last. He thought a King checked by a Parliament was only a King in name.

(*A History of His Own Time*, Geoffrey Burnett, 1643 – 1711)

Extract B Betraying Breda: The Act of Uniformity, 1662

All clergy shall be bound to use the Book of Common Prayer, and shall before the Feast of St Bartholomew, before his congregation declare his consent to the use of all things in that Book.

Extract C Parliament becomes anti-Catholic, 1673

The holder of any civil or military office must take the Sacrament of the Eucharist according to the rites of the Church of England, and make a declaration against the Catholic doctrine of the Mass.

(Test Act, 1673)

Extract D Parliament tries to keep James, Duke of York, off the throne, 1679

The Duke of York being a Papist, and the hope of his coming to the throne, have given the greatest encouragement to present conspiracies, a Bill be brought in to prevent the Duke from inheriting the Crown.

(Exclusion Bill, 1679)

Extract E The Courts accept James II's Dispensing Powers, 1686

There is no law that cannot be dispensed by the lawgiver. We declare that the King may dispense any law, that this is not a trust given to the King by the people, but is the sovereign power of the Kings of England which never yet was taken from them, nor can be.

(Chief Justice Herbert, 1686)

THE YOUNG HISTORIAN AT WORK

Knowledge and understanding

1 (a) Show how Charles II passed laws that **(i)** angered Puritans; **(ii)** angered Catholics.
(b) Why was Charles II forced to pass such laws? **(c)** What were the effects of Charles II's religious policies?

2 Here is a list of reasons for James II's fall: His policies towards Catholics; the birth of his Catholic son; his giving government posts to his friends; bad luck with the wind; politicians' preference for William and Mary rather than James.
(a) Put these reasons for James' fall in their order of importance and explain your choice of order.
(b) Look back at pages 62–3 and 66–7 and make a list of long-term causes for James II's fall.

Interpretation

1 How should we use *extracts A and B* to decide whether Charles II was faithful to the promises he made in the Treaty of Breda?

2 Do you have enough evidence to say that 'James II deserved to lose his throne because he did not learn from the mistakes made by James I and Charles I and II'?

Use of sources

1 How valuable are *extracts C and D* to historians trying to judge the depth of anti-Catholic feeling among many sections of the English people?

2 How reliable is *extract E* in helping us to judge how popular James II's view of kingship was in England? Give reasons for your answer.

Project

1 Look at *picture 2*. Write a conversation between a supporter of James II and a supporter of the bishops, as to whether the King should lose the throne.

2 Look at page 68, picture 2. Draw a cartoon which EITHER **(i)** favoured James II OR **(ii)** was drawn by an opponent of the King.

CROWN AND PARLIAMENT, 1688 – 1750

William of Orange, a firm Protestant, was leading the Dutch War against **Catholic Louis XIV**. He wanted **English aid** and so he accepted the idea of a **joint monarchy**. His wife, **Mary**, **James II's daughter**, provided Parliament with the excuse that it was replacing one Stuart with another.

The Bill of Rights (February 1689) imposed by Parliament, made sure that William and Mary would be unable to rule without its consent. It said:

1 Monarchs could not suspend or abolish **laws** unless Parliament agreed.
2 Taxes could not be imposed without Parliament's consent.
3 There was to be no full-time **army** during peace time.
4 Protestants were allowed to have **armaments** in their homes.
5 Elections were to be free from royal interference.
6 Parliament was to meet 'frequently' and **had to meet** at least once a year to vote the money needed by the monarchs.
7 MPs were to have **freedom of speech and debate**.

Parliament's powers were further increased by **(i)** the **Mutiny Act (1689)** which limited the Crown's power over the army in wartime; **(ii)** the **Triennial Act (1694)** which said that elections had to be held every three years; **(iii) the Act of Settlement** *(extract A)*; on William's death (Mary having died in 1694), the Crown was to go to **Princess Anne**, James II's second daughter. If she died childless, the Crown was then to go the family of **Sophia of Hanover**, James I's granddaughter.

Monarchs had certain powers – they could choose their Cabinets *(extracts B and C)*, but they could govern only with the approval of Parliament. **Queen Anne** (1702 – 14) chose both **Whigs and Tories** for her ministers, as William had done *(extract B)*. She knew that the **Tories** wanted to bring **James II's son** to the throne. Indeed, when she died, they invited him to become King. He would not give up his Catholicism so **George of Hanover** became King. He spoke little English and rarely went to Cabinet meetings: ministers had to choose a chairman, or **first (Prime) Minister**. George feared that the Tories might bring a Stuart from exile so he named **only Whigs** as his ministers.

George II might have tried to take personal charge of government. His wife knew that they were safer with the Whigs *(extract C)*. So from 1714 to at least 1760, the Whigs were in power, popular because **(i)** they **avoided war** and allowed **trade** to grow; **(ii)** they **lowered import and export duties** which lowered prices; **(iii)** they **lowered taxes**, especially land taxes, which pleased the Tory landowners. **Walpole** *(picture 2)*, Prime Minister from 1721 to 1740, knew how to use the **Government's power** to buy the support of many MPs *(extract D)*. Under this 'corrupt' system England had the first industrial revolution.

1 Queen Anne

Extract A The Act of Settlement, 1701

That whoever shall come to the Crown shall join communion with the Church of England. That if the Crown come to anyone not a native of England, this nation be not bound to engage in war for the defence of any territories which do not belong to the Crown. That no one coming to the Crown shall leave the country without the consent of Parliament. That no one born out of these kingdoms shall be a Member of Parliament, or have any office, civil or military, from the Crown.

Extract B Which party can William III trust?

The Tories, friends to the Crown's power, are so friendly to the Jacobites that they cannot be trusted during the war. The Whigs, who support you in the war, will do all they can to lessen your power.

(Godolphin, Chancellor of the Exchequer, to the King, 1693)

2 Robert Walpole

Extract C George II (1727 - 60), Prime Minister and Cabinet

Queen Caroline changed George II's first plan. He meant to have his ministers as mere clerks, not to give advice but to take orders. He meant to listen to all sides. The Queen persuaded him that he should have only one minister, and that it was essential that Walpole be that one. The King's behaviour to Walpole changed; instead of hating him, he employed him, and took every opportunity to declare him his first, or rather his only, minister. He was content to bargain for his two main interests – Hanover and money.

(*Memoirs of the Reign of George II*, Lord Hervey, edited in 1884)

Extract D 'Every man has his price'; the King can buy MPs, 1690

Two hundred MPs gain from friendship with the Government – getting jobs, commissions in the Forces, contracts for supplying the Forces and so on. Think of the votes that this number have in the House, which they are ready to attend, more eager to destroy our constitution than the rest are to preserve it. They do not represent the country, but themselves; they always keep together, vote always the same way as if they were no longer free agents but so many engines turned by a mechanic motion.

(A pamphlet published in 1690)

THE YOUNG HISTORIAN AT WORK

Knowledge and understanding

1 Under William and Mary the powers of the monarchy were limited by a growth in Parliament's power. **(a)** Comment on how those developments were brought about by **(i)** the Bill of Rights; **(ii)** laws about the army and about elections; **(iii)** laws about William and Mary's successors. **(b)** How is modern Britain affected by the changes introduced in the period 1689 – 1750?

2 Queen Anne, George I and George II allowed Parliament to develop its powers. Which groups **(i)** gained and **(ii)** lost during these reigns?

Interpretation

1 Do you agree that the 'revolution' which brought William and Mary and their successors to the throne was a 'Glorious Revolution'? Give the arguments for AND against this description of events.

2 Do *extracts B and D* show that William was a stronger King than the Stuart Kings? Why?

Use of sources

1 How does *extract A* help us to understand **(i)** the power of Parliament in 1701; **(ii)** the failure of the Catholic Stuarts to regain the throne in 1714 and 1745 (pages 74–5); **(iii)** the problems that would have been created in our time if Prince Charles had married the Catholic Princess Marie of Luxembourg (as was once thought to be possible).

2 Is *extract C* a reliable guide to historians writing about George II, Queen Caroline and Walpole? Give reasons for your answer, and show how we could check the reliability of the statements made in this extract.

Project

1 Make a timeline of events between 1688 and 1750, showing the people who helped 'make' modern Britain.

2 Write to your local MP (you can get his/her name from the local library). Ask about the Party to which he/she belongs, and about the work of an MP.

GREAT BRITAIN: THE UNION WITH SCOTLAND

Protestant nobles in the Scottish Lowlands welcomed the new monarchs in **1688**. **Catholic Highlanders** rebelled in favour of James II (James VII of Scotland). Led by **Viscount Claverhouse** ('Bonnie Dundee') they defeated the English at **Killiecrankie** (**1689**). But Dundee was killed; without him, the clans scattered and Scotland settled to rule by James' daughter and her Dutch husband.

In **1691** the monarchs decided that **highland chiefs** had to take an **oath of loyalty**. When **Macdonald of Glencoe** was late in taking the oath, **Campbell of Glenlyon** was sent to punish him *(extract)*. All Highlanders were outraged. **Lowlanders, too**, came to hate William because of the **Darien scheme** (1695). Scots had raised huge sums of money to send colonists to the Darien Isthmus near Panama, hoping to get the sort of profits made by colonists elsewhere. However, the Spaniards, already in Panama, drove the Scots away and **William supported the Spaniards**, his allies in his war against France.

Scotland's hostility was shown by the Scottish Parliament's refusal to pass the **Act of Settlement** (page 72, extract A). It went on to pass the **Act of Security** (**1704**) which said that Scotland would **restore the Stuarts** unless the English helped Scottish trade to develop. In reply the English passed the **Aliens Act** (**1705**): all Scots were to be treated as 'foreigners' and there would be no trade between the two countries until Scotland accepted the Act of Settlement. Politicians in both countries knew that **this hostility ought to end**: Scotland was too poor to fight England and was becoming poorer: England, on the other hand, feared a Franco-Scottish alliance. So, after much negotiating, the **Act of Union** was passed by both Parliaments in 1707 *(picture 1)*. It said that:

1 The Scottish Parliament was to be abolished: Scotland would elect 45 MPs to the Westminster House of Commons and 16 nobles to sit in the Lords.

2 Scotland accepted the Act of Settlement but was allowed to have its own Church and separate legal system.

1 The Act of Union being presented to Queen Anne

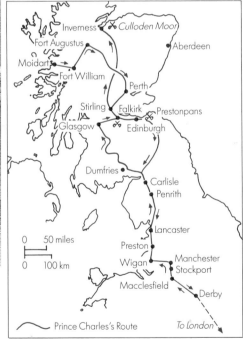

2 'Bonnie Prince Charlie's' campaign, 1745

3 Scottish merchants were to trade freely with England and her colonies.

Highlanders disliked the Act of Union. When Queen Anne died in **1714**, the **Earl of Mar** raised the Stuart standard at **Perth** and named James Edward Stuart as James III. Mar and the Jacobites hoped to get French help: but Louis XIV had just died and his infant son was in the hands of a Regent who was afraid to go to war in case France suffered another humiliation by the English like the one imposed by the Treaty of Utrecht (page 57, extract D). Nor did the silent and ineffective James inspire the Highlanders: after the indecisive battle of **Sherriffmuir**, Mar and James left to live in France.

In **1745** James' son, **Prince Charles Edward**, took advantage of the war going on between England and France to **raise a revolt in Scotland**. The **Highlanders** proclaimed him King at **Perth** and, as the map shows *(picture 2)* he conquered **Scotland**, invaded **England**, won several victories and got as far as **Derby**. **George II** thought he was to lose his throne. But the Scots were discouraged by the lack of support in England and, after several disputes between clan chiefs, they retreated to Scotland.

During the winter of **1745 – 6**, George II's son, the **Duke of Cumberland**, led an English army to Scotland. On 15 April he found the Highlanders' army at **Culloden Moor** near Inverness. Better armed and fed, and with the benefit of surprise, his forces slaughtered the clansmen and their families. Other **rebel chiefs** were captured and either executed or sent to imprisonment in America. All the Highlanders' homes were destroyed, their cattle and horses taken away, all their land given to 'loyal' chiefs. **Clan chiefs** were deprived of their traditional powers and laws were passed banning the wearing of the kilt and the playing of bagpipes.

Charles escaped to France. Many Scots remembered the '**bold Chevalier**' who had gone '**over the sea to Skye**' and they wondered '**will ye no come back again?**' He never did.

Extract The Massacre at Glencoe, February 1692

Glenlyon, one of the (Campbell) Earl of Argyle's regiment, with Lieutenant Lindsay and six score soldiers returned to Glencoe, were billeted and had kind entertainment, living familiarly with the people. But on 13 February about four or five in the morning, Lindsay with a party of soldiers came to Glencoe's house, called in a friendly manner, and got in; they shot his father dead as he was rising from his bed; the mother having got up and put on her clothes, the soldiers stripped her naked and drew the rings from her fingers with their teeth. At Innerriggen, where Glenlyon was quartered, soldiers took nine other men, bound them hand and foot and killed them one by one. The slaughter was made by Glenlyon and his soldiers after they had lived peaceably with the Glencoe men about 13 days; the number slain was about 25 and after the slaughter the soldiers did burn the houses, barns and goods, and carried away horse, cattle and sheep above 1000.

(**Commission into the Slaughter of the Men of Glencoe, 1695**)

THE YOUNG HISTORIAN AT WORK

Knowledge and understanding

1 Show how the following groups reacted to English attempts to conquer them:
(i) Catholic Highlanders, 1688 – 89;
(ii) Lowland merchants after 1695;
(iii) Scottish politicians, 1704 – 5;
(iv) the followers of 'Bonnie' Prince Charles Edward Stuart, 1745 – 6.

2 (a) Make a list of the reasons for the English defeat of the Scots.
(b) Read pages 60–1 and 72–3 and make a list of long-term reasons for the English unwillingness to support the Jacobites in 1745.
(c) How did the English conquest of Scotland affect Scotland **(i)** in the short term; **(ii)** in the long term?

Interpretation

1 Do you agree that the Jacobite cause was bound to fail? Why?

2 Read the *extract*. How differently do you think the massacre was interpreted by **(i)** William III; **(ii)** Catholic Highlanders; **(iii)** Lowlanders like Campbell?

Use of sources

1 Read the *extract*. **(a)** What does it tell you about **(i)** the ruthlessness of William's forces; **(ii)** the nature of Highland society; **(iii)** reasons for the defeat of the Highlanders by the English and their allies?
(b) Do you think that this source is likely to be a reliable account of the massacre? Why?

Project

1 Make a timeline of England's relations with Scotland, using the information on these pages. Show the key events and people involved in the relationship.

2 Look at *picture 1*. Write a conversation between Scots who **(i)** supported; **(ii)** opposed English rule.

UNHAPPY IRELAND, 1689 – 1750

James II appointed Catholics as judges, officers in the army and as ministers in an Irish government headed by the Catholic Tyrconnel, which **refused to accept William and Mary in 1688**. In **March 1689 James II** landed at Kinsale with a French army, hoping to use **Ireland as a base** for the conquest of England and Scotland. The **French hoped to make Ireland an ally** in the war against Protestant William. The **Catholic-Irish and Anglo-Irish nobles** looked forward to their independence from English rule, although the **Ulster Protestants** feared rule by a Catholic government (page 65, picture 3).

In **May 1689**, the Catholic-controlled Dublin Parliament **(i)** cancelled land settlements made by English Kings; **(ii)** declared its independence from the English Parliament; **(iii)** named 2000 Protestants as 'traitors', so increasing Protestant fears.

Between **April and June 1689**, Tyrconnel's army, aided by the French, besieged **Derry** (extract A). After 105 days the Protestants there welcomed the London fleet which broke the boom and relieved the city. In **August 1689** William's army went to fight Tyrconnel: in June 1690 William led his forces to victory over James' army at the **Battle of the Boyne** (extract B) and James fled.

The **English** then set about strengthening their **grip on Ireland** in several ways:

1 Political – the Irish Parliament was allowed to exist, but the Westminster Act (1719) said that its decisions were not legal until confirmed by the English Parliament, while every law passed in Westminster would apply in Ireland (picture 1).

1 The Irish Parliament in session

2 Penal Laws were passed to **punish Catholics**, five-sixths of the population.
Political: along with Presbyterians, they were deprived of the vote.
Social: Catholics were forbidden to **(i)** stand in elections; **(ii)** become army officers; **(iii)** become civil servants; **(iv)** be town councillors; **(v)** send their children to school; **(vi)** wear a sword (the mark of a gentleman); **(vii)** own a horse worth more than £5 – any horse had to be sold to a Protestant who offered £5 for it.
Religious: bishops, nuns and monks were banned; priests had to register with local authorities who tried to stop churches being built (picture 2); Catholics had to pay one-tenth of their income to the local Anglican church.
Land: **(i)** Catholic landowners had to leave their land to be divided between all their children: in time no Catholic would own any sizeable estate (picture 3); **(ii)** Catholic tenants had to accept the harsh terms offered by Protestant landowners (extract C).

3 Protestants as well as Catholics suffered from laws which **(i)** banned the development of any industry which might challenge an English one: the Irish could not have a woollen industry; **(ii)** prevented Irish merchants from trading freely with England, its colonies or the rest of the world.

It is not surprising that, later in the 18th century, Ireland became the centre of more anti-English unrest.

2 Going to Mass in a chapel on wheels

Extract A The siege of Londonderry, 1689
Dublin: June 12

There are fewer than 5000 in the King's camp at Derry, a great many have run away. We hear that some English ships are in the Lough of Derry: a boom of trees is across the river to stop any help arriving. I believe in a while they will be short of clothes, drink and coal. Many Catholics are angry about the French, for the natives are suspicious of them. Putting French officers in place of Irish ones caused great discontent, many soldiers ran away because of it.
(Letter of Intelligence, Somers Tracts, Vol. II)

Extract B James II runs away, July 1690

The attempt to starve out Derry, the last important Protestant stronghold, failed. In August (1689) the Huguenot general Schomberg landed in Ulster and in the following summer (1690) was joined by William himself. James advanced to the Boyne, 30 miles north of Dublin, to give battle. On 1 July the Catholics were defeated. James himself fled in haste: 'I do now resolve to shift for myself,' he told courtiers, and he was at Duncannon, on board ship for France, before William entered Dublin.
(*Illustrated History of the British Monarchy*, J. Cannon and R. Griffiths, 1988)

Extract C The land problem

The terms on which the Irish peasant rented the land were harsh and deprived him of any incentive and security. When his lease expired any improvement he had made in his holding became the property of the landlord. Then the majority were 'tenants at will', that is 'the will' of the landlord. He could turn them out whenever he chose.
(*The Great Hunger*, Cecil Woodham Smith, 1962)

03	90% / 10%
41	60% / 40%
88	20% / 80%
03	14% / 86%
78	4% / 96%

☐ Protestants   ☐ Catholics

3 Transfer of ownership of land 1603-1778

THE YOUNG HISTORIAN AT WORK

Knowledge and understanding

1 (a) Using pages 62–3, 64–5, and 72–3 make a list of long-term causes for the growth of Anglo-Irish hostility. **(b)** Next to each cause, indicate whether the causes were social, political, religious, economic or caused by individuals.
(c) Using pages 70–1, list the short term reasons for the Battle of the Boyne.

2 (a) List, in order of importance, the effects of William's conquest of Ireland in **(i)** the short term to 1719 and **(ii)** the long term, from 1720 until today. Explain your choice of order of importance. **(b)** Do you think there were any years in which anti-Catholic laws were intensified?

Interpretation

1 How do you think the evidence in *pictures 1 and 2 and extract C* were interpreted by **(i)** Irish Catholics; **(ii)** Irish Protestants; **(iii)** English politicians?

2 Do you think the evidence shows that the English found the conquest of Ireland more or less difficult than their conquest of Scotland? Give reasons for your answer.

Use of sources

1 (a) Read *extracts A and B*. How are these useful in explaining **(i)** why the Catholics lost to William; **(ii)** the character of James II?
(b) Do these extracts reveal anything about the points of view of the authors and their reliability? **(c)** How could we check the accuracy of these sources?

2 (a) How does *extract C* provide evidence about **(i)** the viewpoint of the author; **(ii)** Catholic–Protestant relations? **(b)** What primary sources should we use to check the author's statements?

Project

1 Look at *picture 1*. Write the speeches of **(i)** an Irish opponent of English rule; **(ii)** a supporter of English rule.

2 Draw a map of modern Ireland. Mark on the map the major towns and cities, and the part of Ireland still controlled by the British Parliament.

EXPANSION, TRADE AND INDUSTRY: BRITAIN 1750 – 1900

MORE PEOPLE AND NEW PLACES

Picture 1 shows that in 1700 the most populated areas were the South, South-West and East Anglia. Even there, the population was small: in 1700 Middlesex had the **sort of population density found in modern Devon**. Towns were small by modern standards (page 58) and most people lived in villages (page 54).

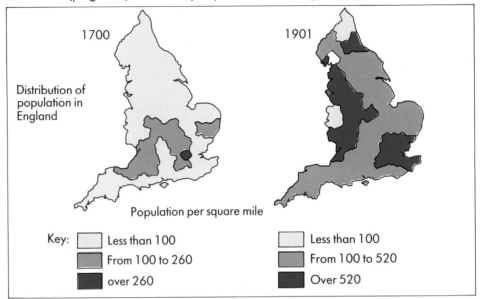

Distribution of population in England

1700   1901

Population per square mile

Key:
- Less than 100
- From 100 to 260
- over 260

- Less than 100
- From 100 to 520
- Over 520

1 Population in England, 1700   **2** Population in England, 1901

Picture 2 shows the distribution of the population in **1901**. Now the most densely populated areas lie around the **coalfields**, sites of the **industrial revolution** (page 82). *Picture 3* is based on official censuses, the first of which took place in 1801. It shows that the **proportion of people living in towns** has grown continually. The following list gives the populations of some towns in thousands: the first figure shows the population in **1801**, the figure in brackets gives the population in **1911**. Notice by how much these towns grew between 1801 and 1911. **Leicester** 17 (212); **Blackburn** 12 (129); **Stoke-on-Trent** 23 (215); **Bradford** 13 (290); **Sheffield** 46 (407); **Manchester** 70 (645); **Liverpool** 82 (704).

The growth of these and other towns was a reflection of the overall growth of **the population** of England and Wales shown in census returns: **1801** 11.5 million; **1831** 17.8 million; **1861** 24.5 million; **1901** 42.1 million. Was the population growth due to an **increase in the birth rate** *(extract A)* or to a **fall in the death rate** *(extracts B and C)*? *Picture 4* shows a decline in the death rate. *Picture 5* shows how, towards the end of the century, the birth rate declined and middle class families were smaller; the **working class** would imitate their 'betters' by having smaller families in the 1930s.

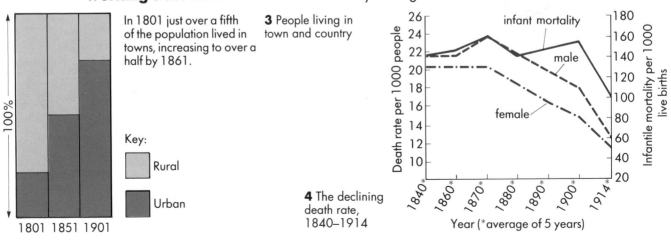

In 1801 just over a fifth of the population lived in towns, increasing to over a half by 1861.

3 People living in town and country

Key:
- Rural
- Urban

1801 1851 1901

4 The declining death rate, 1840–1914

infant mortality

male

female

Death rate per 1000 people

Infantile mortality per 1000 live births

1840* 1860* 1870* 1880* 1890* 1900* 1914*

Year (*average of 5 years)

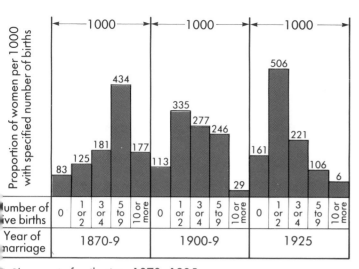

Proportion of women per 1000 with specified number of births		83	125	181	434	177	113	335	277	246	29	161	506	221	106	6
Number of live births	0	1 or 2	3 or 4	5 to 9	10 or more	0	1 or 2	3 or 4	5 to 9	10 or more	0	1 or 2	3 or 4	5 to 9	10 or more
Year of marriage	1870-9					1900-9					1925				

5 Changes in family size, 1870–1925

Extract A Growing towns, 1774

The national wealth increased the demand for labour and raised wages which led to an increase in the birth rate. Why had the population of Birmingham increased from 23 000 in 1750 to 30 000 in 1770? Because there has been an increase in employment, more marriages and, because children are not a burden, more births. As soon as a child can use its hands it can maintain itself, and the parents, too, are fully employed.
(*Political Arithmetic*, Arthur Young, 1774)

Extract B The growth of London, 1800

Much of the growth in population is due to better health conditions, the improvement in medical knowledge, and the improved habits among the people who are cleaner, in homes and habits, than they used to be, partly because of cheaper clothing from our cotton factories, partly because of better knowledge about running the household.
(*Account of Persons Imprisoned for Debt in England and Wales*, Arthur Nield, 1800)

Exract C Growing national population, 1812

The country should be congratulated on the growth in population and on its ability to provide the people with food. (**Parliamentary debates, 1812**)

Extract D The growth of Middlesbrough, 1811-1901

It is surprising when one sees the crowded Middlesbrough of today, to see that in 1831 the population was 154; then the railways were begun and in 1841 the population was 5463. In 1850 ironstone was discovered in the Cleveland Hills within reach of the Durham coal fields, making Middlesbrough an ironmaking centre. The population grew from 18 892 (1861) to 39 284 (1871) and 91 302 (1901). And at the moment of writing, the census of 1911 gives the population as 104 787.
(*At the Works*, Lady (Florence) Bell, 1911)

Extract E Malthus on population growth, 1798

Malthus made three main points:
(i) The supply of food necessarily limits population.
(ii) If population is free from all checks, it will be increased in geometrical progression, i.e. 2, 4, 8, 16 and so on, but food supply will increase only in an arithmetic progression, i.e. 1, 2, 3, 4 and so on.
(iii) Three checks operate to keep population in line with food supply: these are moral restraint, vice and misery.
(Adapted from *An Essay on the Principle of Population*, T.R. Malthus, 1798)

THE YOUNG HISTORIAN AT WORK

Knowledge and understanding

1 (a) Show that the growth of population varied in pace in different parts of England.
(b) Use the text and *extracts A and B* to help make a list of the reasons for the increase in population 1750–1901.

2 (a) Take the list of reasons you made and put them in their order of importance, explaining your choice of order. **(b)** Use the maps, text and extracts to help you write a page about 'the changing face of Britain' in which you show how agriculture, industry and population affected each other.

Interpretation

1 Read *extracts C and E*. **(a)** How would selection of these extracts affect our interpretation of the effects of rising population? **(b)** What reasons can you give for the different interpretations in these two extracts?

2 Read *extract B* and look at the maps. Do these sources support the views expressed in **(i)** *extract C* OR **(ii)** *extract E*?

Use of sources

1 Read *extract D* and look at *pictures 1–3*. How is the extract valuable to historians in a different way from the pictures, as explanations of the effects of a growing population?

2 (a) In what ways are *pictures 4 and 5* valuable to historians trying to discover patterns of family size and mortality rates? **(b)** Are these figures likely to be accurate? Why?

Project

1 Ask your local library to help you find local census returns for your area. When you have them, find what happened to the population of the area at different times between 1750 and 1901. You might be able to use a computer to help you examine the census returns.

2 Make graphs to show the growth of the populations of the towns named on page 78.

CHANGES IN FARMING, 1750 – 1846

Successful British farmers (page 55, extract A) produced enough food to feed the **rising population** (page 79, extract C). They continued to **reduce their costs** and to make their **land more productive**, sometimes because of **falling prices** *(picture 1)*, later to take advantage of **rising prices** and the **export market** *(picture 2)*. In East Anglia and the Midlands most farming followed the **medieval three-field system** *(picture 3)*. **After 1750** most of this land was **enclosed** and strips exchanged to make compact

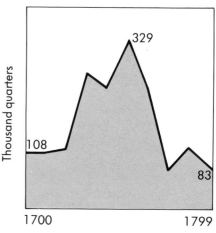

1 Wheat prices, 1750–1879
Figures are in shillings per quarter

2 Wheat and flour exports 1700 –99
Figures are in thousand quarters

farms. Sometimes this was done **by a simple agreement** between those concerned: sometimes it needed a **private Act of Parliament** *(extract A)*. **General Acts** passed in **1801** and after made things simpler. **Some suffered by enclosure**: tenants who **could not prove a legal case** for a tenancy got nothing; others could not pay for the fencing and sold out. The worst off were those who had tilled a few acres on the common; they lost everything *(extract B)*. **Many farmers gained**, especially if they used the Norfolk system *(extract C)*. **Consumers** gained from the **extra supply of food**, including **fresh meat** once stockbreeders had shown how to produce larger animals which were fed through the winter on turnips and the new grasses.

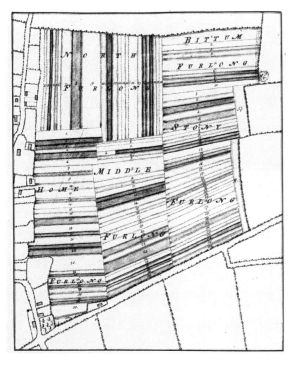

3 Records of the three-field system, Strettington, Sussex

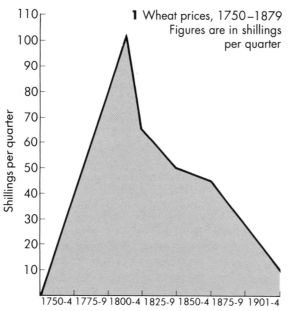

4 Cartoon showing Pitt as the butcher and the starving poor

During the **Napoleonic Wars prices rose** sharply, and life was hard for the lower paid and unemployed *(picture 4)*. **After the Wars**, landowners in the unreformed Parliament (page 88) pushed through **Corn Laws** which banned wheat imports until British prices were very high. When the **middle classes** got their share of political power (page 89) they used it to get **those Laws repealed** *(extract D)*. British farmers did not suffer – at least, at first (pages 98–9).

Extract A An 'Inclosure' Act, 1766

February 3 1766: Mr Cholmley presented to the House a Bill for inclosing and dividing the commons and open fields... in Stillington. Read for the first time.

February 10 1766: A Bill for inclosing... Stillington was read a second time.

February 27 1766: Mr Cholmley reported from the Committee to whom the Bill had been committed. It had examined the Bill, found that the Parties concerned had given their consent, except a few who refused and some who were not at home. No one appeared before the Committee to object. Ordered: the Bill be printed.

March 3 1766: A Bill for inclosing... Stillington was read the Third Time. Resolved: That the Bill do pass.

(Parliamentary Debates, 1766)

Extract B Losers from enclosure, 1799

Time was when these commons enabled a poor man to support his family. Here he could put out his cow and pony, feed his geese and pig. Enclosures have deprived him of these advantages. He now has only 14d per day to keep himself, wife and five or six children when bread is 3d per pound. Now the parish must assist him. Poor rates rise to a terrible height.

(*Walking Tour*, Richard Warren, 1799)

Extract C New farming, Norfolk, 1771

...to give a review of the husbandry which makes this country so famous. Great improvements have been made by means of the following:

First: by inclosing without the assistance of Parliament.

Second: by the use of marl (powdered rock and lime) and clay.

Third: rotation of crops: (i) turnips; (ii) barley; (iii) clover; (iv) wheat.

Fourth: by the culture of turnips well hand-hoed.

Fifth: by the culture of clover and ray-grass.

Sixth: by the landlords granting long leases.

Seventh: by the county being divided into large farms.

(*The Farmer's Tour*, Arthur Young, 1771)

Extract D Against the Corn Laws and for Free Trade, 1833

I am a manufacturer of clothing. Did you ever hear any debates in the House to fix the price of clothing in the market? When I went to Normandy they said to me; 'Admit our corn and then we'll import your clothing. We are millions, willing to buy your clothes, and you have millions of hungry mouths ready to take our corn.' To pay for that corn we would have to increase our exports which would increase the demand for workers and clear the streets of the two million unemployed that now exist.

(*Speeches*, Richard Cobden MP, edited in 1870)

THE YOUNG HISTORIAN AT WORK

Knowledge and understanding

1 (a) Show how 'progress' in agriculture **(i)** benefited some groups but **(ii)** made life worse for others. **(b)** What were the effects of the changes in agriculture on Britain as a whole?

2 (a) How did the following factors affect farmers: war; rising population; the industrial revolution; Parliament; farmers' education? **(b)** How do you think farmers would have listed those factors in order of importance? Why?

Interpretation

1 (a) How would your interpretation of the Enclosure Movement be affected if you studied ONLY *extract B* OR *extract C*? **(b)** How does the use of both these extracts affect the judgement of historians trying to give a balanced view of the effects of enclosures?

2 (a) What did Cobden *(extract D)* expect would happen to corn prices if the Corn Laws were repealed? **(b)** What light does *picture 1* throw on his expectations?

Use of sources

1 Which is the more valuable to historians writing about the effects of high food prices – *extract D* OR *picture 4*? Why?

2 How can *extract B* be used to explain what life was like for farmers on unenclosed land?

Project

1 Write speeches by **(a)** a supporter of AND **(b)** an opponent of enclosures.

2 You are a farmer in 1845. Write a reply to Cobden *(extract D)* explaining why you support the Corn Laws.

THE FIRST INDUSTRIAL REVOLUTION, 1760 – 1830

In the **domestic system**, merchants took raw material to the cottagers and paid them for the finished work *(extracts A and B, pictures 1 and 2)*. This system could not meet the **increased demand** from **colonial trade** (pages 56 and 102) and **the rising population** (pages 78–79), and inventions were made to increase output *(picture 6)*. **Textile changes**. The output of **spinners** was increased with the help of (i) **the spinning jenny** (1764) *(picture 3)*; (ii) Arkwright's **water frame** (1769) which had to be housed in a factory; (iii) **the 'mule'** (1779) *(picture 4)*.

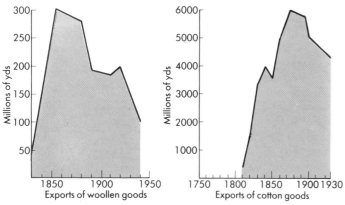

6 The graph shows the export of woollen and cotton goods from 1750 to the 1930s

1 Hand spinning in the 18th century

At first, **handloom weavers** gained from the increased supply of yarn *(picture 2 and extract C)*. They were ruined by the invention of the steam-driven and factory-based **power loom** (1785). **The steam engine** was developed by **James Watt** so that, **after 1786**, it could drive machinery. He was helped by the skill of '**Iron Mad Jack**' **Wilkinson** *(extract D)* who learned to make perfect cylinders while boring cannon for the armed forces: 'from evil something good'.

2 A handloom weaver

Iron and coal were linked by the **Darbys of Coalbrookdale** *(extract F)*. Without their work perhaps none of the other machines could have come about. This shows how one change can lead to other unintended changes.

Capital or money to pay for industrial development came from **families and friends**, **members of the Church** to which industrialists belonged, **local landowners** (page 55, extract B) and from **merchants** (pages 56–7, and page 58, extract A) whose money passed through the **well-developed banking system**.

3 Hargreave's 'Spinning Jenny'

4 Samuel Crompton's 'mule'

Extract A The domestic system

The weaver's workshop was a rural cottage from which he could go to work in his garden if he wanted. The cotton was picked clean by his young children, carded and spun by the older girls and his wife. The yarn was woven by the weaver and his sons. He took in yarn from other spinsters: one weaver could keep three spinners at work.

(*The Philosophy of Manufacturers*, Andrew Ure, 1831)

Extract B Master clothiers cheat the domestic workers

We'll make the poor weaver work at a low rate,
We'll find fault where there is none, and so we will bate (pay less),
If trading goes dead, we will immediately show it,
But if it grows good, they will never know it,
By poor people's labour, we will fill up our purse,
Although we do get it with many a curse.

(*History of Wool and Woolcombing*, John Burnley, 1885)

Extract C The rise and fall of the handloom weaver

They brought home their work in top boots and ruffled shirts, carried a cane and took a coach. They used to walk about the streets with a five pound note in their hat bands... This prosperity did not last. The price for weaving a length of cloth fell to 29 shillings in 1797, and to 6 shillings in 1827. Weavers could not provide for their families although they worked all day.

(*The Life and Times of Samuel Crompton*, Gilbert French, 1860)

Extract D Wilkinson makes cylinders for Watt's engines, 1781

Only after many expensive experiments did Mr Wilkinson achieve perfection in casting and boring which satisfied us. Now we recommend his castings for all our engines.

(Letter from James Watts to a buyer, 1781)

Extract E The marvel of a cotton-spinning factory, 1835

We see a building with a 100 horse-power steam engine with the strength of 880 men, working 50 000 spindles and all the auxiliary machines. It needs only 750 workers to produce as much yarn as would have been spun by 200 000 men: one man now produces as much as 260 did in the old days.

(*History of Cotton*, Edward Baines, 1835)

Extract F The Darbys of Coalbrookdale use coal instead of charcoal

My husband's father tried to smelt iron with coal but it did not work. He then coked the coal into cinders, and this fuel worked. My husband was only six when his father died, but he had his genius and made many improvements. He succeeded in making bar iron from the pig iron using coal. Without these discoveries the iron trade would have died, because wood for charcoal had become very scarce.

(Letter from Mrs Abiah Darby quoted in *Iron and Steel*, Ashton, 1924)

5 The Soho Foundry, Manchester, 1814. Notice the canal – used for carrying goods before the coming of the railways

---

THE YOUNG HISTORIAN AT WORK

Knowledge and understanding

1 Here are some factors which help explain changes in the textile industry. Write them out in their order of importance and explain your choice of order.
Colonial demand; growing population at home; inventions in spinning and weaving; invention of the steam engine; the expansion of the iron industry; war; banks.

2 (a) Show how developments in textiles, iron industry, coal industry and the steam engine all affected one another.
(b) List SIX individuals who played important roles in the first industrial revolution. Which ONE do you think was most important? Why?

Interpretation

1 (a) How would our interpretation of the domestic system differ if we chose to use ONLY *extract A* OR *extract B*? **(b)** How should we check the accuracy of the information in those extracts?

2 Look at *picture 1*. Do you think that it supports the interpretations given in **(i)** *extract A* OR **(ii)** *extract B*? Give reasons for your answer.

Use of sources

1 How can *pictures 4 and 5 and extract E* be used to describe the effects of the first industrial revolution?

2 Which of the sources mentioned in the last question are most valuable for historians writing about **(i)** textile production; **(ii)** child and female workers; **(iii)** the effects of the textile revolution on engineering and on canal transport?

Project

1 You are a handloom weaver (*picture 2*). Give an account of how your life was changed by inventions in **(i)** spinning; **(ii)** weaving. Use *extract C* and the text as guides.

2 You own a textile mill in 1850. Write a letter to a friend abroad explaining why you have become rich. Use *pictures 4 and 6 and extract E* as guides.

FACTORY LIFE AND REFORM, 1780 – 1850

When the factory system was still new, many people wanted a **return to the domestic system** (extract B), in which the cottager chose when to start and end his day (page 82, picture 1 and extract A). **Factory owners** had to force people to accept **fixed times** and to stay by their machines through the day. **Children** were easier to discipline so they were employed (picture 1).

2 Children working in a brickyard

The parish authorities who looked after the poor (page 54) had always sent children to work for master craftsmen (extract A) and they continued to send them to factory owners. It was the fate of these **pauper children** which first roused the interest of reformers. In **1802 Robert Owen and Sir Robert Peel** persuaded Parliament to pass an Act limiting the working day for these children to 12 hours. In **1812 Peel** pushed through an Act which limited the working day for all children working in cotton mills: no child could be employed before the age of nine. But there was **no one appointed to enforce these first Acts**.

1830 – 32 Michael Sadler and Ashley Cooper (later **Lord Shaftesbury**) campaigned for factory reform. A **Parliamentary commission** heard from supporters of reform (extract B), from opponents (extract C) and from good factory owners (extract E).

1833: **the first effective Factory Act** forbade the employment of children under the age of nine and limited older children's working hours (extract D). It also **appointed inspectors** to enforce its conditions. However, it only applied to textile mills. Children still worked in **coal mines** (extract G and picture 3) until the **Mines Act** (**1845**), and in **brickyards** (extract F and picture 2) until education became compulsory in the **1880s**. A **ten hour day campaign** led by **Shaftesbury** forced Parliament to pass Acts in 1844, 1847 and 1850, when, at last, the working day for men and women was fixed at **10 hours**, not including meal times. This was 70 years after Arkwright had opened the first spinning mill at Cromford. **Reform is a slow process**.

1 Children working in a textile mill

Extract A Cruelty to child workers, 1738

It is normal to apprentice poor children to any master living outside the parish; if the child serves him for 40 days we are rid of him for ever. The master may be a tiger in cruelty, beat, abuse, strip naked, starve or do what he will to the poor lad.

(An Enquiry into the Increase of the Poor, 1738)

Extract B Parliament investigates the factory system, 1832

At what age are children employed? Never under five, but some are employed between five and six in woollen mills: they go to work between five and six am; in the summer they work until ten in the evening - as long as they can see. *How do they eat?* They get breakfast as they can; they eat and work - generally water porridge, with a little treacle that they take when they get a minute. *Suppose our Bill forced owners to close down their mills?* This would mean domestic work, the greatest blessing for England; the factory system is slavery.

(Report of the Committee on the Factory Bill, 1832)

Extract C A factory owner writes to Lord Shaftesbury, 1833

My Lord, your Bill will mean that the country will become a wreck of ruined factories. Where are your feelings of humanity when you give a magistrate and an informer power to take an industrious British tradesman from his family and to put him in jail for a few inconsiderable offences which because of sickness or absence he may not know about?

(Letter from a Lancashire cotton-spinner, 1833)

Extract D The Factory Act, 1833

It shall not be lawful to employ in any factory as aforesaid any child who shall not have completed his or her ninth year; children aged between nine and eleven shall not work more than nine hours a day and 48 hours a week... to appoint four inspectors of factories where people under 18 years of age are employed. They shall have the power to make such rules as shall be necessary for the execution of this Act. Every child between nine and eleven employed shall attend some school.

Extract E A reformed factory owner, 1845

From the working of my mills I have learned that as much cloth may be made at the same cost in 11 hours as in 12 hours. I propose to reduce hours to 10 1/2 without suffering any loss. I find the hands work with greater energy and spirit and are more cheerful and happy.

(Parliamentary Papers, 1845)

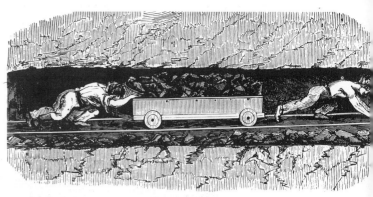

3 Children working in a coalmine

Extract F Child workers in brickyards, 1840

When I was nine years old my work consisted of carrying 40 lbs of clay on my head from the clay heap to where the bricks were made. I did this without stopping for 13 hours a day. Sometimes I had to work all through the night when I would walk about 14 miles. For this I was paid sixpence.

(George Smith of Coalville, Edward Hodder, 1896)

Extract G Child workers in coal mining, 1842

Children aged six or seven go down the pit at four in the morning and stay there for 11 or 12 hours a day. Their work is to open and shut the doors of the galleries when the trucks pass: for this the child sits by itself in a dark gallery for all those hours.

(Report on Mines, 1842)

THE YOUNG HISTORIAN AT WORK

Knowledge and understanding

1 (a) Robert Owen, Sir Robert Peel, Michael Sadler and Lord Shaftesbury all played important roles in the reform of working conditions. Who were the THREE most important? Explain your choice. **(b)** Why was the appointment of factory inspectors important for the success of factory reforms?

2 (a) How did the Factory Reform Movement affect **(i)** children; **(ii)** parents; **(iii)** employers? **(b)** Was the Factory Reform Movement equally successful in every field of working life? Give reasons for your answer.

Interpretation

1 Read *extracts B, C and E.* **(a)** Which groups **(i)** opposed **(ii)** supported reform? **(b)** Why did different people have different views about the factory system?

2 How would reliance on *pictures 1 and 2* and *extracts F and G* provide a different interpretation of the industrial revolution than if we chose to use only *extracts C and E?*

Use of sources

1 How valuable are *extracts C and E* for historians wishing to understand the varied viewpoints of factory owners concerning the Factory Reform Movement?

2 Read *extracts B and D.* **(a)** How far did the 1833 Act respond to the arguments of campaigners for reform? **(b)** Do you think that *extract B* is fully reliable? Give reasons for your answer.

Project

1 Look at *picture 3.* You are the trapper in the picture. Tell the Parliamentary Commission what life is like in your mine.

2 Look at *extract A.* Write a letter from a pauper-child, describing your treatment at work, and what you think of Robert Owen and Robert Peel.

THE STRUGGLE FOR PUBLIC HEALTH REFORM

Old, chartered boroughs had a local council (page 20). **New industrial towns** had no charter and **no local government** *(extracts A and B)*. Even when there were councils, there were **no laws** about sanitary conditions. Everything, including the environment, was to be left to **private enterprise**. Private builders, working for profit, did build **good housing** for those who could afford to pay, but the majority of people were low-paid: their houses were small and **lacking water**, **drainage and toilets** *(extract C)*.

1 Poor people living in a cellar

The poor also had an **inadequate diet** *(extract D)* and they were often ill, saw their children die and had a **shorter life than the better off**. Even rich town-dwellers had less chance of living to old age than the rural poor *(extract F)*.

People and governments were slow to accept the need for **new laws** and for **new administrative bodies** (councils) to implement them. The first **Public Health Act** was passed in **1848** *(extract G)*. It set up a General Board (the forerunner of the Ministry of Local Government) and allowed local ratepayers to elect a Local Board of Health. Few towns wanted such Boards. So the Act allowed the General Board to force such elections – but only after a town had had a very high death rate for seven years *(extract G)*. Even this modest Act was opposed by influential groups *(extract H)* and people continued to drink **dirty water** *(picture 2)* and to live in **poor quality housing** in the world's richest country.

Extract A Local government and the environment, 1818

Sheffield does not have a mayor and corporation. But in 1818 a private Act was passed 'for cleansing, lighting, policing and otherwise improving Sheffield.' Seven improvement commissioners were appointed to put this into effect and they bring offenders before the magistrates.

(*A New History*, Thomas Allen, 1831)

Extract B The environment where there is no local government, 1845

Merthyr is in a sad state of neglect. Because the poorer people, the majority of the population, throw all their refuse into the gutters in front of their houses, parts of the town are networks of filth. There is no local Act for drainage and cleansing. In some places, a toilet was common to 40 or 50 and even up to 100 and more.

(**Health of Towns Commission Report, 1845**)

Extract C Housing in Stockton, 1842

Each house has two rooms, one down and one up, each about three yards wide and four yards long. In one of these houses there are nine people in one family. The cellars are let off as separate dwellings – dark, damp and low, not more than six feet between floor and ceiling.

(**Report on Sanitary Conditions, 1842**)

Extract D Life among the poor, 1838

I visited 83 dwellings, all without furniture, old boxes for tables, stools or large stones for chairs, beds of straw, sometimes covered by torn pieces of carpet, sometimes with no covering. Food was oatmeal for breakfast; flour and water with skimmed milk for dinner; oatmeal and water again for those who had three meals a day. I saw children eating rotting vegetables in the market.

(*Tour in Manufacturing Districts of Lancashire*, William Cooke-Taylor, 1838)

DIPHTHERIA.   SCROFULA.   CHOLERA.

2 Cartoon commenting on the state of London's water

Extract E Disease and the environment, 1842

Careful examination of the evidence leads to these chief
conclusions:
1 That the various epidemics and diseases are caused by
the damp, filthy and crowded dwellings in which the
majority of people live;
2 That where there is drainage, street cleaning, better
ventilation and other improvements, the incidence of
disease drops;
3 That lack of cleanliness is due to lack of good water
supplies.

(Report on Sanitary Conditions, 1842)

Extract F Different ages of death for different classes, 1842

The average age of death	In Manchester	In Rutland
For professional people and gentry	38	52
For tradesmen and families	20	41
For craftsmen, labourers and families	17	38

(Report on Sanitary Conditions, 1842)

Extract G The first Public Health Act, 1848

IV That the General Board of Health in Whitehall shall
control local Boards.
VIII That when one-tenth of the population of a town
dies OR when the death rate (for seven years) has been
more than 23 in 1000 inhabitants, the General Board
shall send an Inspector to examine the sanitary
conditions...

Extract H Opposition to the Public Health Act, 1852

A Briton's privilege of self-government is opposed to
the communistic idea of government for one's
neighbour. The Public Health Act is an attack on this
holy principle. This Act and others have not done much
mischief yet. But if Britons don't take care they will find
their cesspools drained, their refuse carted away and that
sacred principle of 'doing what they like with their own'
trampled under foot by some poking inspector.

(*Punch*, 1852)

THE YOUNG HISTORIAN AT WORK

Knowledge and understanding

1 From the text and *extracts A, B, C, D and G*
show how public health improved in some
ways, but became worse for most people.

2 (a) Read pages 82–3 and 84–5 again.
What are the long-term causes for the growth
of cities and the development of problems of
public health?

(b) Using the text and *extracts E and H*,
describe the attitudes towards public health
reform of **(i)** supporters and **(ii)** opponents of
reform.

Interpretation

1 Read *extracts A, B and C*. **(a)** Show how
selections from these extracts might be used to
support both **(i)** optimistic and **(ii)** pessimistic
interpretations of the state of local government
in towns in 1845. **(b)** How can we check
whether these extracts give a true reflection
of how towns and cities were governed in
1845?

2 Read *extract G* and the text. Do you agree
that the 1848 Public Health Act was 'a land-
mark in the history of Public Health law'? Why?

Use of sources

1 Read *extracts E and F*, and look at *pictures
1 and 2*. **(a)** How valuable are these for
showing the views of supporters of the Public
Health Reform Movement? **(b)** Which of these
primary sources are the most valuable for that
purpose? Why?

2 Read *extract H*. Do you think the writer was
being sarcastic? Give reasons for your answer.

Project

1 Write a newspaper article supporting public
health reform; include a headline and illustrations (from these pages) as part of the article.

2 Read *extracts C, E and F*. Write a list of
questions that might have been asked by the
Commission of Enquiry into Sanitary
Conditions.

PARLIAMENTARY REFORM, 1832

Constituencies (**1830**) *(picture 1)* are the places represented in the Commons. Each county had two MPs regardless of population: most **boroughs chartered** to elect MPs were in the south, where agriculture was the major industry *(extract A)*. In some '**rotten**' boroughs there were few if any voters: the local landowners simply named the two MPs. In other '**pocket**' boroughs a patron (often the government – page 73, *extract D*) controlled the election of the two MPs.

Reformers wanted the new **industrial towns** to be represented *(extract C)*, which would involve a redistribution of seats *(picture 3)*.

The **franchise**, or right to vote, in **county** elections was simple: **borough franchises** were many, varied and, to modern eyes, ridiculous *(extract B)*. Imagine having a vote because you had a fireplace big enough to take a pot of a named size (a **pot-walloper**) or because your house was listed in an ancient charter (**burgage-holder**) or because it was listed as liable to the ancient taxes of **scot-and-lot**. **Reformers** wanted a **simple franchise**, extended to the new classes *(extract D)*.

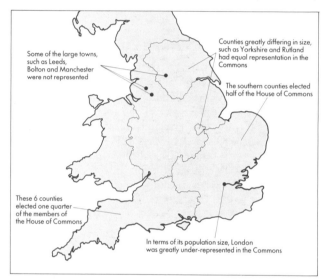

1 Representation in Parliament, 1830

Some of the large towns, such as Leeds, Bolton and Manchester were not represented

Counties greatly differing in size, such as Yorkshire and Rutland had equal representation in the Commons

The southern counties elected half of the House of Commons

These 6 counties elected one quarter of the members of the House of Commons

In terms of its population size, London was greatly under-represented in the Commons

2 Whigs and the King driving the Tories from power

Steps towards reform: Reform Bills had been introduced in the 1780s, but rejected by the Commons. Reformers set up local **political unions** *(extract D)*. Their demonstrations sometimes led to violence (page 92) but finally convinced the **Whig Party** of the need for reform *(extract C)*. The Whigs won the 1830 election, a year in which another French Revolution overthrew the Bourbons yet again. Some Whigs argued that Britain might suffer its own revolution if Parliament was not reformed *(extract E)*. **The King**, on the other hand, feared that reform might lead to revolution *(extract F)* although some people came to see him as a supporter of **Earl Grey's Whig government** *(picture 2)*.

1831 – 2: Two Bills were rejected by Parliament. When the Lords opposed a third Bill, the King agreed to create 100 new peers to push it through. The Lords let the Bill through and it became law on **7 June 1832**.

Before 1832

After 1832

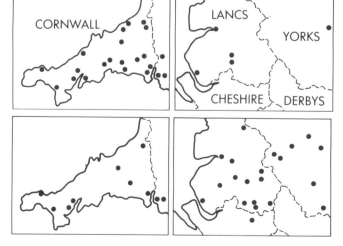

- Boroughs with 1 seat
- Boroughs with 2 seats

3 The distribution of seats in Cornwall and in the industrial North West before and after 1832

Constituencies: **56 small towns** lost both MPs and 31 lost one of their two MPs. 21 seats went to smaller industrial towns and 22 larger towns got two MPs. Extra MPs were given to **more populated counties**, to **Ireland** and **Scotland**. The **franchise for the boroughs** was simple: any male occupier (owner or tenant) of a house valued (for rating purposes) at £10 a year got the vote.

The **county franchise** was extended to tenants of some larger farms. The **results** in the **short term** are illustrated by *extract G and picture 3*. In **the longer run** the importance of the Act was that it made a breach in a traditional system: **in the future** people would ask why the vote should not be given to occupiers of less valuable property or, indeed, to every adult male, or to women.

Extract A Landowners are more important than other people, 1793

I suppose everyone would agree that the landed interest ought to have most weight in our affairs.

(The future Lord Liverpool, in the Commons, 6 May 1793)

Extract B The variety of qualifications for the franchise, 1793

In some places voting is limited to a select body of 30 or 40; in others it may be as much as 10 000. Burgage-holders, scot-and-lot men, pot-wallopers and freeholders, each has the vote in different boroughs. In some places the vote goes to the owner of a piece of land where no one has lived for years.

(Society of the Friends of the People, February 1793)

Extract C This is a new age, 1831

We don't live in the days of barons; we live in the days of Leeds, Bradford, Halifax and Huddersfield.

(Henry Brougham, a leading Whig MP)

Extract D Industrial wealth is as important as landowners' wealth, 1830

The interests of the aristocracy are well represented in Parliament. But the interests of Trade and Industry, the source of the nation's wealth and strength, are unrepresented.

(Birmingham Political Unions, 1830)

Extract E Either reform or face revolution, March 1831

History is full of revolutions produced by causes similar to those now at work in England. A part of the people which had been unimportant, grows, and demands a place in the system. If granted, all is well. If refused, then comes the struggle between the young energy of one class and the ancient privilege of another. Such is the struggle which the middle classes are waging against the aristocracy and the owners of ruins who have powers still denied to cities.

(T.B. Macaulay, in the Commons, 2 March 1831)

Extract F Was the King a 'reformer' or not?

The King admits the need to tackle reform. But he fears that the proposed changes, in these uncertain times, may be greater than the advantages to state and country which the King expects.

(Correspondence of Earl Grey, edited in 1867)

Extract G Elections in Bath – before and after reform

October 1812: Our two MPs were re-elected by 10 aldermen and 20 councillors. January 1833: Bath: Population 38 063. Number of £10 voters, 7314.

(*The Bath Herald*, October 1812. *The Weekly Dispatch*, January 1833)

THE YOUNG HISTORIAN AT WORK

Knowledge and understanding

1 Here are some of the factors that led to the passage of the Reform Act, 1832:
The industrial revolution; a growing middle class; campaigns by political unions; the Whig victory in the 1830 elections.
(a) Which of these factors were **(i)** long-term, and which were **(ii)** short-term?
(b) Are there any other causes for the passage of the Act not listed above?

2 How did the 1832 Reform Act lead to changes in **(i)** the short term and **(ii)** the long term?

Interpretation

1 How different would our interpretation of the Reform debate be if we relied on only ONE of *extracts A and D*?

2 Read *extracts C and E*. What light do they throw on the interpretations noted in your answer to the last question?

Use of sources

1 Read *extracts B and G*. What evidence do they offer for historians trying to show **(i)** why reform was needed and **(ii)** what changes were made in the system by the 1832 Reform Act?

2 (a) How valuable are *pictures 1 and 3* for showing how the Reform Act affected the electoral system? **(b)** How should we check on the accuracy of these sources?

Project

1 Write the newspaper headlines which might have appeared above reports on **(i)** The first Reform Bill, 1831; **(ii)** riots led by the political unions; **(iii)** the passage of the 1832 Reform Bill.

2 Write an interview with the Whig leader, Earl Grey, in which he explains why he pushed through the 1832 Reform Bill.

CHARTISM

Working class leaders who had campaigned for the **1832 Reform Act** were angry with its terms *(extract A)*. Many went on to lead the Chartist movement. Its aims were **totally political** *(picture 1)* although the Chartists really wanted **solutions to workers' grievances** *(extract A)* and were concerned with **social issues** *(extract C)* such as housing, unemployment *(extract B)*, sanitary conditions and education. They knew that **landowners** had pushed through the **Corn Laws** which suited them: they watched the **new middle class voters** working to get those **Laws repealed** (page 81, extract D). Chartists hoped that if the workers had the vote, Parliament would pass laws favourable to them.

Unfortunately, the Movement was divided. **Feargus O'Connor,** an Irish Protestant, believed in **physical force**. His newspaper, **The Northern Star**, called for an armed uprising which alarmed Parliament as well as many workers, *(extract D)* and could never have succeeded *(extract E)*. **William Lovett** (1800 – 76), a cabinet-maker, led the Chartists who believed in **moral force**, arguing that Parliament could be persuaded into reform.

1836 Lovett founded the **London Working Men's Association**.

1837 Chartists submitted their first **National Petition** *(extract A)*.

1838 Napier's army put down **riots in Birmingham** *(extract E)*.

1839 During the continuing **depression** *(extract B)* 500 Chartist groups sent another **petition** to Parliament *(extract F)*. **John Frost** led Welsh miners and ironworkers in an attempt to free the Chartist leader, **Henry Vincent**, from jail in **Monmouth** (page 92, picture 4). Their clash with the army at **Newport** alarmed the government.

1848 was a year of **revolutions** throughout Europe. Chartists held many demonstrations. Leaders of a mass meeting on **Kennington Common** planned to present a **petition** to Parliament *(picture 2)*. The frightened Government prepared to defend London *(extract G)*. Heavy rain cut down the size of the crowd, and **Wellington** allowed the leaders to cross into London with their petition.

This was shown to have many **false signatures** *(extract H)*; some claim that Chartism was 'laughed to death'. Really it was killed by prosperity (page 94).

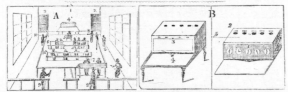

1 The Charter

Extract A Disappointment with the 1832 Reform Act

It was the people's hope that a remedy for their grievances would be found in the 1832 Act. They have been bitterly let down. That Act merely transformed power from one domineering class to another.

(National Petition, 1837)

Extract B How economic depression affects people's lives, 1847

At no period have distress and privation prevailed more heavily on the the working classes. The streets are crowded with paupers. A soup kitchen in Manchester gives out soup and bread daily.

(*The Times*, 17 February 1847)

Extract C 'The knife and fork' question

How could every working man gain the right to a good coat on his back, a good dinner on his table, work that will keep him in good health and as much wages as will keep him in enjoyment of plenty?

(J.R. Stephens of the Anti-Poor Law Movement)

Extract D Chartist divisions by William Lovett, 1845

The physical force agitation is harmful to the movement. Guns are not what are wanted, but education of the working people. O'Connor and Stephens are splitting the movement. Violent words do not slay our enemies.

O'Connor wants to take everything by storm and to pass the Charter into law in a year. The menace of armed opposition leads only to premature risings and our destruction.

Extract E A sympathiser, who leads the army against Chartists, 1838

People should have universal suffrage, the ballot, annual Parliaments and proper education. But by reason and Parliament. Physical force! Fools! We have the force, not they; they talk of their thousands of men. Who is to inspire them when I am dancing around them with cavalry?

(General Sir Charles Napier, 1838)

Extract F Presenting the Charter to the Commons, 1839

The petition started in Birmingham and is now presented to the House with 1 280 000 signatures, the result of 500 meetings. The men who signed it were angry that no effort had been made to relieve their suffering, whether they are handloom weavers or factory workers.

(T. Attwood, MP, in the Commons, 13 June 1839)

Extract G The Duke of Wellington appointed to guard London, April 1848

The Duke's preparations were large and complete. At the Thames bridges were bodies of mounted police and masses of special constables placed on either side. A strong force of military was kept ready.

(*Annual Register*, 1848)

2 Cartoon showing the Charter being presented to Lord John Russell

Extract H Laughing the 1848 petition to defeat, April 1848

Many signatures are in the same handwriting. We also see the names of distinguished people, among them Her Majesty as Victoria Rex. Other names to be seen are the Duke of Wellington and Sir Robert Peel. Many names are obviously fictitious such as 'No Cheese', 'Pug Nose'...

(Spokesman in the Commons, 14 April 1848)

THE YOUNG HISTORIAN AT WORK

Knowledge and understanding

1 There were many reasons for the growth of the Chartist Movement.
(a) Discuss with friends which of those causes were **(i)** political; **(ii)** economic; **(iii)** social.
(b) Do you think that the political causes were the most important? Give reasons for your answer.

2 (a) Using the text and *extracts D, E, G and H*, explain the reasons for the failure of the Chartist Movement in the short term.
(b) Look at *picture 1*. Do you think that Chartism succeeded in the long term? Why?

Interpretation

1 (a) How would selection of ONLY *picture 1* or of ONLY *extracts B and C* affect our interpretation of the origins and aims of the Chartist Movement?
(b) How do *extracts A and E* affect our interpretation of Chartism's origins and aims?

2 Re-read the text and *extracts G and H*. Was the Duke of Wellington right to fear the Chartists *(extract G)*?

Use of sources

1 (a) How valuable are *extracts D and E* in helping to explain the failure of Chartism?
(b) Does the authorship of those extracts add to their value? Why?

2 *Pictures 1 and 2* give a different view of Chartism from that given by *extracts B and C*. Does that mean that the sources become less valuable to historians of the Chartist Movement? Give reasons for your answer.

Project

1 Write a speech by a Chartist supporter in Parliament, asking that the terms of the Charter be accepted.

2 Draw or paint the advertisements for a Chartist meeting by **(i)** a Chartist supporter; **(ii)** someone opposed to the meeting.

VIOLENT PROTESTS

Clashes between **rioters** and the **army and police** were common in this period. There was great **unrest** when the Napoleonic Wars ended (**1815**) *(extract A)*; the author of that extract was present in **1819** at the **Peterloo Massacre** *(picture 1)*.

2 Croppers at work

3 The new shearing machine

1 The Peterloo Massacre

The Luddites *(extract A)* were machine-wreckers. **Croppers** *(picture 2)* were displaced by steam-driven shearing machines *(picture 3)*, as handloom weavers were by the power loom (page 83, extract C). Led by a mythical **Ned Ludd**, workers smashed machines *(extract B)*, murdered their owners and destroyed factories. Another mythical figure, **Swing**, led farm workers in attacks on new machinery *(extract C)*. Between **1850 and 1870**, 'the workshop of the world' provided **more work** for **higher wages for more people**. Skilled workers bought their **homes** *(picture 5)*: their trade unions gave them their own '**welfare state**' *(extract D)*. However, with the **trade depression after 1870**, there was **rising unemployment**. Many felt that society offered no solution to their grievances (page 90, extract A) and they **demonstrated** in London and elsewhere *(extract E and picture 4)*. **Trade unions**, too, became **more militant** and there were violent nationwide strikes.

4 A chartist rising in Newport, 1839

Extract A The threat of an English revolution, 1815 – 16

A series of disturbances began with the Corn Law (1815) and continued until the end of 1816. Riots broke out in London when that Bill was being discussed and lasted for several days; at Bridport and Bideford there were riots over the high prices of bread; at Bury by the unemployed to destroy machinery; at Newcastle by miners; at Glasgow because of the soup kitchens; at Preston by unemployed weavers; at Nottingham by Luddites; at Merthyr on a drop in wages; at Birmingham by the unemployed...

(*Life of a Radical*, Samuel Bamford, 1859)

Extract B A Luddite letter, 1812

Sir, I was asked by my men to give you warning to pull down your detestable shearing frames. If you do not, I shall send 300 men to destroy them and we will burn down your building to ashes... murder you and burn all your housing. Signed by the General of the Army of Redressers, NED LUDD.

(**Letter sent to a Huddersfield manufacturer, 1812**)

Extract C Captain Swing and agricultural rioters, 1830

Sir, Your name is among the Black Hearts in the Black Book and this is to advise you and the like of you, to make your Will. You have been the Blackguard Enemies of the People. Ye have not done as ye ought. SWING.

(Handwritten letter from 'Captain Swing' to a Kent farmer, 1830)

Extract D Contented industrial workers, 1867

The object of this society is to provide mutual support for its members in case of sickness, accident, old age and on the death of members and their wives, for emigration, loss of tools by fire, water or theft, and for unemployed members. They pay one shilling and 3d a quarter.

(William Applegarth for the Amalgamated Society of Carpenters, 18 March 1867)

6 Riots in Trafalgar Square, 1887

Extract E Unemployed rioters, 1887

At three o'clock the men from the East End made towards Trafalgar Square. When the procession reached the end of St Martin's Lane the police, mounted and on foot, charged, striking in all directions. At four o'clock the procession of men from South London reached the Westminster Bridge, and the police made for them: they freely used their weapons and the people, armed with iron bars, pokers, gas-pipes and even knives, resisted.

(*Reynolds' News*, 20 November 1887)

5 The comfortable interior of a miner's cottage, 1893

THE YOUNG HISTORIAN AT WORK

Knowledge and understanding

1 (a) Violent protests occurred for many reasons – economic, social and political. In THREE columns, write down which protests were caused by each of those causes.

(b) Which THREE protest movements do you think were the most important? Why?

2 Towards the end of the 19th century the reactions of prosperous workers *(extract D and picture 5)* differed from those of poorer workers *(extract E and picture 6)*. Comment on the differences and explain them.

Interpretation

1 To what extent do you think that the use of *extract A and picture 1* give historians enough evidence to show the extent of protests in Britain between 1815 and 1819? Give reasons for your answer.

2 Do you agree with the view of the text and the primary sources given here that 'Britain was a violent society' in this period? Why?

Use of sources

1 (a) Read *extracts B and C*. How valuable is the evidence in these extracts in helping to explain the extent of protests in Britain at that time?

(b) How do *pictures 2 and 3* add valuable information to that given in those extracts?

2 Read *extracts B and D*. **(a)** How are these useful in showing **(i)** differences and **(ii)** similarities of response to industrialisation?

(b) Do these differences make these sources less valuable? Give reasons for your answer.

Project

1 Make a series of posters showing support for **(i)** the Peterloo victims; **(ii)** Captain Swing; **(iii)** Trade Unions.

2 Write a letter to a newspaper supporting ONE of the protest movements mentioned on these pages.

SKILLED WORKERS AND INDUSTRIAL CHANGE, 1780 – 1880

Some historians argue that workers suffered because of the industrial revolution. Others argue that they gained, and draw attention to what happened to skilled workers in the 19th century. Such men had formed **trade unions** in the 18th century *(extract A)* and had their own form of **welfare state**. During the French Revolution period governments had seen them as dangerous and had made them illegal in 1799 *(extract B)*. Even after unions were legalised in **1824**, governments, industrialists, magistrates and judges *(extract C)* tried to stop their formation.

However, with the collapse of Chartism (pages 90–1) skilled workers formed legal unions which gave them **welfare benefits** (page 92, extract D) and got them **higher wages** so that they enjoyed **an improving standard of living** *(extract D)*.

This 'aristocracy of labour' demanded a share in the political system *(extracts E and F)*.

The **1867 Reform Act** gave the vote to:

(a) every male householder in a borough constituency;

(b) male lodgers paying £10 a year for unfurnished rooms.

This gave the vote to about **1 500 000 men**. The Act also **redistributed constituencies** so that 45 smaller boroughs lost representation and larger towns as well as more densely populated counties gained seats *(picture 3)*.

The working classes used their **new political power**: there were laws favourable to **trade unions** (1871 and 1875), a **Ballot Act** (**1872**) which provided for secret voting, and the **extension of the borough franchise** to the counties (**1885**) which added **6 000 000** to the electoral registers and made a **further redistribution** of seats *(picture 3)*. Some workers had benefited from the industrial revolution.

1 A skilled worker's home

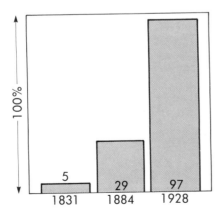

2 Those adults eligible to vote (in %)

Extract A Early unions, 1794

> Jonathan Sowton was asked about the clubs. He said: It is a contribution made by each woolcomber which enables the member to travel in search of work, and to have relief when he is sick and, when he dies, to be buried by the club.
> (*The House of Commons Journal*, 13 March 1794)

Extract B Wilberforce (the slavery reformer) calls for laws against unions, 1799

> Mr Wilberforce said that all combinations of workmen ought to be made illegal. He regarded them as a general disease in our society. Mr Pitt said he would bring in a Bill to remedy the evil of combinations of workmen which has become too general.
> (*Debrett*, Vols. LIII-LIV, 17 June 1799)

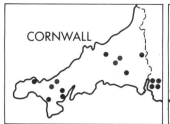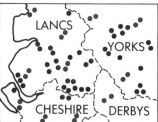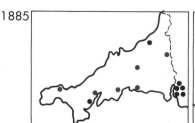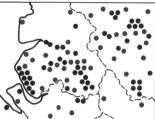

• one Borough member   • one County member

3 Distribution of seats in Cornwall and in the industrial North West in 1867 and 1885

Extract C The illegal punishment of trade unionists, Tolpuddle, 1834

I am not sentencing you for any crimes you have committed or that you were about to commit, but as an example to the working classes of this country.

(Judge Williams, Dorchester Assizes, 19 March 1834)

Extract D Rising living standards for some workers, 1830 – 80

The working classes have enjoyed an improvement in wages in the last 50 years of between 50 and 100 per cent. There has also been a fall in prices. The condition of the masses has improved vastly as shown by the fall in the death rate, the increased consumption of tea, sugar and the like, by the increase of savings bank deposits and other forms of saving. What has happened is a revolution: instead of millions on the brink of starvation we now have new millions of craftsmen and fairly well-paid labourers.

(*Essays in Finance*, Richard Giffen, 1887)

Extract E John Bright demands Parliamentary reform, 1865

The Tories are afraid of 5 000 000 men who are shut out by the present system of representation, but who could vote if they went to live in the Cape, Australia or Canada. I hold this to be dangerous. It was so in 1831-2, when there was the antagonism of the class that then had power to the just claims of the people. Now the same conservatism faces us. It may dam the stream, but the volume is increasing, and the time will come when the waters will burst their banks and sweep away these opponents.

(In Birmingham Town Hall, 13 January 1865)

Extract F Gladstone proposes Parliamentary reform

There has not been a call on the self-improving powers of the workers which has not been fully answered. Thousands of them use the libraries at the Working Men's Free Libraries and Institutes throughout the country. There are 650 000 depositors in the Post Office Savings Banks which we started four years ago. Parliament has been trying to make the workers fit for the franchise. Can anything be more unwise and senseless than to refuse to recognise the increased fitness of the workers for the exercise of political power?

(Gladstone. House of Commons, 12 April 1866)

Extract G Against Parliamentary reform, 1867

will lead to changes, the results of which we cannot predict. In Leeds, for example, there are now 8300 electors. With household suffrage there will be about 35 000.

(Lord Carnarvon to the Duke of Richmond, 11 March 1867)

THE YOUNG HISTORIAN AT WORK

Knowledge and understanding

1 (a) How did the skilled workers improve their position **(i)** economically; **(ii)** socially; **(iii)** politically? **(b)** Why did unskilled workers find it difficult to improve their positions?

2 Name the TWO most important changes that affected the skilled working classes in this period. Give reasons for your answer.

Interpretation

1 Read *extracts A–D*. How would the use of ONLY *extracts B and C* give a different view of trade unions to that given by the use of ONLY *extracts A and D*?

2 How could the use of all four extracts affect the historian's interpretation of the effects of trade unions?

Use of sources

1 How valuable are *picture 1 and extract D* for historians trying to understand the living standards of skilled workers? Why?

2 (a) How valuable are *extracts E, F and G* to historians writing about the attitudes of **(i)** supporters AND **(ii)** opponents of Parliamentary reform?
(b) Do the differences of opinion reduce the value of these extracts? Why?

Project

1 Arrange a debate amongst friends in which they argue for and against the formation of trade unions.

2 Compare the 1867 Reform Act with the 1832 Reform Act (pages 88–9) and show that these Acts were part of a long-term trend, leading to the Electoral Act, 1968.

POVERTY AND POLITICS, 1880 – 1910

Only half the workers enjoyed the changes noted by Giffen in 1887 (page 95, extract D). The **Salvation Army** (founded 1878) worked amongst the worst off *(extract A)* whose lives were described in Charles Booth's **Life and Labour of the People of London**. This showed that **31 per cent of the people** lived below the line fixed at '**an income of between 18 and 21 shillings a week**' *(extract B)*. **Seebohm Rowntree** made his own survey of **York** where he was the main employer. He hoped to prove that Booth's findings did not apply outside London. To his horror '**we find it equalled in York**' (see page 106, extract A).

1 Dockers waiting for work

In **1889** the unskilled and low-paid labourers at **London Docks** *(extract D and picture 1)* won their strike for sixpence an hour. This led to the formation of other unions for unskilled workers *(extract E)*. They could not afford fees for **welfare benefits** (page 93, extract D) nor could their wages pay for decent housing, clothes or food. They needed '**socialism**' *(picture 2 and page 107, extract D)*. Several socialist societies were formed in the 1880s and Keir Hardie formed the **Independent Labour Party** *(picture 3 and extract E)* hoping to get the support of the trade union movement.

In **1900** the **Labour Representation Committee** (**LRC**) was formed by the socialist societies, the ILP and a few unions. **Skilled unions** only joined the LRC when the ability to strike was threatened by the **Taff Vale Judgement** (**1901**) which forced a union to pay £23 000 for damages done to the railway company by a strike. By **1904** two-thirds of all unions had joined the LRC which, independently of the Liberals, *(picture 3)* grew rapidly *(extract F)*.

Extract A Life in Darkest England, 1890

The foul smell of our slums is as poisonous as that of Africa. A population eaten up by every social and physical illness, these are the people of Darkest England, 3 000 000 men, women and children, the Submerged Tenth.

(*In Darkest England, and the Way Out*, William Booth, founder of the Salvation Army, 1890)

2 Socialism shown as the Angel of the labouring man

Extract B Life on a pound a week, 1913

How does a man bring up a family on 20 shillings a week? Four shillings a week is allowed for food for a child boarded out by the poor Law. Assume a family of 4 children. For a woman with 4 children, 4 shillings for food for each child is ridiculous. Even at half of that, food for the children would cost 8 shillings: if we allow the same for the parents, the 6 people spend 12 shillings on food. That leaves 8 shillings; rent may come to 6 or 7 shillings. How can the woman manage on 1 or 2 shillings a week for coal, gas, insurance, clothes, cleaning materials...?

(*Round About a Pound a Week*, Mrs P. Reeves, 1913)

Extract C Children's bone disease and industrialisation, 1889

In areas such as the Clyde district, almost every child was affected by rickets, a disease caused by poverty and malnutrition. A map of the disease's distribution over the whole of England was a map showing the density of the industrial population.

(*Medical Congress Report*, 1889)

Extract D Fighting for a poorly paid job in the Docks, 1889

We are driven into a shed, iron-barred from end to end. Outside the bars a foreman walks about with the air of a dealer in a cattle market. He picks and chooses from the crowd of men, who, anxious to get work, trample each other underfoot as, like beasts, they fight for a day's work.

(*Memories*, B. Tillett, 1931)

Extract E If only the trade unions would support Labour candidates, 1893

Before the London Dock Strike, membership of unions was limited, by the high contributions demanded from members, to about 500 000. Since then, almost every worker can join a union, which increases the power of the trade union organisation. Socialists have tried to set up societies. At a general election unions could put up 2000 voters for every member of a socialist society. Moreover they have the money. A penny a week from every member of a trade union would raise £300 000 and could easily provide £30 000 to support 50 Labour candidates at £600 each. Representation of the working classes at elections will depend on the unions and not on the socialist bodies.

(*Fortnightly Review*, George Bernard Shaw, 1 November 1893)

Extract F A growing Labour Party, 1910

Between the elections of 1900 and 1906, three victories were won: Shackleton was returned for Clitheroe: Crooks won at Woolwich, and I beat both the Tory and Liberal candidates at Barnard Castle. In 1906, 29 of our 50 candidates were successful. In January 1910 we ran 78 candidates and 40 won seats, and formed a separate and independent group.

(*The Aims of Labour*, A. Henderson, 1918)

3 Cartoon showing the refusal of the ILP to dance to the tune played by the Liberals

4 Keir Hardie

THE YOUNG HISTORIAN AT WORK

Knowledge and understanding

1 Show how the following responded to the debate on poverty: **(i)** Charles Booth; **(ii)** Seebohm Rowntree; **(iii)** the skilled workers' unions; **(iv)** leaders of the unskilled workers; **(v)** the Labour Party.

2 What do you think were the TWO most important causes of poverty in this period? Explain your answer.

Interpretation

1 Read *extracts A, B and C* and then re-read extract D on page 95. How would the use of this last extract give a different interpretation about British society to that given by the use of ONLY the extracts on this page?

2 Read *extract D* and look at *picture 1*. **(a)** How do these sources lead to a different interpretation of the strength of trade unions from that given by the use of sources dealing with skilled workers' unions (page 93,

extract D and picture 1 on page 94? **(b)** How complete a picture does *extract D* give of trade union strength?

Use of sources

1 How valuable are *pictures 1, 2 and 3* and *extract E* in showing differing views of the growth of the Labour Party as a vehicle for Socialism?

2 (a) How do *extracts E and F* and the final paragraph of the text explain why the Labour Party became stronger? **(b)** How reliable are the authors of *extracts E and F* to historians of the Labour Party?

Project

1 Write a letter from Charles Booth describing working class poverty in 1900.

2 Make two posters **(i)** supporting and **(ii)** opposing the Labour Party in 1906.

FARMERS AND FOREIGNERS

The Corn Laws were repealed in 1846 (page 81, extract D). Many thought that home farmers would be ruined. Instead they enjoyed 30 good years because of:

1 The continual growth of the **urban population** (pages 78–9) which needed food.

2 The growing demand from **more prosperous townspeople**.

3 The business sense of a **new breed of landowners** (extract A).

4 The **absence of foreign competition** due to high transport costs.

5 Farmers learning to make their land more productive by the use of natural and chemical **fertilisers**, and the use of new methods of **drainage** (extract B).

1 A steam-driven threshing machine

6 The **steam-driven machines** for ploughing, reaping, mowing and threshing (picture 1) which increased output or lowered costs, or both.

7 The **railways** which carried the farm produce cheaply and quickly to market. Too many farmers failed to adopt the new methods (extracts D and E). They did not see that **investment** was, and is, **the key to future success**.

In 1873 everything changed. A series of **bad harvests** was combined with a flood of **cheap foreign food** (extract F and picture 2). Grain was imported cheaply from the **USA** and **Canada**, and meat came in refrigerated steamships from **Argentina** and **New Zealand**. The reasons for the slump in farming were:

1 The development of the **railways in the USA and Canada** which allowed the carriage of wheat grown on **rent-free land**, where many **machines** were used from the start.

2 The development of **larger, lighter and more efficient steamships** which allowed the carriage of the imports at very low cost (extract G).

Not all farmers suffered. Indeed the falls in the prices of wheat, meat and potatoes allowed **many people to buy more and varied food. Dairy, vegetable and fruit farmers** benefited. **Townspeople** also benefited from the sharp falls in food prices (extract H). Well-stocked shops (picture 3) competed for customers, another sign of the **social progress** that follows **industrial change**.

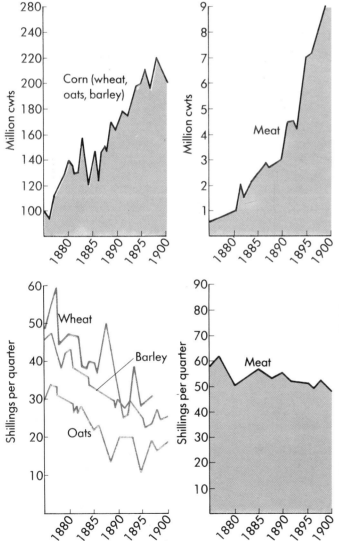

2 The relationship between rising imports and falling prices

Extract A New landowners and agricultural improvements, 1850

The best landlords are capitalists from the towns. They buy estates and manage them with the same attention to business principles as they used in town. They drain land thoroughly, erect good buildings, then let the land to good tenants. The rents are high but these farms can pay a good rent, much better than can a poor estate pay even a moderate rent.

(*Letters*, Sir James Caird, 1850)

Extract B The importance of drainage

Until land is free from stagnant water and made able of yielding its best to the efforts of the farmer, all other outlay is useless. Wherever it is applied it always pays off – land is more suitable for plants and animals and so much easier to work.

(*English Agriculture*, Sir James Caird, 1850 - 1)

Extract C The railways - the farmers' friend, 1868

During the last year the Great Eastern Line brought 306 000 sheep to London from the Eastern Counties, 41 900 pigs, 610 330 sacks of flour, 277 740 quarters of wheat..., malt, beer, potatoes, poultry, fruit and vegetables.

(*Quarterly Review*, October 1868)

Extract D Too much undrained land

Out of 20 000 000 acres needing drainage only 3 000 000 have been drained; of all kinds of improvement needed, only one-fifth has been done.

(A Report, Select Committee of the House of Lords, 1873)

Extract E Too little machinery, 1873

Even the best new machines are not yet in general use. Some farmers haven't had a chance to see them, and most machine-makers live in the four Eastern counties where most machines are used.

(A Report, Lords Select Committee, 1873)

Extract F The agricultural depression, 1882

The two important causes are bad seasons and foreign competition, made worse by the heavy loss of animals. Once, the farmer suffering from bad seasons would have benefited from the higher prices for the smaller crop. Now the foreign supply comes in at greatly reduced prices. (Royal Commission, 1882)

Extract G Railways, shipping and the farmer, 1882

The cost of building a steamship is much less than it was 10 years ago. The cost of working ships has fallen with the better engines – less coal is burned, fewer

3 A well-stocked shop around 1900

men are required, steam winches have replaced hard labour. Ships used to carry 2000 tons from America: now they carry 4000 tons and such ships are worked at much less than double the cost of the smaller ones. Transport costs fall. Every line of railway built in America brings another farming area to compete with ours. The cost of transport is very small. For practical purposes, Chicago is as near London as is Aberdeen.

(Royal Commission, 1882)

Extract H Depression and human happiness, 1887

The last 10 years of depression have contributed more to solid progress and true happiness than the booms of the past.

(*Contemporary Review*, Alfred Marshall, March 1887)

THE YOUNG HISTORIAN AT WORK

Knowledge and understanding

1 (a) In what ways was the period 1850 – 1900 one of both **(i)** prosperity AND **(ii)** decline for British farmers? **(b)** How did both the prosperity and decline in agriculture affect people who were not farmers?

2 How did the development of technology **(i)** help the growth of some parts of British agriculture but **(ii)** cause the decline of other parts?

Interpretation

1 (a) How do *extracts F and H* give different interpretations of the fortunes of agriculture? **(b)** How do you explain these differences of interpretation? **(c)** Which interpretation does *extract C* seem to support?

2 (a) How far do *extracts A, B, D and G* give a complete picture of **(i)** why agriculture prospered and **(ii)** why it ran into difficulties? **(b)** Why do you think these extracts do not give full explanations of the changing fortunes of the agriculture industry?

Use of sources

1 Look at *picture 1*. **(a)** What sort of technology does this source reveal? **(b)** What were the long-term reasons for the growth in agricultural technology?

2 (a) How valuable are the graphs (*picture 2*) in explaining **(i)** the difficulties facing some farmers; **(ii)** the improvement in living standards of many British people (page 95, extract D)? **(b)** How reliable is *picture 3* as a guide to the living standards of British workers in 1900?

Project

1 Write the diary of a farmer who has had good and bad years.

2 Write an interview with the workers shown in *picture 3*, in which they talk about their work.

SLOWER INDUSTRIAL GROWTH LEADS TO RELATIVE DECLINE

In **1851**, a '**Crystal Palace**' was built in Hyde Park to house the **Great Exhibition**, which showed off Britain's industrial power. Britain **produced** most of the world's goods and also **loaned money** to foreigners to help them buy her railway lines and engines and textile machinery *(extract A)*. This increased output, employment and exports.

In **1900** the French organised the **Paris Exhibition**. British scientists saw that **foreign industry** had overtaken Britain's. Because of that, Britain's **share of world trade** had declined *(picture 1)*.

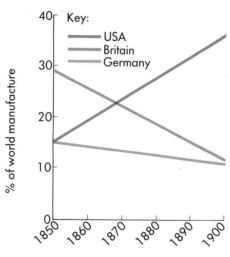

1 Britain's decline of trade, 1850-1900

What had happened? New inventions and new discoveries had led to the growth of **new industries** such as the chemical and electrical engineering industries. These relied less on physical power (as did coal and iron) and more on the work of **scientists**, **trained workers** and **expensive machinery**. Britain was slow to adopt these rapidly-growing industries: she relied on the old and slow-growing ones. Others outstripped Britain in steel production *(picture 2)* while she relied on increasing textile exports to an expanding Empire (pages 104–5). **Who was to blame?** Some blamed **foreign countries** which used import duties to keep out British goods *(extract A)* while benefiting from Britain's **free trade policy** *(picture 3 and extract F)*. Some blamed **industrialists** *(extracts B and D)*, others blamed **governments** and the **educational system** *(extracts C and D)*.

Because of the decline, Britain had a smaller share of world trade *(picture 1)*, **exported less** *(extract E)* and **imported foreign goods** *(extract F)*. This led to **increased unemployment**, even for skilled workers, which helped drive them into the infant **Labour Party** (page 96). It also led to the call for **an end to Free Trade** *(extract G)*. It was a long way from the free trade days of 1851.

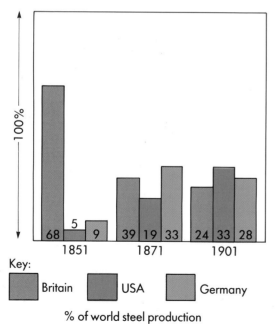

2 Steel production, 1851-1901

Extract A Foreign competitors and British trade, 1881

In 1851 England had a monopoly of the manufacturing industries of the world. She produced more than she used, other nations produced almost nothing. The world had to buy from her; they could not buy anywhere else. Now, France, America and Belgium have our machinery, our workmen and our capital. Each year they send us their goods which drive out our own, and every year they close their markets to our goods.
(*Nineteenth Century*, Edward Sullivan, 1881)

Extract B Industrial investment leads to lower prices, 1904

Automatic machinery is more used in America than here. Up-to-date factories have enabled the Americans, paying the highest wages known in the world, to produce steel plates at a cost of three shillings per ton for labour and averaging 225 tons per shift. Our mills cannot do this.
(**Tariff Commission, 1904**)

Extract C The need for more education, 1903

One of the evil consequences of our educational failure is the slow progress we have made in the industries which are based on recent scientific discoveries. These depend on the appreciation, by capitalists and industrialists, of the way in which science promotes industrial development. We are also in need of general education: our competitors have reaped the benefit of their awareness of the value of knowledge as a basis for industrial prosperity.

(Sir J.W. Swan, 1903)

Extract D Who is to blame? 1918

The decline in British industries is due to workers who tried to limit output, to manufacturers and to Government. Employers have neglected new processes and inventions; they relied on cheap labour rather than on efficient organisation.

(*The British Dominions Year Boo*k, 1918, Sir L. Money MP, 1918)

Extract E A slow-down in our foreign trade, 1903

Since 1872 our export trade has grown by £22 million, something like 7 1/2 per cent. Since 1872 our population has grown by 30 per cent. In that time USA exports have grown by £110 million and German exports by £56 million. Our export trade has been practically stagnant for 30 years.

(Joseph Chamberlain, 6 October 1903)

Extract F Importing foreign manufactured goods, 1896

Some of your own clothes were probably woven in Germany: more surely were some of your wife's clothes. Go through the house and the foreign mark will greet you everywhere – the piano, the mug on the dresser, your drainpipes, the paper wrappings for your book. You put those in the fire – with a poker forged in Germany.

(*'Made in Germany', The New Review*, E.E. Williams, 1896)

CAUGHT NAPPING !

3 A cartoon showing Germany taking Britain's trade

Extract G The end of free trade? 1881

We propose a tariff of 10 per cent on all foreign goods to be used when bargaining with countries, from whom we import, to admit our goods as freely as we admit theirs.

(*Fair Trade*, William Farrer Ecroyd, 1881)

THE YOUNG HISTORIAN AT WORK

Knowledge and understanding

1 The following have been blamed for Britain's industrial decline: industrialists; dependence on old industries; foreign imports; government; the education system; failure to adopt new industries. **(a)** What do you think were the THREE most important causes of Britain's decline? Why? **(b)** In what ways was the decline due to **(i)** long-term and **(ii)** short-term causes?

2 How did the relative decline of British industry affect the British people?

Interpretation

1 The extracts on these pages offer a variety of explanations for the decline of British industry. **(a)** Do you think that any ONE extract gives the best explanation for that decline? Explain your answer. **(b)** How complete as a whole are the extracts in explaining Britain's industrial decline?

2 Do you think that Britain's industrial decline was caused by **(i)** many factors; **(ii)** a few; **(iii)** only one? Explain your answer.

Use of sources

1 Are the graphs *(pictures 1 and 2)* and the cartoon *(picture 3)* useful to historians trying to explain the decline in British industry? Why?

2 In what ways is *extract F* different from other extracts as regards **(i)** style of writing and **(ii)** reliability as evidence?

Project

1 Write a speech by a tariff reformer arguing for an end to free trade.

2 Write the interviews you might have had at the Paris Exhibition with people commenting on the British failures and the success of the USA and some European countries.

COLONIES, TRADE AND THE INDUSTRIAL REVOLUTION

Britain had gained some colonies in the 17th century (page 56). The most important were the **13 colonies** in North America *(picture 1)*, each of which had its own elected Parliament. However, a British governor could set aside any decisions made by a State (or colonial) Parliament. The British Government made sure that:

1 Colonies did not start any industry to compete with an English one: so no American woollen or iron industries, and no Irish woollen industry were founded.

2 Colonies **supplied Britain** with goods which could not be produced in England. **America** supplied timber, tobacco and pig iron; the **East Indies and India** *(picture 2)* sent spices, coffee, tea and silks; from the **West Indies** came sugar, rum and timber. Many of these goods were made into **manufactured** products near Bristol (page 57, picture 5), Liverpool (page 58, extract A), Glasgow or London, which became important industrial centres. More people were **employed** – in harbour work, warehouses, manufacturing and transport – at or near these ports. They then had money to spend on home-made goods and so provided one spur to the first industrial revolution (page 82).

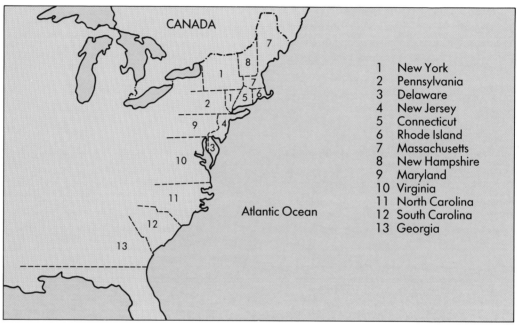

1 The American colonies, 1770

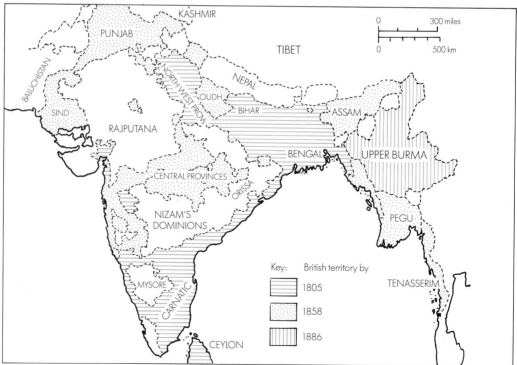

2 British territory in India

Many of the imported goods were **re-exported** to Europe. This further increased employment in shipping. The re-export trade also increased the **demand for banks** to look after the financing of import and export trades. The growth of local banking systems was an important help to the first industrialists (page 82. See also page 25, extract A).

Europe had once been the main market for British goods but the colonies grew in importance as markets *(extract A)*. This was a **second spur to the first industrial revolution**: the domestic system (page 82, extract A) was unable to provide enough goods. This colonial trade was a major reason for the growth of some industrial towns and for the high levels of employment there *(extracts B and C)*.

The **West Indies** grew in importance *(extract A)*. The sugar plantations there, like the cotton and tobacco plantations of North America, depended on the work done by the **millions of slaves** carried from Africa in British slave ships (page 56, picture 4). This slave trade was not abolished until 1807 and slavery itself was abolished in the Empire only in 1833.

The profits made in colonial trade were an essential part of the capital available for the first industrialists to invest in industry.

Extract A British exports and imports (%)

	Exports			Imports		
	1750	1770	1797	1750	1770	1800
Europe	77	49	38	55	45	43
North America	11	25	22	11	12	7
West Indies	5	12	25	19	25	25
East Indies & Africa	7	14	13	15	18	25
Total in £ mill.	9.5	9.6	21.6	7.7	12.2	28.3

(Compiled from custom house ledgers, PRO customs)

Extract B The importance of the American market, 1812

Those in Birmingham that are totally employed in the American trade are 50 000 excluding the nail trade which employs another 20 000 in the American trade. About two-thirds of all people are employed in the export trades, including trade to the United States.
(Joseph Shaw, Chairman of Birmingham Chamber of Foreign Commerce in evidence to a Parliamentary Committee, 1812)

Extract C Sheffield and the American trade, 1821

What is the population of Sheffield? According to the 1811 census about 53 000. *How many are employed in the American trade?* 4000 men and 2000 women and children: about 6000 in all.
How many work in the home trade? 6000 men and 1000 women and children. *How many work in the foreign trade, excluding the American trade?* 2000 men and 1000 women and children. This trade includes trade with Spain, Portugal, the West Indies, South America and Canada.
What proportion of Sheffield goods go to America? About one-third of all our manufactures; the home market takes about one-half.
(John Bailey, Sheffield exporter and home producer to a Parliamentary Committee, 1812)

THE YOUNG HISTORIAN AT WORK

Knowledge and understanding

1 (a) Show that the colonies were an important cause of change in Britain as **(i)** markets for goods; **(ii)** suppliers of materials. **(b)** How did colonial trade affect **(i)** the development of ports; **(ii)** the growth of a banking system; **(iii)** the start of the first industrial revolution?

2 What do you think were the two most important effects of the colonies on Britain? Explain your answer.

Interpretation

1 Look at page 56, picture 4. How might this be used to **(i)** condemn the slave trade; **(ii)** excuse and explain it?

2 What use could be made of *extract A* to defend British involvement in the slave trade?

Use of sources

1 (a) How valuable are the maps for showing the extent of British expansion in India and America? **(b)** What other sorts of evidence do you need if you wish to discover how the growth of the Empire affected people in Britain and in the colonies?

2 Read *extracts B and C*. **(a)** Do these show that Adam Smith was right in describing England as 'A nation of shopkeepers' (1776) interested mainly in 'buying and selling'?
(b) How reliable do you think the statements in these extracts are likely to be and how do you think they can be checked?

Project

1 Write a speech by an MP demanding the abolition of the slave trade.

2 On a map of the world draw the trade routes from British ports to the West Indies, Africa and America, showing the types of goods exported and imported.

AN AFRICAN EMPIRE, 1880 – 1902

1 An engraving showing Britannia and her armies

The Tory leader, Disraeli, called colonies '**millstones around our necks**'. Why then, by 1900, were the Tories for 'Queen and Empire' *(picture 3)* in Africa?

1 Markets for British goods would provide employment *(extracts A and F)*.

2 Money would come from investment in colonial development *(extracts A–C and H)*.

3 Materials – colonies were a secure source of raw materials.

4 Arrogance – the lawyer Dicey *(extract E)* spoke for many people of the time.

The **making of a colony** began with the work of **trading companies**, as it had in India *(page 57, extract C)*. Companies were given **charters** *(page 56, picture 2)* giving them the sole right to trade in a certain area: **Nigeria**, **Kenya**, **South Africa** and so on. Company agents signed **treaties** with chiefs, ensuring the company's rights *(extract D)*. The **Government** gave these charters, encouraged investors *(extract B)* and, when needed, **fought to defend the companies** *(picture 1 and extract H)*. And, if a company failed, the Government **annexed** the area concerned: **Uganda**, **Kenya and Nigeria** were annexed in this way.

Chamberlain, Colonial Secretary, 1895 – 1903, encouraged expansion in Africa *(extracts A and B)*. He also tried to unite the 'white colonies' (**Australia**,

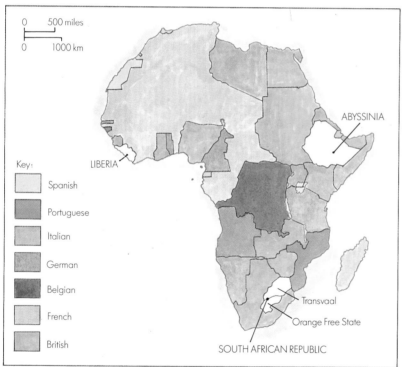

2 The division of Africa

Key:
- Spanish
- Portuguese
- Italian
- German
- Belgian
- French
- British

(Map labels: ABYSSINIA, LIBERIA, Transvaal, Orange Free State, SOUTH AFRICAN REPUBLIC)

New Zealand, Canada and, after 1902, South Africa). He asked them to put a **lower tariff on British goods** than on the foreign goods: in return he proposed an **import tariff on non-colonial food imports** into Britain. Because this would push up prices *(picture 3 and extract G)* this tariff campaign failed. Expansion of the Empire gave markets for **old-fashioned goods**: the export of capital meant a **lack of investment** in Britain in new industries *(page 100, picture 2)*. Britain's decline continued.

3 Chamberlain speaking in Birmingham, 1904

Extract A Colonies as markets needed investment, 1895

Our colonies cannot be developed without our assistance. I will consider any case in which investment of British money may help to develop colonies. In such development I see a solution of our social problems: there is no way of securing more employment than by creating new markets and developing old ones.

(Joseph Chamberlain, speaking in 1895)

Extract B The need for investment, 1895

Our profit is in the prosperity of our people and in the development of new markets. This involves risk. But if we are not willing to invest our wealth in the colonies, then I see no future for them, and it would have been better never to have gone there.

(Chamberlain, 1895)

Extract C How was the investment used?

About £100 million a year was invested abroad – South Africa, Egypt, colonies on the coasts of Africa, India, Australia... for railways, docks, water and gas works, mining concerns and plantations.

(*The Export of Capital*, C.K. Hobson, 1914)

Extract D The acquisition of Rhodesia, 1889

A company has been formed to develop the Bechuanaland and countries to the north. Mr Rhodes of the Cape Colony, representing the holders of the concession from Lobengula, promises to cooperate. The example of the East Africa Company shows that such companies save the Government much expenditure. The company for Bechuanaland will render valuable help in South Africa.

(Colonial Office to the Foreign Office, 16 May 1889)

Extract E The pride of imperialists, 1877

Englishmen are bound by a manifest identity to found empires abroad and to make themselves the dominant race in countries in which they wander.

(*The Nineteenth Century*, Edward Dicey, 1877)

Extract F A British tariff, imperial unity and employment, 1903

Tariff reformers believe that a British tariff may secure a lowering of foreign tariffs and a fairer exchange of goods than we have now. More importantly, they might secure, by arrangements with our colonies, a great development of Imperial trade, so adding greatly to the employment of our ever growing population.

(Chamberlain, 4 November, 1903)

Extract G Chamberlain mocks the attack on his tariff campaign, 1904

Liberals say that a tariff on imported wheat would make the loaf dearer, or, if the price stayed the same, smaller. Here, in one hand, is a 'free trade loaf' and, in the other, 'a tariff reform loaf'. Can you tell the small difference between them? Of course not.

(Chamberlain in Birmingham, 1904)

Extract H Investment leads to Government support

It is not too much to say that modern British foreign policy is mainly a struggle for profitable markets for investment. People who enjoy the income from this investment try to extend the fields for their investment and to safeguard their existing investments. This is the most important fact in modern politics.

(*The Exports of Capital*, C.K. Hobson, 1914)

THE YOUNG HISTORIAN AT WORK

Knowledge and understanding

1 Here is a list of factors which led to the growth of the British Empire in Africa. Place them in order of importance and explain your choice of order:
Need for new markets; need for sources of raw materials; the demands of investors; British arrogance; the work of some individuals; the long-term effects of the industrial revolution.

2 Outline and explain the rôle of Britain towards Africa **(i)** when British interests were attacked; **(ii)** when Chamberlain was Colonial Secretary.

Interpretation

1 Read *extracts A and H*. **(a)** Show how they offer differing interpretations of the relationship between Britain and her colonies. **(b)** What light does *extract B* shed on these differing interpretations?

2 Read *extracts B, C, D and H*, and the text, to help you decide whether colonies were 'millstones around our necks' OR **(ii)** aids to British prosperity.

Use of sources

1 (a) How might historians use *extract E* when writing about British attitudes towards Africa? **(b)** How does *picture 2* add to the implications made in *extract E*?

2 (a) Read *extracts F and G* and look at *picture 3*. Do you think that Chamberlain's arguments were reliable? Why? **(b)** How can you check their reliability?

Project

1 Write the speeches by MPs **(i)** supporting; **(ii)** opposing tariff reform.

2 Find out how Kenya, Nigeria and Zimbabwe are developing in the 1990s.

RELIGIOUS CHANGE AND SOCIAL REFORM

Walpole and the Whigs (page 72) remembered how religion had led to Civil Wars (page 66) and the overthrow of James II (page 70). They **appointed bishops** who behaved more as **politicians** than religious leaders. **Local clergy** were left to do much as they liked: some became lazy and **failed to look after their parishes**. The Anglican Church also failed to deal with the **growth of industrial towns**: in many there were no churches; in others, the parish was too big for the clergy. **John Wesley**, an Anglican clergyman, and his friends were nicknamed '**Methodists**' because of their methodical lifestyle (prayer, study and work). He went to the people to **preach** (in the open), to help them start schools and local churches where **non-clerics** (lay preachers) held services. At first some clergy led mobs to attack Wesley. By 1820 many **Anglicans** had come to imitate him and brought the Gospel (**Evangel**) to the masses. Some became active in social reform: **Wilberforce** led the anti-slavery movement; **Shaftesbury** worked for factory reform. Methodists saw that **ordinary people** could **run a local church**; some went on to **run trade unions** (pages 92 and 94) and saw **skilled workmen** become well-housed, well-dressed and 'respectable'.

However, as has been seen, the **mass of the people** were trapped in a **cycle of poverty** *(extract A)* and had poor housing and food, and a high death rate (page 86, extracts A–F). Some religious people thought that the **poor ought** to imitate the skilled workers by saving and **providing for themselves** *(extracts B and C)*. They **condemned** 'Socialism' *(extract D)*, and the poor had to wait before a start was made on the creation of a welfare state.

Extract A The cycle of poverty, 1900

The labourer's life is marked by alternating periods of want and plenty:

1 In **early childhood** he probably will be in poverty.

2 When he and the other children **earn money,** they add to the father's wages to raise the family above the poverty line.

3 Then, when he is **earning money and living at home,** he will have more money than is needed for lodgings, food and clothes. This is his chance to save.

4 If he has saved enough to furnish a cottage, this prosperity may continue after marriage, until he has two or three children when **poverty comes again.**

2 Mealtime at a workhouse in St. Pancras, 1900

5 This poverty lasts until the first child is 14 and begins to earn: if there are more than three children it will last longer.

6 While the children are earning and living at home, the man has **prosperity**.

7 He sinks **back into poverty** when his children have married and left home, and he himself is **too old to work**.

(*Poverty*, S. Rowntree, 1902)

Extract B The poor should save and so provide

The poor should meet the ORDINARY problems of life, relying not on charity but their own thrift and self-help. The worker knows that:

1 temporary sickness will sometimes visit his household;

2 times of slackness of work will occasionally come;

3 if he has a large family his resources will be taxed to the utmost;

4 old age will make him incapable of work.

All these are the **ordinary problems** of life. If the worker thinks they will be met by State aid he will make no effort to meet them himself.

(**Annual Report of the Charity Organisation Society, 1876**)

1 A pawnshop

Extract C An aging Prime Minister and the need for workers' self-help, 1884

People think that the Government can do this and that and everything. If the Government does what a man ought to do for himself, it will do more harm to the man than good. The spirit of self-reliance should be developed among the masses of the people.

(**William Gladstone, Edinburgh, September 1884**)

Extract D Chamberlain, as a Radical Liberal, challenges Gladstone, 1885

It is ridiculous for a political Rip Van Winkle to wake up and tell us that these reforms are to be excluded from the Liberal programme. We have to grapple with the misery of the people. Now that we have a Government by the people we will make it the Government for the people, to secure for every man his rights to a fair enjoyment of his existence. I shall be told that this is Socialism.

Of course it is. Most local government work is Socialism. The Education Act is Socialism and every Act by which we show care for the poor is Socialism. It is none the worse for that. Our aim is the elevation of the poor – a levelling up – to remove the great inequality in social life.

(**Joseph Chamberlain, Warrington, 8 September 1885**)

THE YOUNG HISTORIAN AT WORK

Knowledge and understanding

1 Why did many working class people **(i)** abandon the Anglican Church; **(ii)** become Methodists; **(iii)** take up Socialism as a cause?

2 In what ways did Anglican Evangelicals, Methodists and Socialists imitate each other?

Interpretation

1 Do you agree that the evidence in the extracts and in the text shows that religion was an unimportant force in the 19th century?

2 (a) How do *extracts A and B* offer differing interpretations of the life of the poor? **(b)** How do *extracts C and D* contribute to those interpretations?

(c) Why do you think there were these differences of interpretation?

Use of sources

1 How are *pictures 1 and 2* useful to historians writing about **(i)** the effects of poverty on people's lives; **(ii)** the reasons why people campaigned against poverty *(extracts A and D)*?

2 Read *extract A*. You have already read about Rowntree, the author of this extract (page 96). Do you think that this extract, from this author, is a reliable source for historians writing about the nature and extent of poverty in 1902? Why?

Project

1 Write an interview with a follower of John Wesley about **(i)** his life and work and **(ii)** the difficulties he faced.

2 Write a speech by a social reformer campaigning for Government help for the poor.

BRITAIN AND THE GREAT WAR: 1914 – 1918

1914: A WAR PLANNED BY SOME AND WELCOMED BY MANY

On **28 June 1914**, the heir to the Austrian Crown was murdered in **Sarajevo**, capital of Bosnia *(picture 1)* which the Serbs claimed was part of 'larger Serbia'. **Austria** declared **war** on Serbia (**on 26 July**) when she was refused the right to send troops into Serbia to find the murderers. **30 July**: **Russia** mobilised her army, showing her wish to defend Serbia. **1 August**: **Germany** (Austria's ally) declared war on **Russia and her ally**, **France**.

1 The Balkans in 1914

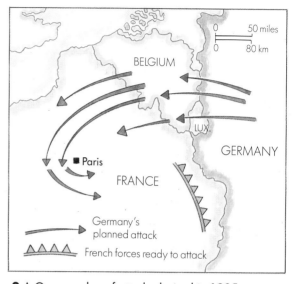

2 A German plan of attack, devised in 1905

3 A British view of Germany's threat to Belgium, 1914

BRAVO, BELGIUM!

4 The revised German plan, 1914

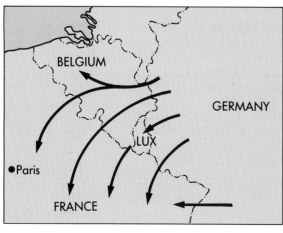

Germany had planned a war against France *(picture 2)* by going through **Belgium**. **2 August**: Britain asked Germany to honour the Treaty of Neutrality of Belgium **1839** (page 118, picture 2). When she refused, **Britain declared war (4 August)**. **German plans were ruined** by **(i)** the need to take troops from France to fight in Russia; **(ii)** the British *(extract C)*. Paris was never encircled *(picture 4)* and a second plan, to capture the Channel ports, also failed *(extract D)*.

In Britain, millions volunteered for the army *(extracts E–G)* in response to **Kitchener's** call *(picture 5)*. Later, military service was made compulsory. A few people refused to serve: these **conscientious objectors** were harshly treated by the authorities, and seen as cowards by the mass of people. Both the objectors and their harsh critics were victims of **propaganda** (pages 118–19).

Extract A A Czech writer in the streets of Prague, 26 July 1914
I noticed a crowd gathered around a shop window where there was a telegram in the window. 'War declared'. No one spoke for a minute. Then I heard 'Thank God'. The speaker was an Austrian army officer.
(Quoted in *The Army*, P. Lane, 1978)

Extract B From the British Ambassador, Berlin, to the British Foreign Secretary, 6 August 1914

The German Chancellor (Prime Minister) was very angry. He said that the step taken by the British government was terrible, and only for a word – 'neutrality' – just for a scrap of paper, Britain was going to war against a kindred nation which only wanted to be friends with her. It was like attacking a man from behind when he was fighting for his life against two enemies.

Extract C The first Battle of Mons, August 1914

About 100 000 British soldiers had their first taste of battle at Mons. Here the Germans faced the rapid British rifle fire. It was so fast and so accurate that the Germans thought the British had thousands of machine guns. A German wrote 'They were well dug in and hidden. They opened a murderous fire. Our casualties increased. Our rushes became shorter. Finally the whole advance stopped, but only after bloody losses'.

(*The Army*, P. Lane, 1978)

Extract D Ypres, November 1914. The Germans fail to reach the coast

The supreme memorial to the British regular Army.

(The military historian, B.H. Liddel-Hart)

Extract E From a young English soldier to his parents, July 1916

I could not pray for a finer death, and you my dear Mother and Dad, will know that I died doing my duty to my God, my Country and my King.

(Letter from E. James Engell of the 16th London Regiment)

5 A famous – and successful – recruiting poster

Extract F A young recruit explains to his mother why he volunteered to fight

I have no wish to remain a civilian any longer. Although the idea of war is against my conscience, I feel that in a time of national crisis like this I have no right to my ideas if they are against the best and immediate needs of the state. (Letter from Harold Parry to his mother as he left to join the King's Royal Rifles)

Extract G A young public schoolboy explains why he volunteered to fight

What really made me volunteer was less a feeling of patriotism than the wish to please my schoolmates. To have a conscientious objector at my school – even if I had wanted to be one – would have been unthinkable.

(G. Alan Thomas of the 6th Royal West Kent Regiment)

THE YOUNG HISTORIAN AT WORK

Knowledge and understanding

1 Why did Austria, Germany, Russia and Britain go to war in 1914?

2 Explain how each of the following prevented Germany gaining the quick victory she had expected: **(i)** Russian mobilisation; **(ii)** British resistance *(extract C)*; **(iii)** the Battle of Ypres *(extract D)*.

Interpretation

1 Read *extracts E, F and G*. **(a)** How does each *extract* give a differing interpretation of why people supported their government's entry into the War? **(b)** Explain these differences.

2 *Extracts E, F and G* were written by soldiers. **(a)** Which one do you think welcomed the Kitchener poster *(picture 5)*? **(b)** Which one least welcomed that poster? **(c)** Which one was most influenced by public opinion?

Use of sources

1(a) Why did the Germans fail to achieve a quick victory in 1914? **(b)** How valuable are *pictures 2 and 4 and extract C* in helping to answer that question? **(c)** Do these three sources give a complete answer to the question?

2 What does *picture 3* tell you about British attitudes towards **(i)** Germany and **(ii)** Belgium in 1914?

Project

1 Write the newspaper headlines which might have appeared above reports of the outbreak of War in **(i)** Germany; **(ii)** France; **(iii)** Britain.

2 You have fought at the defence of Paris and Ypres. Write a letter telling your parents about your first few months as a soldier.

TRENCH WARFARE, 1914 – 18

For many men, the War began and ended in trenches defended by **barbed wire**, **machine guns and individual rifles**. Even the best trenches *(extract A)* became **mudholes** because of **rain** and **artillery bombardment** *(extract B)*, ordered by **distant commanders** who thought that 'one more attack would win the War'. **Rupert Brooke** *(extract E)* had died in 1915 in the Dardenelles. Perhaps, if he had lived, he would have shared most soldiers' views about **the lunacy of trench war** and **the idiocy of most generals**. **Wilfred Owen** wrote *Apologia Pro Poemate Men* in which he gave thanks for servicemen's friendship but **bitterly attacked civilians** at home who had not shared their suffering *(extract G)*.

1 The reality of the trenches

2 A typical postcard from the 1914–18 War

JUST BEFORE THE BATTLE, MOTHER (2).
Farewell, Mother, you may never, you may never, Mother,
Press me to your heart again;
But oh, you'll not forget me, Mother, you will not forget me,
If I'm numbered with the slain.

Extract A Life in the trenches, World War I

A good trench was about six foot deep, so that we could walk in safety from rifle-fire. In each bay of the trench we built fire-steps about two feet off the bottom. This allowed us to put our heads over the parapet. During the day we had an hour's sleep, on a wet and muddy fire-step, wet through to the skin. When anyone had to visit the company on our right he had to walk through thirty yards of waterlogged trench, chest deep in water in some places. The duckboard track was always being shelled. In some places over a hundred yards had been blown away. It was better to keep off the track, but then sometimes you had to walk through very heavy and deep mud.
(*Old Soldiers Never Die*, F. Richards, 1933)

Extract B The Somme, July 1916

For a week about 300 guns poured shells onto the Germans. The noise seemed to throb in our veins even during the quiet of the night. Then, again, in the morning, the guns opened up. For a mile, our trenches belched out dense columns of green and orange smoke. It rose, curling and twisting, blotting everything from view. It seemed impossible that men could stand up to this terrible onslaught. The air was full of a vast and agonised violence, bursting into groans and screaming and pitiful whimperings... (Quoted in *The Army*, P. Lane, 1978)

Extract C A French officer's diary just before he died

Mankind is mad! It must be mad to do what it is doing. What slaughter! What scenes of horror and killing! Hell cannot be so terrible. Men are mad!

(Lt. Alfred Joubaire, quoted in *Eye-Deep in Hell*, J. Ellis, 1976)

Extract D

I know a simple soldier boy, Who grinned at life in empty joy
Slept soundly through the lonesome dark And whistled early with the lark.
In winter trenches, cowed and glum, With crumps of lice and lack of room,
He put a bullet through his brain. No-one spoke of him again.

(*Suicide in the Trenches*, S. Sassoon, 1915)

Extract E

Now, God be thanked Who has matched us with His hour,
And caught our youth, and wakened us from sleeping.

(*Peace*, R. Brooke, 1915)

Extract F

'Good morning; good morning' the General said,
When we met him last week on our way to the line.
Now the soldiers he smiled at are most of 'em dead,
And we're cursing his staff for incompetent swine.
'He's a cheery old card,' grunted Harry to Jack
As they slogged up to Arras with rifle and pack...
But he did for them both with his plan of attack.

(*The Generals*, S. Sassoon, 1915)

Extract G

Nevertheless, except you share with them in hell the sorrowful dark of hell,
Whose world is but the trembling of a flare, And heaven but as the Highway for a shell,
You shall not hear their mirth, You shall not come to think them well content
By any jest of mine. These men are worth
Your tears. You are not worth their merriment.

(W. Owen, 1915)

THE YOUNG HISTORIAN AT WORK

Knowledge and understanding

1 Soldiers on both sides faced similar conditions in the trenches. Use the text and the extracts here and on pages 108–9 to explain **(a)** why trench warfare lasted for so long; **(b)** the nature of the conditions endured by soldiers; **(c)** why no one seemed able to improve them.

2 (a) How was the War affected by the technological changes resulting from the industrial revolutions, studied earlier in this book? **(b)** What weapons were developed in an attempt to bring trench warfare to an end?

Interpretation

1 (a) Read *extracts C, D and F*. How do these extracts give a different interpretation of the War from that given by *extract E* here and extract E on page 109? **(b)** Use *extracts A and B* to explain those differences of interpretation.

2 Why do you think people at home glorified war, while the men at the Front tended to become hostile to it?

Use of sources

1 How can *picture 1 and extracts A–D* be used to help explain **(i)** what life was like in the trenches and **(ii)** how men reacted to those conditions? **(b)** Do you agree that *picture 1* is less reliable than *extract A* to historians trying to reconstruct life in the trenches? Give reasons for your answer.

2 What message is *picture 2* trying to convey? Explain your answer.

Project

1 Write a newspaper report about your life in the trenches and about battles on the Western Front.

2 Use *extract A and picture 1* to help you draw a sketch of a typical trench.

SUBMARINE WARFARE

Before 1914 Britain had been angered by the German building of a large navy. In spite of this, however, there were **few large naval battles** during the War. On **31 May 1916**, the two fleets did meet at **Jutland**. After a day's fighting the German fleet withdrew: Jellicoe, the British Commander, did not pursue them because he feared German minefields. **The Germans claimed a victory**: they had **lost fewer ships** than the British, a tribute to their gunpowder, armour and seamanship. **The British claimed a victory** because the Germans remained bottled up in Kiel *(picture 1)*.

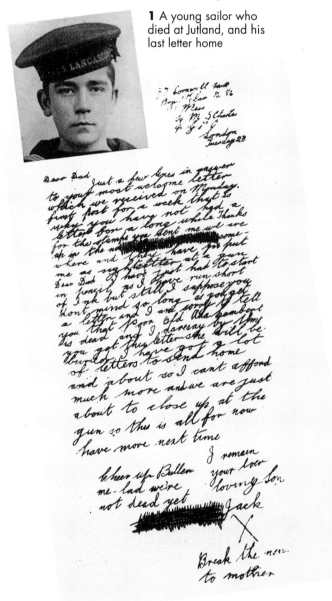

1 A young sailor who died at Jutland, and his last letter home

The British Navy was used to **protect troops** crossing to France and going to fight in the East and the Dardenelles. It was also used to **blockade Germany** to prevent goods being imported. In 1914 this blockade led to the demoralisation of the German people. Short of food, clothing, heating and other necessities, they demanded an end to the War while their troops were still in retreat, but on French soil. The British Navy had also to **protect shipping** bringing goods to Britain, which was heavily dependent on imported food (page 98, picture 2). Both sides used mines and submarines against the enemy. In **February 1915** the Germans announced an **unrestricted campaign** by which they threatened to sink all shipping around the British coast *(extract A)*. This was called off in May **1916** after the USA had protested over the sinking of the passenger liner, the **Lusitania**, with the loss of American lives *(extract B)*.

2 Cartoon showing the Germans with their 'baby', the U-boat

Submarines continued to attack British merchant shipping; the British lost many ships, lives and imports *(extract A)*. Some people thought that this campaign would lead to a German victory. However, a change of government brought **Lloyd George** as Prime Minister and a more vigorous **anti-submarine campaign** *(extract A)*. Because of the new **convoy system**, the Germans lost many submarines, while a system of **food rationing** lessened the demand for imports.

In **February 1917** the Germans announced a resumption of the **unrestricted campaign**. The German Foreign Secretary, **Zimmermann**, had warned his diplomats about this *(extract C)*. His 'Telegram' was published in the USA and led to a demand for American entry into the War. With the **US declaration of war** on Germany (**April 1917**) the Allies received the benefit of fresh troops and large supplies of munitions, plus added protection for Atlantic convoys.

Extract A Submarine warfare, 1916 – 18

At first they relied on cruisers and mines and other normal ways of attacking our merchant ships. When their last cruiser had been destroyed, the Germans used their 'little swordfish' which had already destroyed more of our ships in a month than their cruisers had sunk during a year. Then they built many more and much larger submarines. By the end of 1916 their submarines had sunk 738 of our ships, nearly one-fifth of all the ships we had had in 1914. No wonder we thought that we could not continue to fight for much longer. And I found that no one on our side had prepared any system for defeating the submarines.

Once the new government was formed in December 1916, the problem of the submarines was the first one we looked at. We considered several suggestions for dealing with the situation:

1 A system of convoys for merchant shipping in the danger zones;

...7 An increase in home supplies of food, timber and ore, and a reduction in consumption.

(*War Memoirs*, D. Lloyd George, 1933 – 36)

Extract B The sinking of the liner *Lusitania*, May 1915

The horror of the sinking of the *Lusitania* stirred the people more deeply than any other murderous acts committed by the Germans. The lives lost number over 1400 and every one foully murdered. It makes clear the hideous policy of brutality which has placed the whole German race outside the pale. The Germans have shown that they are determined to wage war under conditions of cold-blooded murder. Never before has a whole race, many millions of people, been organised for wholesale murder and destruction.

(*The Times*, 10 May 1915)

Extract C The Zimmermann telegram, 16 January 1917

We intend to begin unrestricted submarine warfare on 1st February. We shall try to keep the USA neutral. If this fails we offer Mexico an alliance – to make war together... and with our help, Mexico to reconquer Texas, New Mexico and Arizona. The unrestricted use of submarines will force England to make peace within a few months.

(**Zimmermann to German Ambassador, Washington, 1917**)

Extract D The USA declares war against Germany, 2 April 1917

The new policy has swept every restriction away. Ships of every kind have been sunk without warning. I advise that Congress declares this to be nothing less than German war against the USA, and that Congress takes immediate steps to put the country in a state of defense and to use all its power to bring the end to the War.

(**President Wilson to US Congress, April 1917**)

THE YOUNG HISTORIAN AT WORK

Knowledge and understanding

1 Explain the varying effects of British control of the sea by commenting on **(i)** Jutland; **(ii)** the blockade of Germany; **(ii)** the protection of troopships; **(iv)** the convoy system; (v) the entry of the USA into the War.

2 Name the THREE most important effects of naval warfare on the outcome of the War. Explain your answer.

Interpretation

1 How can *extracts B and C* be used to explain US policy towards the War as outlined in *extract D*?

2 Do you think that the extracts in these pages give enough evidence to explain why Germany ultimately failed to win the War at sea? Explain your answer.

Use of sources

1 (a) What does *picture 2* tell you about British propaganda? **(b)** What does such propaganda tell you about **(i)** the attitude of the British government; **(ii)** the attitudes of the people who read or looked at it at that time?

2 How valuable is *picture 1* to historians writing about **(i)** attitudes of sailors towards the War; **(ii)** what people at home knew about the War; **(iii)** censorship?

Project

1 Write an eyewitness account of the sinking of the *Lusitania*.

2 Interview Zimmermann about his policy towards Mexico *(extract C)*.

WARTIME TECHNOLOGY AND POST-WAR TRAVEL

In 1915 and again in December 1916, Governments were driven from office because of **industry's failure** (pages 100–101) to produce enough **ammunition** *(extract A)*. **Lloyd George's Government** (1916 – 18) dealt with the **submarines** (page 113, extract A) and the **industrial problem**. Some industries were **nationalised**; all had their **supplies controlled** by the Government, which made them produce what was wanted. **US methods of mass-production** were introduced, as was **US machinery** *(extract B)*.

After the War, William Morris used these methods to produce the **first cheap British car**, benefiting also from the development of **stronger engines**, needed to drive tanks and aeroplanes. **A new transport revolution** began in 1919 *(extracts C–D)*.

The air age also dawned because during the War governments had paid for the development of **stronger engines and steel frames** for aircraft. The first **crossing of the Atlantic** was by **two RAF pilots** flying a **former RAF bomber** – a tribute to the effects of the War and a foretaste of the future *(extract F)*.

1 Assembly line in the Singer Car Works, Birmingham, after the War

2 Pilots had to simultaneously fire at the enemy pilot and fly the 'plane

Extract A British industry fails to deliver the munitions, 1915

We had insufficient high explosives to destroy the enemy's parapets. This lack of an unlimited supply of explosives was a fatal bar to our success.

(*The Times*, **14 May 1915**)

Extract B The introduction of mass-production methods, 1916 – 18

The gun, aeroplane and tank factories of 1918, in their equipment and lay-out and in their methods of organisation, bore little resemblance to most British factories of 1913.

(*Economic effects of the World Wars on Britain*, A. Milward)

Extract C William Morris explains his success, 1924

The success of Morris Motors happened because we took steps to achieve a continually improving product, a reduction of cost and falling prices. The best way was to get specialists on every separate unit of the job. Today we have contracts with over 200 firms for various parts. At Oxford we only assemble the cars.

The firm that makes only one important part for us is probably making larger quantities than we would make ourselves. It is interested in nothing except that part and can keep its best brains on it. So it is better made. We ask firms to do work at prices that they think, at first, are too low. They haven't realised the savings made by mass production. (**Quoted in** *Life of Lord Nuffield*, Andrews and Brunner, 1955)

Extract D The post-war effects of the motor car revolution

Science made the car which made the roads which made the whole country accessible to everyone. No one is so poor that he cannot afford an occasional charabanc outing: so the country is brought to the town.

Formerly the people of a village had a strong sense of 'belonging to it', and even people from neighbouring villages were 'furriners'. Villagers did most of their shopping in the village. Today they still buy most of their groceries in the village shop, but their clothes and household furnishings are bought in the big shops in nearby towns. From the towns, too, come fresh fish and meat, bread, groceries and greengroceries are brought to the village by lorry or van. Village schoolchildren are carried to town in school buses and no longer suffer educational disadvantage.

(*The Century of Science*, F.S. Taylor, 1940)

Extract E Flying, 1914

The first time I saw a German plane in the air, both the pilot and myself were completely unarmed. We were taking photographs of the enemy's trench system when I suddenly saw a German two-seater about 100 yards below us. The German observer was not shooting at us. We waved a hand to him and went on our way. The enemy did likewise. But afterwards, just for safety's sake, I always carried a gun with me. In the next two or three months I had an occasional shot at a German machine. But these encounters could hardly be called 'fights'. If we saw the enemy we would fly towards it and fire half-a-dozen shots. We didn't expect to shoot him down; but it was a pleasant break from the monotony of reconnaissance and artillery observation.

(*War in the Air*, H.A. Jones, 1928)

Extract F The first flight across the Atlantic, 1919

Our plane had two Rolls-Royce engines of 350 horse-power. It cruised at ninety mph, but with a following wind we averaged 120. We came across the Atlantic in 16 hours, but it wasn't pleasant. We had no radio to guide us. We had fog nearly all the way and I saw the sky once for long enough to fix our position by the stars. We sat in an open cockpit with the sleet driving at us and obscuring the windscreen. Then ice began to form on the wings and clogged the aileron hinges, putting us into a dangerous spin from which we came out just above the waves. We went on until we saw Ireland and we crashed into a bog. My first words were 'Well, that's the start; they'll soon be coming over in dozens.' (Whitten-Brown quoted in *Scrapbook for 1919*, L. Bailey, 1919)

THE YOUNG HISTORIAN AT WORK

Knowledge and understanding

1 Show how the First World War was important in accelerating the developing technology for **(i)** arms production; **(ii)** road transport; **(iii)** aeroplanes.

2 Explain how the War **(i)** showed up the long-term failure of British industry; **(ii)** changed the role of government; **(iii)** led to the Americanisation of British industrial practices; **(iv)** promoted new groups into political life.

Interpretation

1 (a) How do *extracts A and B* confirm the interpretation of the pre-War failure of British industry? **(b)** Are there other explanations of that failure, not mentioned in these extracts?

2 How do *extracts C and D* reveal evidence for the view that the War had major long-term effects on **(i)** the car industry and **(ii)** society as a whole?

Use of sources

1 What do *extracts E and F* tell historians about **(i)** the nature of early aircraft; **(ii)** their uses in the First World War; **(iii)** how far aeroplanes had developed during the War; **(iv)** the long-term significance of the development of aircraft technology?

2 Do you agree that *extracts C, D, E and F* are reliable primary sources for historians investigating the growth (and its effects) of the car and aircraft industries? Why?

Project

1 Write the interview you had with a car worker *(picture 1)* in the 1920s, in which he compared old and new methods of car making.

2 How do you think aeroplanes *(picture 2)* could have been used to break the stalemate on the Western Front?

NEW ROLES FOR GOVERNMENT, WORKERS AND WOMEN, 1914 – 18

Control of labour. Britain's peace-time army was destroyed in 1914 (page 109, extracts C and D): millions of volunteers died in 1915 – 16 (page 109, extracts E–G). In **May 1916** all unmarried men aged between 18 and 41 (and widowers with no dependants) had to sign a register making them liable for **military service**. **27 Liberal MPs** voted against this interference with '**men's freedom**'. This registration showed how unhealthy the people were *(extract A)*.

Control of food. The **submarine campaign** made the Government bring in the **Corn Production Act** (1917) which guaranteed farmers fair prices for their products. Many Liberals opposed this **interference with market forces**. They were more angered by the introduction of **food rationing** (1918), which ensured that everyone had the right to the same weekly ration of basic foods. In wartime many homes had higher incomes than in 1913, and many people were better fed as a result *(extract B)*.

Workers' hopes. Unions gave up their right to strike, and let unskilled workers do the work usually done by skilled men. **Three Union leaders** became Government Ministers in 1916, and **many others** joined committees formed to raise production levels. Unions hoped that, in peacetime, they would continue to have a share in **decision-making** and that **living standards** would improve *(extract B)*.

Votes for women. In 1913 Lloyd George had opposed **Mrs Pankhurst** and her campaign for votes for women. In 1914 she demanded '**the right to work**': Lloyd George accepted this and millions of women joined the workforce. In **1918** a **Parliamentary Reform Bill** was amended to give **women over the age of thirty the right to vote** (along with all men aged 21 or over) *(extract D)*.

Extract A The unhealthy results of a century of industrialisation

Of every nine men of military age in Great Britain, *three* were perfect, fit and healthy, *two* were of a poorer quality of health and strength because of some disability or some lack of development, *three* were unable to do any real physical work and could best be described as physical wrecks, and the remaining one was a permanent invalid with only a slight grasp on life. (A Government report on conscription, 1917)

1 A 1915 propaganda poster

Daddy, what did YOU do in the Great War?

Extract B The wartime improvement in working class diet

We have found that in June the working classes as a whole were able to buy as much food as they had bought in 1913. Indeed, our figures show that the families of unskilled workers were slightly better off in 1918 than they had been in 1914. This finding is confirmed by reports from School Medical Officers. From London comes the report that the proportion of children in a poorly fed condition is less than half what it was in 1913.

2 The opening of a communal kitchen in 1918—all were rationed to the same amount of food

Parents are now better able to give their children the better food they need. This can be seen from the figures of children who need to claim free meals from the education authorities. The figures for 1917 show that, compared with the figures for 1914, there has been a fall of about four-fifths in the numbers of 'necessitous children'.

(A Government report on working class diet, 1919)

Extract C Women and munition workers, 1915

On July 18 1915 there was the great Women's War Pageant. Thousands of women marched for miles along London streets. They brought me, as Minister of Munitions, a deputation which expressed their welcome of the National Register, and offered their services to help the country. Their leader, Mrs Pankhurst, also asked for wage conditions which would safeguard their standard of living and prevent them from being exploited by manufacturers. I gave a guarantee that they would have a fair minimum wage for time work, and that they would have the same rates as the men for any piece work. These conditions were strictly imposed by the Ministry throughout the war. This had a permanent effect on the status of women workers in this country.

(*War Memoirs*, D. Lloyd George, 1933-36)

Extract D An opponent describes how women first got the right to vote, 1918

Let me describe how gradually, but how inevitably we descended the slippery slope. First of all it was not proposed to include women (in the 1918 Reform Act). Then an important member of the House of Commons said that it was impossible to exclude from the franchise the brave men who had fought in the War. That argument was enthusiastically welcomed, and soldiers were admitted.

AT LAST!

3 'Votes for Women' – a 1918 *Punch* cartoon

Then another MP said; 'if you are giving the vote to the brave soldiers, what about the brave munition workers?' That argument had to be accepted once you had accepted the argument about the 'brave soldiers'. Then a cunning MP said; 'What about the brave women munition workers?' And, once we had given in to the argument about men munition workers, it was impossible to resist the claims of the women.

(Lord Birkenhead, formerly F.E. Smith, MP, in the House of Lords, 1928)

THE YOUNG HISTORIAN AT WORK

Knowledge and understanding

1 Read the text and *extracts A–D*, and look at *pictures 1 and 2*. Show how the War was a force for change in **(a)** the short term and **(b)** the long term. You might refer to **(i)** conscription; **(ii)** food supply; **(iii)** diets; **(iv)** the rôle of women; **(v)** trade union expectations.

2 Although the War had major effects on the British people, these changes did not occur at a regular rate. Explain **(a)** what events and **(b)** which individuals caused some changes to occur very quickly.

Interpretation

1 Read page 111, extract G, again. How does the attitude which Wilfred Owen revealed in that extract become more understandable after you have read *extract A* on this page?

2 (a) How can *extract C* be used to show the importance of **(i)** women and **(ii)** Lloyd George during the First World War?
(b) What interpretation does *extract D* provide about the effects of the War on women's demand for the vote?

Use of sources

1 *Picture 1* is an example of government propaganda. Do you agree that this source is a valuable piece of evidence about the messages that the Government was giving to the people during the War? Why?

2 How valuable is *picture 3* to historians examining the campaign for women to have the right to vote?

Project

1 Find out more about Mrs Pankhurst and the Suffragette Movement.

2 Make a poster supporting the campaign 'Votes for Women', 1918.

POETRY, PROPAGANDA, POSTERS AND PRAYER

In 1917, a US Senator said '**The first casualty when war comes is truth**'. Look at *picture 1* and then read *extract A*. Someone was lying.

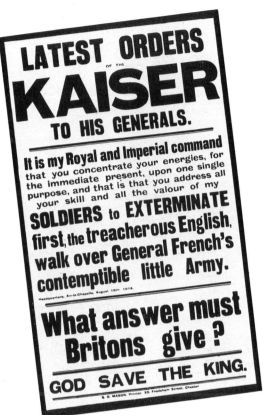

1 A propaganda poster from 1914

Extract A The German Kaiser's comment on the British poster (*picture 1*)
'I never made such an order. On the contrary, I always stressed the high value of the British Army and warned against underestimating it.'
(William II, Chancellor of Germany, 1914)

Another **wartime 'casualty'** was the **patriotic idealism** which inspired Rupert Brooke (below and page 111, extract E) and many other men (page 109, extract E).

Extract B Brooke's welcome for a 'patriotic' death
If I should die, think only this of me:
That there's some corner of a foreign field
That is for ever England. There shall be
In that rich earth a richer dust concealed
A dust whom England bore, shaped, made aware,
Gave, once, her flowers to love, her ways to roam,
A body of England's, breathing English air,
Washed by the waves, blest by the suns of home.
(*The Soldier*, R. Brooke, 1915)

The slaughters of **1914 – 16** (pages 110–11, extracts A–D) **killed that idealism**. Even **later volunteers** seemed less 'patriotic' (page 109, extracts F and G). **Sassoon**, 'a patriotic volunteer', became critical of the War and of his leaders (page 111, extracts D and F). **Owen was even more bitter** (page 111, extract G and below):

2 An enlistment poster, mentioning the 1839 Treaty

Extract C On the horror of fighting
If in some smothering dreams, you too could pace
Behind the waggon that we flung him in,
And watch the white eyes writhing in his face...
My friend, you would not tell with such high zest
To children ardent with some desperate glory,
Dulce et decorum est,
Pro patria mori.
(*Dulce Et Decorum Est*, W. Owen, 1915)

Propaganda took various forms. Soldiers were supposed to be roused by the **Kaiser's contempt** for them (*picture 1*) and by his **attack on 'little Belgium'** (*picture 2* and page 108, picture 3). **Popular songs** influenced opinion:

Extract D Music-hall encouragement to volunteers
We don't want to lose you, But we think you ought to go,
For your King and your Country, Both need you so...

Posters were used **to attract** volunteers (page 109, picture 5), **to shame** the less willing (page 116, picture 1 and page 109, extract G), and **to blind relatives** as to the true nature of trench warfare (*picture 3* and page 110, picture 2). **Prayer** for victory in '**the holy War**' turned many against religion.

Extract E A nurse's attack on 'holy war'
I wish that people who write about 'a holy war' could see a case of mustard gas, the poor men burnt and blistered, with blind eyes and always fighting for breath, their throats closing and they know they will choke.
(*Eye-Deep in Hell*, J. Ellis, 1976)

Extract F Soldiers mock popular hymns
Forward Joe Soap's army, Marching without fear
With our old commander, Safely in the rear...
(To the tune of *Onward Christian Soldiers*)

Extract G A poet on 'cursing God'
But War – as war is now and always was
A dirty loathsome, servile murder – job:

Men, lousy, sleepless, ulcerous, afraid,
Toiling their hearts out in the pulling slime...

Men stunned in brainlessness, and gibbering
Men driven to death and worse than death...

Cursing with their last breath, the living God
Because He made them, in His image, men.
(G. Frankau, 1917)

3 A totally misleading representation of life at the front

4 The cartoonist has drawn a crying child ('1940 class') to predict a future war

And for what? In 1919 the politicians wrote the **Treaty of Versailles** as the end of '**The War to end All Wars**'. But even then some people saw that the flawed Treaty contained **the seeds of future wars** (*picture 4*).

THE YOUNG HISTORIAN AT WORK

Knowledge and understanding
1 Read *extracts B and C*. Can you explain why these two poets had differing attitudes towards the War? You should re-read page 11, where you will also find other examples of these writers' poems.

2 What do the primary sources given on these pages reveal about the effects of War on **(i)** patriotism; **(ii)** propaganda; **(iii)** religious belief; **(iv)** the power of governments over people?

Interpretation
1 (a) Which of the *extracts* on these pages seem to **(i)** support patriotic calls to serve in the War; **(ii)** be opposed to patriotism?
(b) Do you think that the selection of *extracts* on these pages is biased **(i)** for OR **(ii)** against war and patriotism? Explain your answer.

2 (a) Do you believe that dying for one's country was *Dulce et Decorum* ('sweet and beautiful') (*extract C*)? **(b)** How does *picture 4* seem to bear out Owen's warnings about war?

Use of sources
1 How valuable are *pictures 1 and 2* to historians investigating **(i)** the purpose of propaganda and **(ii)** its effects on the British people?

2 (a) How does *picture 3* differ from the truth about life in the trenches as shown in the pictures and extracts on pages 110–11?
(b) Does this make *picture 3* less reliable as a picture of life in the trenches? **(c)** Is *picture 3* of any value to historians investigating wartime propaganda?

Project
1 Make two posters: ONE calling for recruits; ONE condemning the War.

2 Write a poem about the effects of war on soldiers and their families.

THE ERA OF THE SECOND WORLD WAR

THE LEGACY OF THE FIRST WORLD WAR

The Allied peacemakers had to deal with the problems linked to the collapse of the Empires of Russia, Austria and Germany *(picture)*. They also had to try to arrange a treaty to finish 'the war to end all wars'. **Wilson** (USA) was mainly concerned to get a League of Nations set up (page 124, extract A), **Clemenceau** (France) wanted to punish Germany *(picture and extract D)*, **Orlando** (Italy) to gain territory for Italy (page 124, extract B), **Lloyd George** (Britain) to get a lasting peace *(extracts A–C)*. The pressure from British public opinion and from France forced Lloyd George to agree to a punitive Treaty which carried the seeds of future troubles (page 119, picture 4).

Former territory of Imperial Russia

Plebiscite areas

Lost by Germany 1919

Austria-Hungary until 1918

Saar: League of Nations control 1919–1935

Pre 1919 borders in black

Demilitarised Rhineland

FINLAND

ESTONIA

LATVIA

LITHUANIA

USSR

SWEDEN

DENMARK

EAST PRUSSIA

POLAND

HOLLAND

GERMANY

BELGIUM

Saar

CZECHOSLOVAKIA

FRANCE

AUSTRIA

SWITZERLAND

HUNGARY

ROMANIA

YUGOSLAVIA

ITALY

SERBIA

BULGARIA

0   300 miles

0   500 km

1 Frontier changes in Europe after 1918

Extract A A just and lenient Peace Treaty?

We (British) seek no selfish and greedy aims; we have only one purpose – to obtain justice for others. We do not seek to destroy Germany or to diminish her boundaries: we do not seek to enlarge our Empire. **(D. Lloyd George, 5 January 1918)**

Extract B Still looking for a lasting peace, early 1919

It is easy to patch up a peace which will last for thirty years. It is hard to draw up a peace which will not provoke a fresh struggle when those who have gone through the War are dead. You may strip Germany of her colonies, reduce her army to a mere police force and her navy to that of a fifth-rate Power; but if she feels she has been unjustly treated, she will find ways of getting revenge on her conquerors.
(D. Lloyd George in a memorandum)

Extract C German anger at the final Treaty, 7 May 1919

Lloyd George went to Versailles to present the Peace terms to the Germans. I do not think David realised, before he went, what an exhausting event it would be. He came back quite exhausted with emotion. The Germans were arrogant and insolent. He says that it has made him more angry than any incident of the War, and if the Germans do not sign, he will have no mercy on them. He says for the first time he feels the same hatred for them that the French feel. I am glad they stirred him up so that he may keep stern with them: if they had been submissive he might have been sorry for them.
(Diary extract by Frances Stephenson, Lloyd George's secretary and, later, wife)

Extract D Extracts from the Treaty of Versailles, May 1919

42 Germany is forbidden to have any fortifications on either side of the left bank of the Rhine or on the right bank to the west of a line fifty kms to the east of the Rhine.

43 In the area defined above, the assembly of armed forces of any kind is forbidden.

45 As compensation for the destruction of the coal mines in north France, Germany cedes to France the coal mines in the Saar Basin.

51 The territories ceded to Germany in 1871 are restored to France.

80 Germany will respect the independence of Austria.

119 Germany renounces, in favour of the Allied Powers, all her overseas possessions.

160 The German Army must not exceed 100 000 men including officers and men at depots. It shall be devoted exclusively to the maintenance of order within the frontiers.

231 The Allies confirm and Germany accepts the responsibility of Germany and her allies for causing all the loss and damage to which the Allies and their peoples have been subjected as a consequence of the war imposed on them by the aggression of Germany and her allies.

232 Germany will make compensation for all damage done to the civilian population of the Allies and to their property.

233 The amount of the above damages shall be fixed by an Allied commission.

THE YOUNG HISTORIAN AT WORK

Knowledge and understanding

1 Explain the reasons for the harsh punishment of Germany after World War One.

2 What were the short- and long-term effects of the harsh treatment of Germany?

Interpretation

1 How do *extracts A and C* differ in their interpretation of Lloyd George's attitudes to how Germany should be treated in 1919?

2 Why did these differences occur?

Use of sources

1 What do *extracts B and D* tell you about how Germany was affected by the Versailles Treaty **(i)** economically; **(ii)** socially; **(iii)** politically?

2 Do you agree that the *picture* is a valuable source to historians wishing to understand how Europe changed after World War One?

Project

1 Write the speech of **(i)** a French politician and **(ii)** a German politician about the Treaty of Versailles.

2 'The Allies were wrong to be harsh towards Germany after World War One'. Do you agree? Give reasons for your answer.

THE COLLAPSE OF GERMAN DEMOCRACY

When the German Kaiser abdicated in 1918, Germany became a **Republic**. The new government was blamed by the army and the nationalists for accepting the humiliating **Treaty of Versailles** (page 121, extract D). It became even more unpopular in 1923 when the French occupied the Ruhr industrial basin and when **inflation** saw the price of a loaf of bread rise from 2 marks (1921) to 470 billion marks (1923). Because of international cooperation, Germany had a period of stability and recovery (1924 – 9) before the Wall Street collapse of 1929 began a **world trade recession** which saw a massive rise in unemployment *(extract C)*. It was this which led to support for the **National Socialist (Nazi) Party** led by Hitler *(extract C)*. He had a para-military 'army' of brownshirted **Stormtroopers** modelled on **Mussolini's Blackshirts** (page 124–5, extract C and picture 1). These frightened many, but attracted the support of many others *(extract A)*. Hitler also used '**the big lie**' *(extract B)* as part of his propaganda to gain support among those angry with Versailles (page 126, extract A) and unemployment *(extract C and picture 1)*. Industrialists welcomed the promises to crush socialism and the unions and to spend money on armaments (page 126, extract B). In **January 1933 Hitler became Chancellor** (Prime Minister) in a coalition government. He used his new power *(extract D)* to increase his political power. He also used his power to frighten other parties to vote for him to have dictatorial powers *(extract E)*.

1 This Socialist Party poster reads 'Our Last Hope, Hitler'

Extract A The Nazi Anthem

Hold High the banner! Close the hard ranks serried!
SA (Stormtroopers) marches on with sturdy stride.
Comrades by Red Front and Reaction killed, are buried.
But march with us in image at our side.
Gang way! Gang way! Now for the Brown Battalions!
For the Storm Troopers clear roads o'er the land!
The Swastika gives hope to our entranced millions,
The day for freedom and bread's at hand...
(By Stormtrooper Horst Wessel, 1925)

Extract B Hitler on the use of propaganda – and lies, 1924

Most of the people have little intelligence, so propaganda must consist of a few points in a few simple words, repeated again and again until even the most stupid know them. In the big lies there is always a certain force of credibility. The masses easily fall victim for the big lie rather than the small one, because they themselves often use small lies but would be ashamed to try a big one. The huge lie always leaves traces behind even after it has been shown to be a lie. (*Mein Kampf*, Adolf Hitler, 1924)

2 A Nazi rally

Extract C Unemployment and the rise of the Nazis to power: 1919 – 33
Figures in brackets show percentage of votes for each party

	1919	1920	May 1924	Dec 1924	1928	1930	July 1932	Dec 1932	March 1933
Nationalists	42 (10)	65 (15)	106 (20)	103 (21)	79 (14)	41 (7)	40 (6)	51 (8)	53 (8)
Centre Party	71 (20)	68 (14)	65 (13)	69 (14)	61 (13)	68 (12)	75 (12)	70 (12)	73 (12)
Social Democrats	163 (38)	113 (22)	100 (21)	131 (26)	152 (30)	143 (25)	133 (22)	121 (20)	120 (18)
Communists	— —	2 (2)	62 (12)	45 (9)	54 (11)	77 (13)	89 (14)	100 (17)	81 (12)
National Socialists Nazis	— —	— —	32 (7)	14 (3)	13 (3)	107 (18)	230 (37)	196 (33)	288 (44)
Unemployed (millions)					1.8	2.8	3.2	4.8	6.0

Extract D Using government power to help win the election in March 1933

February 3 1933. I talk about the start of the election campaign with the Leader. The struggle is an easy one now, since we are able to use all means of the State. Radio and Press are at our disposal. The Leader is to speak in all towns having their own broadcasting stations. We transmit the broadcast to the entire people and give listeners a clear idea of all that occurs at our meetings. I will introduce the Leader's speech and I shall try to give the hearers the magical atmosphere of our huge demonstrations.

(*My Part in Germany's Fight*, J. Goebbels, 1935)

Extract E A cowed Reichstag gives Hitler total power, 24 March 1933

Hitler said that it would be against the spirit of national resurgence if he had to bargain with the Reichstag for every action. So he needed the Enabling Law. Its rejection would be taken as a sign of 'Now, gentlemen, you may choose peace or war'. Only 535 of the 747 deputies were present: others were in concentration camps. Due to the full weight of Nazi pressure and terror, the Enabling Law passed with a vote of 441 in favour. This marked the real seizure of control by the conspirators. The Reichstrat (Upper House) met immediately after and approved the Law without debate.

(Adapted from reports in *The Times*, March 1933)

THE YOUNG HISTORIAN AT WORK

Knowledge and understanding

1 (a) Put the following factors, which led to Hitler's rise to power, in order of their importance: the Versailles Peace Treaty; the Wall Street Crash; Hitler's personality and policies. **(b)** Explain your choice of order.

2 What other factors, not mentioned above, do you think help to explain Hitler's rise to power?

Interpretation

1 Read *extracts A and C*. How do these *extracts* give **(i)** a different interpretation of Nazi popularity before 1933 AND **(ii)** a similar interpretation?

2 What do you think opponents of the Nazis thought of Horst Wessel's interpretation of the Nazi movement? Give reasons for your answer.

Use of sources

1 Read *extracts B, D and E*. How do these extracts help historians understand the importance of Nazi propaganda and intimidation of opponents?

2 Study *pictures 1 and 2*. What do these pictures tell us about how the Nazis were trying to win support from the German people?

Project

1 Do you agree that Hitler's rise to power was inevitable? You might like to discuss this with friends.

2 Make a timeline from 1918 to 1933, showing the key events in the story of Hitler's rise to power.

ITALIAN FASCISM, THE LEAGUE OF NATIONS AND ABYSSINIA

Italy had been **united** only in 1870 and its democracy was still young. In 1919 there was great **discontent**: ex-soldiers faced unemployment; nationalists were angry at **Orlando's failure** to gain much at **Versailles** *(extract B)*; millions hoped for a Russian-style Communist revolution. **Mussolini**, an ex-socialist, founded the **Fascist Party** in **1919**: he was supported by industrialists (frightened of a Bolshevik Revolution), by the unemployed (hoping for work, and willing to join his **Blackshirts**, *picture 2 and extract C*) and ex-soldiers. In 1922 his threatened 'March on Rome' led the weak king to make him **Prime Minister** and he used his new powers to get himself made dictator. His aggressive foreign policy was meant to please Italians and distract attention from their poor conditions at home. His invasion of Abyssinia *(picture 3 and extract D)* might have been stopped by the League of Nations *(extract A)*. But the main powers – Britain and France – were unwilling to act *(picture 4)*: they saw him as a possible **ally against Hitler**. Mussolini realised how lucky he had been *(extract G)*. Hitler realised that the League would never act – and so he became an **expansionist**.

1 *Evening Standard* cartoon. Japan trampling on the League of Nations; Britain repairs its face

Extract A The League of Nations promises united action against aggressors, 1918

Should any member of the League resort to war, all members undertake immediately to break off all trade relations. It shall be the duty of the Council of the League to recommend what effective military, naval or air force the Members of the League shall contribute to the armed forces to be used to protect the Covenants of the League (against aggressors).

(The Covenant of the League of Nations, Article 16)

Extract B Why many Italians supported Mussolini's Fascists, 1919

When I returned from the War I found the politicians had betrayed the soldiers, reducing Italy to a shameful peace. Many, even the most generous, tended to Communism. In my opinion, three-quarters of Italian youth would have become Bolsheviks: a revolution at any cost! Mussolini gave youth that programme which they searched for.

(*Recollections*, Air Marshal Balbo, 1932)

2 A group of Blackshirts

3 Invasion of Abyssinia

Extract C Mussolini's Blackshirts frighten many into submission

If you met them in the daytime they would be humble and fawning. By night, and together, they were wicked and evil. They have always been at the disposal of anyone who gave orders, and always will be. But recruiting them into a special army, with special uniform and arms, is something peculiar to the last few years. Such are the Fascists. Their boldness had another explanation, too. Each of us would have been a match for three of them. But what chance did we have in their midst? What was to bind us together? What linked us? There we were in the middle of the square, all born in Fontamara. Everyone thought only of himself, of the best way of getting out of that square of armed men. We all thought first of our families. (*Fontamara*, I. Silone, 1965)

Extract D Mussolini excuses his attack on Abyssinia, 1 August 1935

There must be no misunderstanding upon this task which I assign to Italians. There is no question of territorial conquests: but of a natural expansion which will lead to a collaboration between Italy and the people of Africa. We ask from those who have made good by earlier conquests that they should not take pains to block the expansion of Fascist Italy. I think for Italy like the great Englishmen who made the British Empire thought for England. (*The Times*, 1 August 1935)

Extract E The League seems ready to act against Mussolini, October 1935

When the Council met on 5 October 1935 I told them that since war had broken out we must act speedily: a Committee of six gathered a few minutes after the end of the Council's meeting. By the evening of 6 October the Fascist Government's action was condemned: 'The Committee concludes that the Italian government has restored to war in disregard of its obligations under the Covenant of the League'. The Assembly met on 9 October, and on 10 October 50 states had agreed to apply sanctions. (*The Eden Memoirs*, A. Eden, 1962)

THE AWFUL WARNING.

FRANCE AND ENGLAND (*together?*). "WE DON'T WANT YOU TO FIGHT, BUT, BY JINGO, IF YOU DO, WE SHALL PROBABLY ISSUE A JOINT MEMORANDUM SUGGESTING A MILD DISAPPROVAL OF YOU."

4 *Punch* cartoon suggests Anglo–French 'mild disapproval'

Extract F The League's members do not keep their promises

We have to admit that the purpose for which sanctions were imposed has not been realised. The League put sanctions on some goods only, because the incomplete membership of the League made it impossible to make all sanctions effective. Oil could not be made effective by League action alone. It has to be said that sanctions did not succeed.

(Foreign Secretary Eden in the Commons, 18 June 1936)

Extract G Mussolini admits that he was lucky

If the League had extended economic sanctions to oil, I would have had to withdraw from Abyssinia within a week.

(Quoted in *The Diaries of O. Harvey*, 1937 – 40)

THE YOUNG HISTORIAN AT WORK

Knowledge and understanding

1 Explain why Mussolini gained the support of **(i)** the unemployed; **(ii)** industrialists; **(iii)** nationalists; **(iv)** soldiers; **(v)** the young.

2 What were the causes and consequences of the failure of the League of Nations to stop Mussolini's invasion of Abyssinia?

Interpretation

1 Read *extracts A, E and F*. Illustrate and explain why there are differing interpretations of the strength of the League of Nations here.

2 Read *extracts D and G*. Why do these extracts provide differing interpretations of Mussolini's strength during the invasion?

Use of sources

1 Look at *extract C and picture 2*. How reliable are these sources to historians wishing to write an accurate history of the Blackshirts?

2 What do *pictures 1 and 4* tell us about **(i)** Italian and Japanese foreign policy and **(ii)** attitudes in Britain towards these events?

Project

1 Write a speech of **(i)** a supporter and **(ii)** an opponent of Mussolini in 1922.

2 Draw a cartoon which one of Mussolini's supporters might have produced at the time of the Abyssinian War.

HITLER'S EXPANSIONISM

1 German expansion, by March 1939

Once in power **Hitler ignored** the terms of the **Versailles Treaty** (page 121, extract D); he built up the army, the navy and the air force and spent massive sums on re-armament *(extract B)*. When Mussolini defied the League over **Abyssinia** (pages 124–5) Hitler 'invaded' the Rhineland and the League failed to act *(extract C and picture 2)*. Like Mussolini in Abyssinia (page 125, extract G), Hitler knew that he could not have defied League action in 1936 *(extract D)*. In 1938 he **again broke the Treaty** of Versailles when he **invaded Austria** (picture 1). Then, with the connivance of the British, French and Italians he divided the Versailles state of **Czechoslovakia** *(picture 3 and extract E)*. He had outlined these **expansionist** plans in his book, **Mein Kampf** (1923 – 4), so his policies ought not to have surprised people in Europe.

Extract A Hitler condemns the Treaty of Versailles, 1924

What use could be made of the Treaty! Each one of the points could be branded in the minds and hearts of the Germans until 60 million find their souls aflame with rage and shame, and a torrent bursts forth as from a furnace, and a will of steel is forged from it, with the cry; 'We will have arms again'.

(*Mein Kampf*, **Adolf Hitler, 1924**)

Extract B Aggression will pay for German living standards, 1943

Our armaments have swallowed fantastic sums: either these debts will be put on the people in the shape of taxes, or they will be paid by the profits from the occupied territories.

(**Hitler, speaking in 1943**)

THE GOOSE-STEP.
"GOOSEY GOOSEY GANDER,
WHITHER DOST THOU WANDER!"
"ONLY THROUGH THE RHINELAND—
PRAY EXCUSE MY BLUNDER!"

2 'The Goose-Step', *Punch* cartoon, 1936

Extract C The Rhineland: a small case study, 1936

11 March 1936: The French know that the invasion of the demilitarised zone was against the advice of the German Generals; they feel that if we show firmness, we may discredit Hitler with his people. If we do nothing, the League will cease to have any meaning. But the country will not let us take action in what they see as a purely French interest.

12 March 1936: The French say that the Covenant has been broken and they ask us to fulfil our obligations under the Covenant and the Treaty of Locarno. The French are right. Hitler gambled. If we send an ultimatum to Germany she will climb down. What is the good of that? It will mean communism in Germany, which is why the Russians are keen on it. So we have to swallow the humiliation.

(*Diaries and Letters*, **Harold Nicholson, 1930 – 39**)

Extract D Hitler on the Rhineland crisis, 1936

7 March 1936: In the train going to Munich this evening, Hitler said: 'We had no army worth mentioning; it would not even have had the strength to maintain itself against the Poles. If the French had taken any action, we would have been easily defeated; our resistance would have been short-lived.'

(*Inside the Third Reich*, **Albert Speer, 1970**)

Extract E Czechoslovakia: another small case study, 1938 – 9

19 September 1938: After meeting Herr Hitler at Berchtesgaden, I told the Czechs to be ready to make sacrifices. The maintenance within their boundaries of the Sudeten Germans cannot continue without imperiling peace which cannot be assured unless these areas are transferred to Germany.

28 September 1938: I met Herr Hitler again on 22 September at Godesberg. He told me that our plans for Czechoslovakia were too slow and that he was prepared to risk a World War over the Sudeten lands.

29 September 1938: This means peace in our time; the Munich agreement is a symbol of our two peoples' determination not to go to war again.

(Adapted from N. Chamberlain's letters and diaries, 1938 – 9)

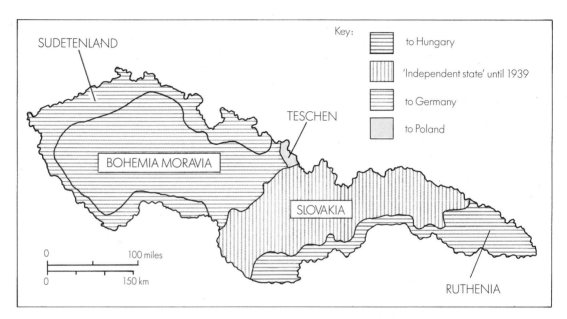

3 The destruction of Czechoslavakia

THE YOUNG HISTORIAN AT WORK

Knowledge and understanding

1 Explain the reasons why the majority of German people supported Hitler in his foreign policy before 1939.

2 Make lists of the ways in which **(i)** Hitler broke the Treaty of Versailles and **(ii)** other countries' politicians reacted.

Interpretation

1 Do you agree that the evidence shows that Hitler's foreign policy was a complete success by 1939? Give reasons for your answer.

2 Do Albert Speer's memoirs confirm or reject Harold Nicholson's interpretations of Hitler's strength in 1936? Explain your answer.

Use of sources

1 How reliable do you think *extract A* is as a guide to German attitudes to the Versailles Treaty?

2 What can historians learn from *pictures 1–3* about Hitler's policies?

Project

1 Make a timeline showing how and when Hitler expanded Germany's borders.

2 How do you think Mussolini's policies compare with Hitler's?

GERMANY AND 'SOLVING THE JEWISH PROBLEM'

Hitler blamed **the Jews** for all the evil in the world: for the defeat of Germany in the First World War *(extract A)*, for taking jobs from Germans, for having too much success in the professions, banking and trade... By 1945 the Nazis had **killed 70 per cent** of European Jews (about 6 million people). Hitler attacked them in election manifestos, in speeches and, through his **Stormtroopers** (page 122, extract A), encouraged physical attacks on Jewish people and property *(picture 2 and extract B)*. At a huge rally in Nuremberg in 1935 (page 122, picture 2) Hitler announced a series of **anti-Jewish laws** aimed at making life almost impossible for them. One of his colleagues, Julius Streicher, edited an almost pornographic newspaper, **Der Stürmer**, which attacked and misrepresented Jews and their religion *(picture 1)*. During the War, Jews in occupied countries were gathered into **concentration camps**, some of which were earmarked as extermination camps *(extract D and picture 3)*. This '**Holocaust**' remains a blot on German, and European, history.

1 The front page of Der Stürmer, May 1934

Extract A Hitler blames the Jews for the German defeat, 1918

If, at the beginning and during the War, someone had only subjected about 12 or 15 000 of these Hebrew enemies of the people to poison gas, then the sacrifice of millions at the front would not have been in vain. (*Mein Kampf*, A. Hitler, 1924)

2 Elderly Jews are forced to scrub pavements for the amusement of the Nazis

Extract B Speedy action against Austrian Jews, June 1938

I met an Austrian yesterday who had just got away from Vienna, and what he said made me ill. They rounded up the people walking in the Prater on Sunday last, and separated the Jews from the rest. They made the Jewish men take off all their clothes and walk on all fours on the grass. They made the old Jewish ladies get up into the trees by ladders and sit there. The suicides have been appalling. (*Diaries and Letters*, H. Nicholson, 1930 – 9)

Extract C Hitler demands an anti-Jewish campaign, 1942

The Fuhrer once more expressed his determination to clean up the Jews in Europe pitilessly. There must be no more squeamish sentimentalism about it. Their destruction will go hand in hand with the destruction of our enemies. (*Diaries*, J. Goebbels, 1943)

Extract D The Auschwitz Extermination Camp, by its Commandant

The 'Final solution' of the Jewish question meant the complete extermination of all European Jews. I was told to set up extermination facilities at Auschwitz in June 1941. There were already three other such camps: Belsen, Treblinka and Wolzek. At Treblinka the Commandant told me that he had liquidated 80 000 in half a year, mainly from Warsaw. He used monoxide gas... not very efficient. At Auschwitz I used Cyclon B, a crystallised prussic acid dropped into the death chamber. It took from three to fifteen minutes to kill the people in the chamber: we knew they were dead when they stopped screaming. After the bodies were removed, special commandos took off the rings and extracted the gold from the teeth of the corpses. We built our gas-chambers to take 2000 at one time.

(Evidence given at the Nuremberg Trials, 1947-9)

Belsen concentration camp, 1945

Extract E A British Medical Officer at Belsen, 1945

I visited the human remains lying on the straw mats, covered with filthy blankets. At first we were unable to define their sex. Their heads shorn, the agony of their sufferings showed clearly in their expressions, their eyes sunken and listless, cheek bones prominent, too weak to close their mouths, their arms extended in an appalling manner. The floor was filthy, straw littered with human excrement. **(Statement made in 1945)**

Extract F SS Commander Himmler praises the exterminators, October 1943

I now want to mention, quite openly, before you all, a difficult subject. Among ourselves it can be discussed, but never mentioned in public. I mean the extermination of the Jews. Any member of the Party will tell you 'the Jews will be exterminated. It's part of our programme.' But not one has seen it done. You will know what it means to have a hundred corpses lying there, or 500 or 1000. To have seen this through has made us hard and is a page of glory in our history.

(Himmler to SS Generals in Poland, 10 October 1943)

THE YOUNG HISTORIAN AT WORK

Knowledge and understanding

1 Explain in detail how Nazi persecution of the Jewish people become increasingly extreme from 1935 to 1945.

2 Make a list of reasons, in order of their importance, for the popularity of these policies amongst many German people.

Interpretation

1 How and why do you think that the writers of *extracts C and E* differed in their interpretation of Nazi destruction of the Jews from the authors of *extracts B, D and F*?

2 Why do you think that Nazis used anti-Jewish propaganda as in *picture 1*?

Use of sources

1 Which extracts do you find most useful in understanding what it was like to be a Jew under Nazi domination?

2 How can we use *pictures 2 and 3* to understand the effects of Nazism?

Project

1 You are a war journalist. Write a newspaper article describing what it was like to find a concentration camp at the end of the War.

2 On a map of Europe mark the location of concentration camps and the numbers of Jews who died in each country.

GERMAN SUCCESS, 1939 – 42

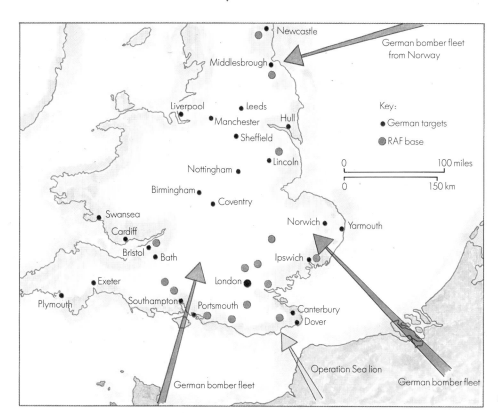

1 The Battle of Britain, August–October 1940

In 1938 the British and French allowed Hitler to take most of **Czechoslovakia** (page 127, extract E). In doing so, they ignored the Soviet Union, which had an alliance with Czechoslovakia. This may help to explain why **Stalin made a Pact with Hitler in 1939**. **Hitler** may have seen that Pact ('a major turn about') as part of his long-term plans for conquest of the east. That conquest was made easier by his **invasion of Poland in September 1939** – which plunged Europe into **war**. The conquest of Poland, like later conquests of Norway and Holland (extracts B and C), was speedy – the combined use of air force, tanks and mobile infantry in a 'blitzkreig' allowing German troops to overcome less-prepared opposition (extract B). With the **collapse of France in 1940**, only Britain remained unconquered: the **Battle of Britain** (picture 1) failed to bring Britain to the negotiating table. In June 1941 Hitler invaded the Soviet Union expecting a quick victory (extract E). By December 1941 he seemed to have almost succeeded: later advances in 1942 (picture 3) saw his troops advance on Moscow and Stalingrad, in spite of the snow (picture 2).

2 German soldiers on the Eastern Front

Extract A The 'Phoney' War, September 1939 – April 1940

My soul revolted at what was happening. France and Britain stood still while Germany swallowed Poland. We waited to be attacked. If this was war, I did not understand it.

(Field Marshal Montgomery, with the troops in France, 1940)

Extract B The British, unprepared, defeated in Norway, April-May 1940

The troops lacked aircraft, anti-aircraft guns, anti-tank guns, tanks, transport and training, snow shoes and skis... a ramshackle campaign.

(W. Churchill on the Norway campaign, 1940)

Extract C The Germans, prepared, overwhelm Holland in 'blitzkreig', May 1940

The avalanche of fire and steel rolled across the frontiers, and an overwhelming onslaught was made from the air. The whole country was in a state of confusion. (Churchill, after speaking to Dutch Government Ministers, 1940)

Extract D The first of Churchill's great speeches, May 1940

I would say to this House as I said to those who had joined the government, 'I have nothing to offer but blood, toil, tears and sweat. You ask what is our policy? It is to wage war, with all our might and with all the strength God can give us. You ask what is our aim? In one word: Victory.' (Churchill to the House of Commons on becoming Prime Minister, 1940)

Extract E Hitler's confidence on invading Russia, June 1941

You only have to kick in the door and the whole rotten structure will come crashing down.

(Hitler to von Rundstedt, Commander of the Forces in the Ukraine)

Extract F Have the Germans taken on too much? Russia, August 1941

We reckoned on about 200 enemy divisions: but we have already counted 360. And time favours them, for they are near their own resources, while we are moving further away from ours. Our troops, spread out over an immense front line, without any depth of support, face constant enemy attacks.

(General Halder, in his diary, 11 August 1941)

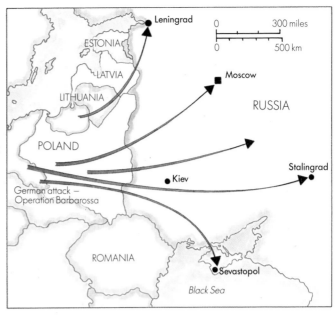

3 German advances into Russia, 1941 – 42

Extract G Russian stubborness and 'General' winter, December 1941

Now when Moscow was in sight, the mood of the commanders changed. With amazement we discovered in late October that the Russians were unaware that, as a military force, they had ceased to exist. Then the weather broke and the full force of the Russian winter was upon us.

(General Blumenritt, December 1941)

Extract H The first months of the siege of Leningrad, 1941

November 1941 arrived; icy wind drove powdered snow through the slits of dugouts and the broken windows of hospitals. The constant shortage of food, the cold weather and nervous tension wore the workers down. Few people paid any attention to the German shells that had shocked them before. In those days death loomed menacingly: lack of food and cold sent 11 000 to their graves in November. But the operetta company remained and the people loved them: the ballerinas were so thin it seemed they must break in two if they moved.

(Pavlova's eyewitness account of the siege, 1941)

THE YOUNG HISTORIAN AT WORK

Knowledge and understanding

1 How were Hitler's successes helped by **(i)** the British and the French; **(ii)** Stalin; **(iii)** his military forces; **(iv)** Hitler's own daring?

2 Show why 'progress' for the Germans meant disaster for Europe.

Interpretation

1 Do you agree that *extract E* gives a different interpretation of the War from *extract G*? Give reasons for your answer.

2 Do *extracts F and H* support *extract E* or *G's* interpretation? Why?

Use of sources

1 What do *extracts A, B, C and picture 3* tell us about why the Germans succeeded in 1939 – 42?

2 *Extracts D and F and pictures 1 and 2* give evidence of resistance to the German invaders. Which of these sources are **(i)** most and **(ii)** least useful? Why?

Project

1 Write a letter from a German soldier describing conditions at war in Russia.

2 Find out more details about the Battle of Britain.

JAPANESE SUCCESS, 1937 – 42

Japan's long-term plans for the conquest of Asia had led to the invasion and **conquest of Manchuria** (1931) and the **invasion of China** (1937) when she signed a Pact with Hitler and Mussolini. After the collapse of France in 1940, **Japan occupied part of French Indo-China** *(picture 1)*. The USA stopped trading with Japan in the hope of forcing her out of China and Indo-China. While negotiations about this were going on in Washington, Japanese forces attacked the US naval base at **Pearl Harbour** *(extract C)* and brought the USA into the War: even pro-German isolationists such as Lindbergh *(extracts D and E)* saw that this was inevitable. Hitler's foolish **declaration of war on the USA** made the War world-wide.

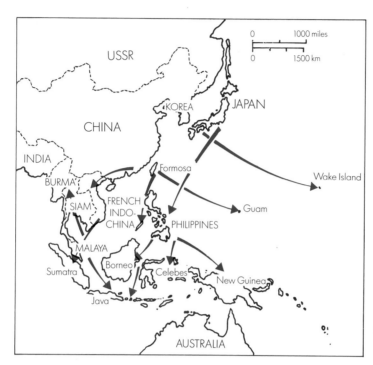

1 Japanese advance through South-East Asia, 1942

Even before this, the USA had been friendly to Britain *(extracts A and B)* and supplied her with **arms and supplies**. This did nothing to stop the headlong advance of the Japanese throughout Asia *(picture 1)* in 1942: from bases in New Guinea and the Celebes they **threatened Australia**. The Allied naval victory at the **Coral Sea** *(extract F)* prevented an invasion of Australia and marked the high point of Japanese success. In December 1941, Churchill and Roosevelt *(picture 2)* had agreed that the defeat of Japan would have to wait until Hitler had been defeated – a surprising decision by the USA, considering the reasons for its involvement in the War.

Extract A President Roosevelt's 'Four Freedoms' for the future, 1941
In the future days, which we seek to make secure, we look forward to a world founded on
(1) Freedom of speech everywhere; (2) Freedom of everyone to worship God in his own way;
(3) Freedom from want for every nation; (4) Freedom from fear for every nation...
(Roosevelt's speech to the people, January 1941)

Extract B A summary of the Atlantic Charter, August 1941
The President and the Prime Minister (state) certain common principles on which they base their hopes for a better future for the world: They promise that their countries will not try to seize any land anywhere. They agree that all people have the right to choose their own form of government. All conquered countries should have their independence restored. 'After the final destruction of the Nazi tyranny' all nations should join together to try to ensure greater prosperity for all and to protect peace.
(Adapted from the Joint Declaration by Churchill and Roosevelt, 1941)

Extract C Japan's plans for the attack on Pearl Harbour, 1941
A gigantic US fleet has massed in Pearl Harbour. This will be crushed with one blow at the beginning of hostilities. The success of our surprise attack will be the Waterloo of the war to follow. The Imperial Navy is massing ships and planes to ensure success. By attacking and seizing all key points at one blow while America is unprepared, we can swing the scale of later operations in our favour.
(Japanese Chief of Staff to Strike Officers, 10 November 1941)

2 Churchill and Roosevelt, December 1941

Extract D An anti-British pacifist on US entry into war, December 1941

Monday, 8 December: I am not surprised the Japs attacked. We have been prodding them into war for weeks. They have simply beaten us to the gun. The President spoke at 12.00, asked for a Declaration of War. Senate passed it unanimously; only one 'no' in the House. If the President had asked for war before, Congress would have turned him down with a big majority. But now we have been attacked. I see nothing to do except to fight. If I had been in Congress I would have voted for war.

(Wartime Journals of Charles Lindbergh)

Extract E Extending the War, 1941

Thursday 11 December: Germany and Italy have declared war on the US. All that I feared would happen has happened. We are at war all over the world.

(Wartime Journals of Charles Lindbergh)

Extract F The first check to the Japanese advance: Coral Sea, May 1942

Friday, 15 May 1942: The Battle of the Coral Sea has resulted in the destruction of many Japanese warships and transports... by aircraft. This action (is) one of the most important which has yet taken place. The Japanese can't replace their losses as Britain and America can; and as their aggressions depend on sea transport, they must come to an end. Burma has fallen, but no move of any kind has taken place this week. The Battle of the Coral Sea may have been preparatory to an invasion of Australia.

(*Journal of the War Years*, *Vol. II*, A. Weymouth, 1948)

THE YOUNG HISTORIAN AT WORK

Knowledge and understanding

1 Make a list of **(i)** long-term reasons and **(ii)** short-term reasons for the outbreak of war between USA and Japan.

2 How did Japan's policies affect Manchuria, China, Asia, Germany, the USA and Australia?

Interpretation

1 Do you agree that *extract F* shows that *extract C* does not give a fully accurate interpretation of Japanese naval strength? Why?

2 How does *extract D* provide evidence of both **(i)** support for and **(ii)** opposition to USA policies?

Use of sources

1 How reliable do you think *extracts A and B* are as guides to American and British foreign policies? Give reasons for your answer.

2 How may *picture 1 and extract F* be used to illustrate the extent and causes of **(i)** Japan's successes and **(ii)** the limits to Japan's advances?

Project

1 Write a speech that Roosevelt might have written after the Japanese attacked Pearl Harbour.

2 Why was Hitler's declaration of war on the USA 'foolish'?

GERMAN DEFEATS, 1942 – 5

Churchill called 1942 '**the turning point**' in the War. The Japanese were defeated at the Coral Sea, and later at **Midway**. The Russians halted the Germans at **Stalingrad** in September 1942: the severe Russian winter came to the defenders' help (page 130, picture 2) and in February 1943 the Germans surrendered to the Russians *(extracts B)* – the first major set-back for the Axis Powers in Europe. By then the British had won the Battle of **El Alamein** *(extracts A)* and were driving the Germans and Italians across North Africa *(picture 1)*.

In **June 1944 Allied forces** landed on the beaches of northern France where, in spite of stiff resistance, they were successful *(extracts C and D)*. The **liberation of France, Holland and Belgium** was followed by a drive to Berlin from the west, while the conquering Russians advanced from the east *(extract E and picture 1)*. German cartoonists tried to show that the Americans were allowing the British and Russians to do most of the fighting *(picture 2)*: which was to ignore the major rôles played by US forces in Europe.

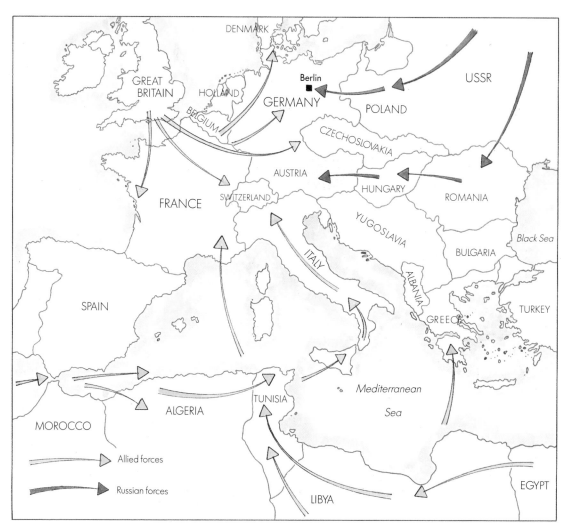

1 The defeat of the Axis Powers, 1943–45

Extracts A Turning point Number 1: El Alamein, November 1942
A real hard bloody fight has gone on now for eight days. I think Rommel is now ripe for a real hard blow that will topple him. If we succeed it will be the end of his army.
(**Field Marshal Montgomery to General Alanbrooke, 1 November 1942**)

Dearest Lu, very heavy fighting; not going well for us. The enemy's superior strength is slowly levering us out of war positions. That will mean the end. Air raid after air raid after air raid.
(**General Rommel to his wife, 2 November 1942**)

Extracts B Turning point Number 2: Stalingrad, January 1943
The Russians are finished. In four weeks they will collapse. (**Hitler, September 1942**)
Every seven seconds a German soldier dies; Stalingrad – mass grave. (**Moscow Radio, January 1943**)

Troops without ammunition, food, dressings or drugs for wounded. Further defence useless. Army requests permission to surrender to save the lives of the remaining troops.

(General von Paulus to Hitler, 24 January 1943)

Surrender is forbidden. 6th Army will hold position to last man and the last round.

(Hitler to von Paulus, 24 January 1943)

Carrying out your orders, on 2 February 1943 we completed the destruction of the encircled enemy forces at Stalingrad.

(General Rokossovsky to Stalin, February 1943)

Extract C France welcomes the invading Allies, 8 June 1944

The first evidence of French feeling came from a village woman. 'God has sent the British and Americans,' she said tremblingly. The Germans are afraid. They told me as they came through here; "The Allies have so many men, so much material the sea is filled with their ships". Then at Bayeux, men, women and children lining the streets. It was a hysterical welcome. They stood in the cobbled streets from which the Allies had just driven the Germans with tears streaming down their faces, flags from every balcony. No people were ever more justified in hysteria.

(BBC commentary, 8 June 1944)

Extract D Rommel advises negotiations with the Allies, 15 July 1944

The situation on the Normandy front is becoming more difficult every day. Because of the fierce fighting, the large amounts of material used by the enemy in artillery and tanks, and the impact of the enemy air force which is in full control, our own losses are so high that they seriously reduce the effectiveness of our divisions. The supply situation is also difficult because of the destruction of the railways and the vulnerability of the roads up to 150 kms. behind the front. The enemy front line receives new forces and supplies every day. (Rommel, 15 July 1944)

Extract E Berlin under attack, 9 March 1945

The capital will be defended to the last man and bullet; every building, every house, every floor, every hedge, every shell-crater will be defended to the utmost.

(Order issued by Berlin's Commanding Officer, 9 March 1945)

2 A German view of the Allied effort, 1944

THE YOUNG HISTORIAN AT WORK

Knowledge and understanding

1 (a) Show how Germany's defeat was brought about by the following events: defeat in Russia; USA entry into the War; defeat at El Alamein; invasions in 1944 – 5. **(b)** Place these factors in order of importance.

2 What factors in the defeat of Hitler are not mentioned above?

Interpretation

1 How full an explanation of Germany's defeat is offered in *extract D*?

2 Do you agree that the map *(picture 1)* and the text and *extracts* show that the cartoon *(picture 2)* does not give an accurate picture of the Allied war effort? Give reasons for your answer.

Use of sources

1 How reliable are the statements in *extracts A, B, and E* by the leading soldiers and politicians on both sides in the War?

2 In what ways does *extract C* provide more valuable evidence than *extract D* to historians writing about life in Normandy in 1944?

Project

1 Describe the welcome you would have given to the Allied troops if you had been a villager near Bayeux in 1944.

2 Make up interviews with German soldiers and civilians about their experience of war.

JAPANESE DEFEATS, 1942–5

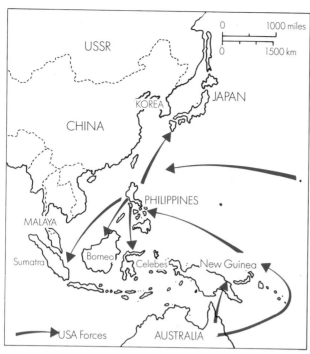

1 The defeat of Japan, 1943–45

The German cartoonist (page 135, picture 2) used his skill to misinterpret the US contribution to Allied successes. The USA had more **factories** than any other country – and **all free from enemy attack**. She also had more raw materials than any other country. During 1941 (while still at peace), America's output of munitions was doubled and over 2000 aircraft produced each month. In 1942 over 60 000 aircraft and 45 000 tanks were produced. By the end of the War the USA had produced 86 000 tanks, 296 000 aircraft, 64 000 landing craft, 6500 naval vessels and 54 000 transport ships. Much of this output was given to the **British** and the **Soviet Union** to help their smaller and often attacked industry.

Much of it went to ensure the **defeat of Japan** (picture 1) whose forces had to be pushed from one island after another in a costly advance by US forces. In August 1945 President Truman ordered the dropping of the **first atomic bomb** (extracts B, C and D) after first warning the Japanese of what was to happen if they continued to fight (picture 2). **The destruction of Hiroshima** (picture 3) was followed by the atomic attack on **Nagasaki** and the **Japanese surrender**. Few people, in 1945, opposed the use of the atomic weapon.

We are in possession of the most destructive weapon ever designed by man. A single one of our atomic bombs equals the explosive power carried by 2000 of our Super-Fortresses ... Before using this bomb again and again to destroy every resource which your military leaders have ... we ask you to petition your Emperor now to end the war.

2 American leaflet warning of their imminent attack by atomic bomb

Extract A The Japanese (like the Germans) in retreat, 1943
The Japanese are now speaking of the successful evacuation of Salamua in New Guinea. These successful evacuations are getting common with the Axis. In the course of one year we have done so much successful evacuating that a large part of our former war potential has been lost.
(*Diaries*, J. Goebbels, 1943)

Extract B Truman's decision to use the atomic bomb, August 1945
The final decision of where and when to use the bomb was up to me. I regarded the bomb as a military weapon and never had any doubt that it should be used. My military advisers recommended its use and Churchill unhesitatingly told me he favoured its use if it might aid the end of the War.
(*Year of Decisions*, H. S. Truman, 1955)

3 After the Bomb, Hiroshima, 1945

Extract C The Hiroshima bomb, 6 August 1945

Suddenly a glaring light appeared in the sky accompanied by an unnatural tremor and a wave of suffocating heat and a wind which swept away everything in its path... thousands in the streets scorched by the searing heat... others screaming in agony from the pain of their burns. Everything standing upright was annihilated and the debris carried up into the air... trams, trains... flung like toys. About half an hour after, a fine rain began to fall caused by the sudden rise of over-heated air to a great height where it condensed. Then a violent wind rose and the fire extended with terrible rapidity. By evening the fire died down. There was nothing left to burn, Hiroshima had ceased to exist.
(*Warrior Without Weapons*, M. Junod)

Extract D A prisoner of war welcomes the news of Hiroshima

If the atom bombs had not been dropped the War would have dragged on. Those terrible bombs must have seemed as supernatural to the Japanese as they seemed to me when I first heard of them in the darkness and danger of our own prison. For me, selfish as it may sound, there was the certain knowledge that if the bomb had not been dropped, the Japanese would have fought on and hundreds of thousands of prisoners would have been killed. Even if we had not been massacred, we were near our physical end through lack of food. (*Night of the New Moon*, L. van der Post, 1970)

Extract E Why did the Allies win? Why did the Axis powers lose?

They became stretched out far beyond their basic capacity for holding their gains. For Japan was a small island state with limited industrial power. Italian incompetence was a constant drain on Hitler's resources. (The military historian, B. H. Liddel-Hart)

THE YOUNG HISTORIAN AT WORK

Knowledge and understanding

1 Explain why the USA was an important war ally for Britain.

2 Why did few people in the USA and Europe oppose the dropping of the atom bomb on the people of Hiroshima and Nagasaki?

Interpretation

1 Does the account of the dropping of the bomb at Hiroshima *(extract C)* offer a different interpretation to *extract D*? Give reasons for your answer.

2 Do you think that *picture 1 and extracts A and E* show that the atom bomb was not essential for the defeat of Japan?

Use of sources

1 How valuable are *pictures 2 and 3* in adding to the description of the effects of the bomb given in *extract C*? Give reasons for your answer.

2 Do you think that *extract B* is a fully reliable source for historians? Give reasons for your answer.

Project

1 Find out about the long-term effects of the bombing of Hiroshima.

2 Make a poster for a British newspaper on the victory over Japan.

WARTIME BRITAIN

1 A cartoon of 1944

As in the First World War, the government controlled the nation's economic life – controlling industry as well as manpower. When **Churchill** became **Prime Minister** in May 1940 he brought Labour politicians into his Cabinet and they '**ran the War at home**' so that workers better accepted the loss of trade union power, wages control and higher taxes since they came from 'their' leaders. The **severe bombing** of many cities *(extract A)* led to the destruction of millions of homes, factories, ports and business centres, all of which had to be rebuilt after 1945. But the War brought the people together *(extracts B and C)*: better-off people in safer suburbs took in children from bombed cities *(picture 3)* and learned to sympathise with their poverty: soldiers had education classes *(extract D)* in which they called for a **post-War unity** in a fight against pre-War problems such as unemployment *(picture 1)*. The **coalition** government produced a series of plans for a better Britain: the most important of these was the **Beveridge Report** *(extracts F and G)* which called for a major social revolution *(picture 2)*. 'From the evil of war, some good came.'

2 'Make way for Socialism', *London Express* cartoon

Extract A A destructive war

London people lost much sleep and suffered anxiety and discomfort, but there was no panic except in the small heavily bombed areas. After a few days the first horror of raids wore off and people adjusted to shelter life. Disorganisation was more serious. The network of railways was cut at many places, hundreds of bridges put out of action, roads blocked by craters and debris, water and gas mains broken, telephone exchanges put out of action, factories destroyed or damaged, and millions of homes rendered unfit for use. (**Cabinet Papers 67/9**)

Extract B Togetherness

People were much more together. They met in the air-raid shelters, in the tubes at night, in the Home Guard, or in food queues. They lost a lot of inhibitions about talking to their neighbours. When the raids were over they used almost to celebrate in the morning, and this was the spirit that I think a lot of people hoped would continue after the War.

(Prof. A. Ling, quoted in *Now the War is Over*, P. Addison, 1985)

Extract C Evacuees learn new habits – and the sympathy of their host families

My sister whispered for days. Everything was so clean. We were given face flannels and toothbrushes – we'd never cleaned our teeth before. And hot water came from the tap: and there was a lavatory upstairs. And carpets. And clean sheets. It was all very odd. I didn't like it.

(*The World is a Wedding*, B. Kops, 1973)

3 London children were evacuated to the safety of the countryside

4 Workers could often afford more food in wartime than when unemployed

Extract D And soldiers learn from one another

As in all wars there were periods of violent action but long periods of boredom during which people had time to read, argue and discuss. Troops were much concerned with what Britain was going to be like after the War... a great deal of discussion about war aims. (*The Day Before Yesterday*, A. Thompson, 1971)

Extract E Fair shares of food for all

The War forced us to adopt a food policy based on the needs of the people. Estimates were made of minimum food requirements. Then a scheme was designed to provide the food to meet those needs. The available food was distributed with special measures being taken to ensure that the highest needs of mothers, children and of heavy workers would be met. The poorest part of the population is actually better fed than before the War. (*Food and the People*, J. B. Orr, 1943)

Extract F Looking ahead, 1942

Now, when war is abolishing landmarks of every kind, is the opportunity of using experience in a clear field. A revolutionary moment in history is a time for revolutions and not for patching. (W. Beveridge, 1942)

Extract G The far-reaching Beveridge Report, 1942

His report was greeted as a blueprint for future society and became a best seller. He noted that there were five giant evils: Want (poverty), Ignorance (poor schooling), Squalor (bad housing), Disease (ill-health) and Idleness (unemployment). He called on the Government to do more for education (which the 1944 Education Act set out to do), for Full Employment (as a 1943 White Paper promised), for a National Health Service, for a huge housing programme and for a Ministry of Social Security. (*Post-War Britain*, P. Lane, 1979)

THE YOUNG HISTORIAN AT WORK

Knowledge and understanding

1 Rank in order of their importance the **(i)** political; **(ii)** social; **(iii)** economic effects of the War on Britain. Explain your order.

2 According to the text, *extracts C and E and picture 4*, how did the War affect the workers in a different way from better-off people?

Interpretation

1 Do you agree that *extracts A to F* offer differing interpretations of the effects of the War? Explain these differences.

2 Do you agree that the extracts and text back up the statement that 'out of the evil of war some good came'? Give reasons for your answer.

Use of sources

1 In what ways are *pictures 1 and 2* useful in helping to understand the effects of the War on the hopes of many people for the future?

2 How reliable do you think *extracts F and G* are as evidence for the benefits of the War for the British people?

Project

1 Write a speech supporting the policies of Beveridge *(extracts F and G)*.

2 Draw a cartoon on the theme of the bombing of the cities of Britain.

POST-WAR FRONTIERS

Churchill and **Roosevelt** held several wartime meetings (page 132, extract B and picture 2). In January 1943 they met in Casablanca and announced that the War would go on until the Axis Powers had '**surrendered without conditions**'. There was going to be no repetition of the mistakes made in 1918 – 19 which had allowed some Germans to claim that their army had never been defeated. They met Stalin in Teheran in November 1943 and discussed the future of post-War Europe. That discussion continued when the three met at **Yalta** in **February 1945** at what was, perhaps, the most important conference. They agreed to **divide Germany between the Allied powers**, each having an agreed 'zone'. They agreed that the liberated countries would be free to **choose** the kind of **government** they wanted and they finalised their agreement on the setting up of the **United Nations Organisation** (page 142).

Stalin's army liberated Eastern Europe *(extract A and picture 1)*. But, instead of allowing free elections, the invaders imposed Communist governments on most of the liberated countries *(extracts C and E)*. This disappointed Churchill who had defended Stalin's reputation *(extract D)*, Labour's Foreign Minister, Bevin, *(extract E)* who had hoped that 'left would talk to left', and the Americans, who had hoped to bring their troops home from Europe once the War ended. Instead, Stalin's aggressive policy in Europe and the Middle East led to increased US involvement in post-War Europe *(extract G)*. **The Iron Curtain** *(extract F)* was a symbol of the Cold War in which Germany, and particularly Berlin, were centres of crisis until the 1970s.

Extract A The Red Army liberates Eastern Europe – at a price

First came the tank divisions, the guns, the lorries, the parachute divisions, then hundreds of thousands of columns of marching soldiers, men and women. Then the lorries belonging to the Political Commissars and the NKVD (secret police).

(*East Wind Over Prague*, J. Stransky, 1950)

Extract B The Yalta Agreement and the Polish question

A new situation has been created by the liberation of Poland by the Red Army. This calls for a Polish Provisional Government more broadly based than was possible before this liberation. The Provisional Government now in Poland should be reorganised on a democratic basis with the inclusion of democratic leaders from Poland itself and from Poles abroad.

(Yalta Agreement, February 1945)

1 Russian control of Eastern Europe, 1944 – 7

Extract C Yalta – a 'free' Agreement?

By February 1945 Poland and all East Europe, except Czechoslovakia, was in the hands of the Red Army. As a result it was not a question of what Britain and the USA would permit, but of what they could persuade the Soviet Union to accept. (US Secretary of State writing shortly after the signing of the Agreement, 1945)

Extract D Churchill's optimism about Russia's post-war policies

I know of no government which stands to its obligations more solidly than the Russian Soviet government.
I decline absolutely to embark here on a discussion of Russia's good faith.

(House of Commons debate on the Yalta Agreement, 27 February 1945)

Extract E Britain's suspicions of Soviet policy, January 1946

Russia's foreign policy is as imperialistic as Peter the Great's. She is seeking to put around her a group of satellites with the view of controlling every place in contact with her.

(E. Bevin, Foreign Secretary, January 1946)

2 The division of Germany and enlargement of Poland

Extract F Churchill's 'Iron Curtain' speech, March 1946

From Stettin in the Baltic to Trieste in the Adriatic an iron curtain has descended across the continent. Behind that line lie all the capitals of the ancient states of Central and Eastern Europe. The Russian-dominated Polish Government has made wrongful inroads upon Germany. The Communist Parties in all these Eastern States have been raised to pre-eminence and power far beyond their numbers and seek to obtain totalitarian control... there is no true democracy.

(Speech at Fulton, Missouri, 5 March 1946)

Extract G Truman's anti-Communist 'Doctrine'

At the present moment every nation must choose between alternative ways of life. The choice is too often not a free one. One way of life is based upon the will of the majority. The second is based on the will of a minority imposed on the majority. To ensure the peaceful development of nations, we took a leading part in the establishment of the UNO, to make possible lasting freedom and independence for all its members. We shall not gain our objectives unless we are willing to help free people to maintain their free institutions against aggressive movements that seek to impose on them totalitarian regimes which undermine the foundations of peace and hence the security of the USA. (President Truman to US Congress, 12 March 1947)

THE YOUNG HISTORIAN AT WORK

Knowledge and understanding

1 Show how **(i)** Stalin affected the map of Europe and **(ii)** how the events of the War may have influenced Stalin and his followers in the USSR.

2 Explain how British and American politicians came to be disappointed by events in Europe after 1945.

Interpretation

1 How do you explain the fact that *extract D* gives a differing interpretation of the USSR's policies from *extract F*?

2 How do *extracts A and E* compare with *extract D* in their interpretation of USSR policy?

Use of sources

1 How valuable are *extracts C and G and pictures 1 and 2* to historians wishing to explain and assess the success of USA foreign policy?

2 Is *extract B or C* the most reliable source to historians writing about the Yalta treaty? Why?

Project

1 How has the rôle of the USSR changed in Europe since 1988?

2 Discuss with friends whether Britain and the USA could have avoided the domination of Eastern Europe after 1945.

THE UNITED NATIONS ORGANISATION, HUMAN RIGHTS AND REFUGEES

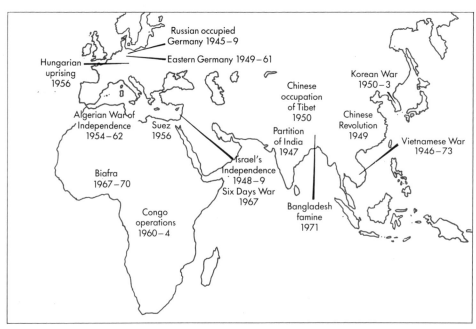

1 World refugee problems since 1945

The League of Nations had failed the world in the 1930s (pages 124–7). Allied leaders made wartime plans for a wider-ranging organisation (extract A). Its Charter was first discussed in January 1942 and approved in June 1945 (extract B), and the first meeting of the 51 member nations took place in January 1946.

The **United Nations Organisation** (UNO) had several important agencies, such as the UN International Children's Emergency Fund (**UNICEF**). Other agencies are linked to UNO – the World Health Organisation (**WHO**), the Food and Agricultural Organisation (**FAO**) and the International Monetary Fund (**IMF**). These and other organisations are symbols of statemen's hopes for a more united world. In 1948 the UN produced its **Declaration on Human Rights** (extract C) which extended the idea of 'rights' into many areas other than political and religious. Some people argue that the Declaration was, and is, incapable of implementation (extracts D and E). However, it remains an ideal at which people can aim.

The United Nations Relief and Rehabilitation Administration (**UNRRA**) was set up in 1943 to plan help for European refugees made homeless by the War. Since then it has had to cope with the ever-growing flood of refugees, from many countries (pictures 1 and 2), which TV and the press have helped many of us to understand.

2 Refugees in Biafra

Extract A The original idea, August 1941

The President (Roosevelt) and Prime Minister (Churchill) desire to bring about the fullest collaboration between all nations in the economic field with the object of securing, for all, improved labour standards, economic advancement and social security.

(The Atlantic Charter, August 1941)

Extract B The UN Charter, June 1945

We, the people of the United Nations, determine to save succeeding generations from the scourge of war, and to reaffirm our faith in fundamental human rights, in the dignity of the human person, in the equal rights of men and women and of nations large and small, and to establish conditions under which justice and respect for obligations can be maintained, and to promote social progress and better standards of living, tolerance and peace, promise to unite our strength to maintain peace and to ensure that armed force shall not be used save in the common interest, and to employ international machinery for the promotion of the economic and social advancement of all peoples...

(Signed 26 June 1945 to come into operation 24 October, 1945)

Extract C The Universal Declaration of Human Rights, 1948

23 (1) Everyone has the right to work, to free choice of employment...favourable conditions of work and protection against unemployment.
(2) Everyone has the right to equal pay for equal work.
(3) Everyone has the right to remuneration ensuring for himself and family an existence worthy of human dignity, supplemented by other social protection.
24 Everyone has the right to leisure and holidays with pay.

25 (1) Everyone has the right to a standard of living adequate for the health of himself and his family... food, clothing, housing and medical care and the right to security in unemployment, sickness, widowhood, old age...
26 (1) Everyone has the right to education... free... compulsory,
(2) Education shall be directed to the full development of the human personality... respect for human rights and freedoms... tolerance among nations, racial or religious groups...

Extract D The absence of human rights in Latin America

I was born in a small peasant family. None of us children had any schooling. I lost my job when the land went to raising cattle instead of crops. My wife and I lived in a poor hut, and soon after she died of typhoid - drinking polluted water. There was nothing else to do except emigrate to the big city and hope I could pick up work.

(Quoted in *Rich World, Poor World*, G. Lean, 1978)

Extract E The fight for human rights

In Latin America today it is not possible to feed, clothe or house the majority of people. Those who are in power are an economic minority that dominates because it controls those who have political and military power. This minority will not make decisions against its own interest. This is called revolution. If it is necessary, the Christian must be a revolutionary. His priestly love for fellow men may force him to this if he is to be true to God.

(*Revolutionary Priest: Camilo Torres*, J. Gerassi, 1971)

THE YOUNG HISTORIAN AT WORK

Knowledge and understanding

1 Explain how the formation of the United Nations was intended to improve the lives of the peoples of the world.

2 Explain briefly the roles of (i) the War and (ii) individual politicians in the formation of the United Nations.

Interpretation

1 Do you agree that the text, *extracts*, and *pictures* show that the formation of the United Nations has been a failure? Why?

2 How do you explain the differences between the ideals set out in *extracts A to C* and the problems illustrated in *extracts D and E*?

Use of sources

1 How reliable are *extracts B and C* to historians writing about the effect of the United Nations after 1945? Why?

2 Look at *extracts D and E and pictures 1 and 2*. Compare the value of each source to historians writing about the social problems of the world.

Project

1 Find out how the United Nations have dealt with any one crisis since 1961.

2 Draw a cartoon or symbol to represent the aims of the United Nations.

THE ROMAN EMPIRE

ROMAN ROOTS: FROM LEGEND TO FACT, 753 – 510 BC

1 Italy around 800 BC, showing positions of various tribes

2 A typical mosaic, 3rd century AD

Around 800 BC many tribes lived in Italy *(picture 1)*. The most important were **the Etruscans** who had come from **Asia Minor** and occupied much of northern Italy. They were great traders and earned the money to build large walled cities where they recreated much of **Greek civilisation** *(pictures 2–4)*.

Roman legend says that twin boys **Romulus and Remus** were sons of an Alban princess and the God Mars. A cruel uncle, King Amulius of Alba, tried to drown them in the **Tiber**, but they were saved by **a she-wolf** who suckled them *(picture 5)*. Later, they threw their uncle off the Alban throne and restored their grandfather to power. He let them found a city of their own. Romulus killed Remus in a quarrel over the location of their city, which he built on **the Palatine Hill**. He invited Alban friends and refugees from other tribes to start settlements on other nearby hills. The site of the new 'city' (in the centre of the peninsula) was the crossing point over the **Tiber for north–south trade routes** and the start of the **west–east salt trade route**.

We know nothing about the first four legendary kings of Rome (753 – 616 BC). We know more about the **three Etruscan kings** who ruled from **616 – 510 BC.** Their system of **government** was **aristocratic**. **The common people** (plebs) chose a Popular Assembly (**Curiae**): the older and original families (**patricians**) chose a permanent Council (**Senatus**) and formed **a noble class** which owned the land, had its own religious rites and controlled the government. The **plebs** had their own religious rites, did most of the commercial work which enriched Rome, but had little power. They were forbidden to marry into the patrician class.

By 510 BC Rome had expanded. Marshes had been drained, and temples and other buildings made from the volcanic rock which was so hard that they lasted almost for ever. The Servian Wall enclosed Rome's seven hills.

The last Etruscan King, **Tarquinius Superbus** ('The Proud') was expelled from Rome in a revolt caused by his rape of **Lucretia**, wife of a leading patrician.

3 Chariot racing in a stadium: Roman mosaic at Bardo, Tunis

4 Fresco portrait of a girl
from Pompeii,
1st century AD

5 Romulus and Remus with the she-wolf

THE YOUNG HISTORIAN AT WORK

Knowledge and understanding

1 Make a list of the reasons why **(i)** the Etruscans were the most powerful of the tribes
in 800 BC; **(ii)** Rome's location in Italy helped the city to become wealthy.

2 (a) Explain how, in early Roman art, 'the nobles', 'common people' and 'slaves'
were divided. **(b)** Make lists of the differences and similarities between Roman
Society and England's Feudal Society (pages 12–23).

Interpretation

1 The story of Romulus and Remus is a legend. **(i)** What is the difference between
historical fact and legend? **(ii)** How do you think the stories about how Rome was
founded were told and written?

2 Why do historians (e.g. Livy) not have a clear idea of how Rome began in the
8th century BC?

Use of sources

1 (a) What do these pages tell you about **(i)** how Italy was divided in the 8th century BC;
(ii) who the Etruscans' enemies were? **(b)** How different was Italy in the 8th century BC
from Italy in the 1st century BC (see picture 1 on page 152)?

2 (a) Do you agree that *pictures 2, 3 and 4* are valuable to historians wishing to
study the Etruscan way of life? Give reasons for your answer. **(b)** What evidence is
there of Greek influence on the Etruscans?

Project

1 Look at *pictures 3 and 5*. Write Romulus' story of his early life and how he began to
build Rome on the Palatine Hill.

2 Make some sketches for a frieze on 'The Etruscan way of life and the beginning of
Rome'.

FROM CITY STATE TO ITALIAN POWER, 510 – 260BC

Instead of kings, **republican Rome** had **two consuls**. They held office for one year only. They were **elected** by the whole people, although **only patricians** could stand for election until the law was changed in **367 BC**. Consuls presided over **the Senate** and commanded **the army**, although they may not have had military experience. That was why, in **510 BC**, the post of **Dictator** was created (*extracts A and B*). Each **purple-robed consul** had a guard of twelve **lictors**, **in red robes**, to walk before him carrying a bundle of rods (**fasces**) tied with **a red strap**. When consuls left Rome the fasces contained **an axe** as a further mark of power. Only the temporary Dictators showed the axe in the city itself.

The first years of the Republic were dangerous ones. The last King, **Tarquinius**, led the Etruscans against Rome and might have taken the city but for '**brave Horatius**' (*picture 2*) who '**kept the bridge**' until it was chopped down, making invasion impossible. In time the **Etruscans were defeated** by Greeks from **Sicily** and by invading **Gauls** (*picture 1*) who also defeated Roman armies and captured all the city except for the Capitoline Hill. However, they were badly organised and, slowly, were pushed back to the area of **Cisalpine Gaul** ('Gaul on this side of the Alps'). While defeating them, the **Romans captured Etruscan cities** and confined the Etruscans to the area now known as **Tuscany**.

Rome then had a period of **expansion**. They defeated the **Samnites** (342 – 290 BC) and took control of most of the south. The Greeks at **Taranto** asked their kinsman, **Pyrrhus**, King of Epirus, to help them. He lost so many men in beating the Romans (*extract C*) that he went home and **Taranto surrendered to the Romans**.

The Romans allowed the conquered peoples to become **Roman citizens** and to enjoy **greater prosperity**. They gave Italy a good **legal system**, uniform **weights and measures**, Roman **numerals**, a common **language** and a common **calendar** in which the first month was March (after the god **Mars**, *picture 4*). April was named after **Aprilis**, another name for Venus, goddess of love, May was named after **Maia**, a mother-goddess, and June after **Juno** (*picture 5*), the wife of Jupiter, the King of the gods. Most other months were named after **Roman numbers**: e.g. **December** comes from the Latin **decem** meaning **tenth**.

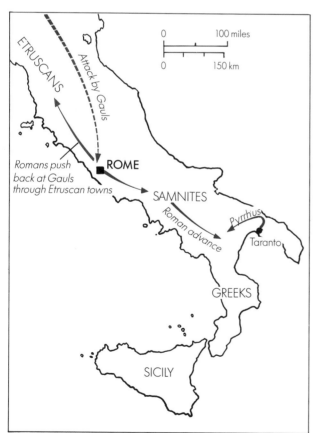

1 The Etruscans were defeated by invading Gauls

2 An impressive Horatius, on the bridge of Rome

3 January was named after Janus, the God of the doorway

4 March was named after Mars, the God of war

5 June was probably named after Juno, the wife of Jupiter

Extract A Why the young Republic created Dictators, 501 BC

In seasons of great peril
'Tis good that one bears sway;
Then choose we a Dictator,
Whom all men shall obey...
Then let him be Dictator
For six months and no more.

(*The Battle of Lake Regillus*, in *Lays of Ancient Rome*, T.B. Macaulay, 1859)

Extract B Cincinnatus, consul in 460 BC, becomes Dictator, 458 BC

After the defeat by the Aequi, the senate sent deputies to Cincinnatus to invite him to come and be Dictator. He was then at work in his field, and, being his own ploughman, was dressed in a manner fit for that work. When he saw the deputies coming, he stopped his oxen, not knowing what such a number of persons could want with him. One of the deputies approached him, and asked him to put on more suitable dress. He went into his hut, put on other clothes, and came to those who were waiting. They immediately invested him with the purple robe: the lictors stood in front of him and asked him to follow them to Rome. Troubled at this sight, he for some time shed tears in silence. Then he said only: 'My fields will not be sown this year.' However, when the enemy were defeated, he went back to his farm, having been Dictator for only sixteen days. (*The Percy Anecdotes*, Byerley and Robertson, 1820 – 23)

Extract C King Pyrrhus of Epirus defeats the Romans twice, but at a cost

Another such victory and we are lost. (**After his victory at Heraclea, 280 BC**)

THE YOUNG HISTORIAN AT WORK

Knowledge and understanding

1 Make a list of the ways in which Rome was affected by **(i)** Consuls; **(ii)** the Senate; **(iii)** the Etruscans; **(iv)** the Gauls.

2 How did Roman military power affect the tribes in Italy in **(i)** the short term; **(ii)** the long term?

Interpretation

1 Read *extracts A and B*. How do these **(i)** agree and **(ii)** differ in their interpretation of how a man became Dictator?

2 Using *extracts A and B* suggest why there are bound to be differences in accounts of how Dictators were chosen.

Use of sources

1 How can the text and the map be used to show **(i)** how the Romans overcame their opponents; **(ii)** why Roman success was not inevitable?

2 Look at *picture 2*. **(i)** Do you think the picture is a primary or a secondary source? Give reasons for your answer. **(ii)** Does this source have any use for historians writing about the Roman–Etruscan war?

Project

1 Look at *picture 3*. Find out the Roman origins for the months of February; July; August; September; October; November.

2 Imagine you were an eyewitness of the battle shown in *picture 2*. Write a report on the battle, describing the swords, other weapons, general atmosphere and the result.

THE ROMAN ARMY

Rome's expansion owed a great deal to its army. At first **every man** between the ages of 17 and 46 was liable for military service. Later, as the Empire expanded, it became **a full-time professional army** of men who signed on for **25 years** of service. At the heart of the army were **the legions**, each with its **own number**, **standard** (page 152, picture 4), and commander (a **legate**). The first legions consisted of **2100** men, but later they consisted of **6000**. Each legion was divided into **groups of 80–100**, each commanded by a **centurion** (picture 1 and extract A). There were **heavy infantry** and **light** (**velites**) (picture 2). In battle a legion was drawn up in three lines, each containing some heavy and some light infantry. (See page 151, extract C).

Recruits were carefully chosen (extract B) and a legionary's skills were developed by **constant training** (extract C). They had to be strong enough to carry not only their **armour** but about **27 kilos** of other equipment (extract D). A day's march (extract D) always ended in a well-prepared **camp** (picture 3) where men could rest and repair their weapons (extract E).

Legions might be stationed in **small fortresses** (page 165, picture 5) or in larger, more comfortable **fortified 'towns'** (page 164, picture 2).

Retired soldiers were often given land to help them settle as part of a **Roman 'colony'** in a part of the Empire where they helped in the **Romanisation** of their new homeland.

Extract A The qualities needed to be a centurion

They are not so much bold and adventurous as men with an ability to command, steady and of a deep-rooted spirit... who, in the face of superior numbers or great pressure, would endure and die in the defence of their post.

(*History*, the historian Polybius, 204 – 122 BC)

Extract B The qualities needed to be a legionary

Choosing men is like choosing horses. A young soldier should have alert eyes and hold his head upright. He should be broad-chested with powerful shoulders and brawny arms, his fingers long rather than short. He should not be pot-bellied; his calves and feet should not be flabby but made entirely of tough sinew. When you find these qualities in a recruit, take him on even if he is on the short side. It is better for soldiers to be strong rather than tall. The well-being of the Roman State depends on the recruits you choose.

(*On Military Affairs*, Vegetius, 4th – 5th centuries BC)

1 The tombstone of a centurian

2 Roman troops and barbarians from the 2nd Century AD

Extract C Training and success

As if born holding swords in their hands, they never rest from training. Their training is as strenuous as real warfare. Every soldier, every day, exercises as eagerly as if he were in action. That is why they make light of fighting. No confusion drives them out of their usual formation. They are not paralysed with fear or exhausted by hard work. Victory is inevitable, for their enemies can never equal them. (The Jewish historian, Josephus, who fought against the Romans in Palestine in AD 67)

Extract D Roman soldiers on the march

They move forward in silence and in good order. Each man keeps to his position as if he were fighting. Foot-soldiers, armed with breast-plate, back-plate and a helmet, carry two swords, one on each side. The one on the left is longer than the other. The one on the right is not much more than a dagger. Soldiers in the general's bodyguard have a spear and

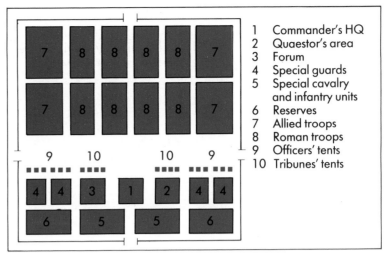

1	Commander's HQ
2	Quaestor's area
3	Forum
4	Special guards
5	Special cavalry and infantry units
6	Reserves
7	Allied troops
8	Roman troops
9	Officers' tents
10	Tribunes' tents

3 The layout of a Roman camp

a round shield. The ordinary soldier carries a javelin and a tall oblong shield. He also carries a saw, a basket, a mattock, an axe, a sickle, a chain, and rations to last him for three days. He is not very different from a pack mule. The cavalry wear a long sword on the right and hold a long thrusting spear in the hand. Their large shield rests on the horse's back. They have a quiver with three or four pointed weapons for throwing, as long as spears. They wear the same helmets and plates as the foot-soldiers.

(Josephus)

Extract E Craftsmen travel with the legion

A legion has builders, carpenters, masons, blacksmiths, painters and all the craftsmen needed to build their winter quarters, to make equipment, towers, fences and siege machines, and to build and repair weapons, waggons and artillery. There are workshops for shields, breast-plates and bows, where they also make arrows, missiles, helmets and other types of armour. Whatever the army needs is always available in the camp.

(Vegetius)

THE YOUNG HISTORIAN AT WORK

Knowledge and understanding

1 (a) How did the Roman army both **(i)** change and **(ii)** remain the same through the years?
(b) Why do you think **(i)** these changes took place and **(ii)** the organisation of the Roman army stayed basically unchanged?

2 Read *extract E* and the text. How did the Roman army affect the development of the world which it helped to conquer?

Interpretation

1 Read *extracts A and B*. Write down **(i)** two statements of fact and **(ii)** two statements of opinion found here.

2 (a) How does *extract A* both **(i)** agree and **(ii)** differ from *extract B* in the interpretations of the qualities needed by a Roman soldier? **(b)** Why do these *extracts* contain such differences of opinion? **(c)** Does *extract D* confirm or deny the views given in *extracts A and B*?

Use of sources

1 Using *extracts C and D*, write an account of the difficulties which a Roman soldier had to overcome.

2 Do you agree that these two primary sources are more valuable to historians writing about the Roman army than a textbook account written in 1992? Give reasons for your answer.

Project

1 Using *pictures 1–3* and other pictures copied from books or magazines about Rome (from your home, school or library) make a frieze on *Roman Army Life and Organisation*.

2 Places in Britain with names ending in '– ester' were the sites of Roman towns or camps (castra). Colchester is one such example. Find TEN such places.

THREE WARS WITH CARTHAGE, 261 – 146 BC

1 A battleship with soldiers

2 Hannibal

Carthage had a large **Empire** (picture 3) and a well-led, skilled army. **In 261 BC Messina** (picture 3) was at war with the **Greeks** from **Syracuse**. Some Messinians asked Rome for help, others asked Carthage, and the two city states went **to war**. The **Carthaginian navy** repeatedly defeated the Roman navy, until **Rome built a new, larger fleet** modelled on a Carthaginian wreck. The Romans then added a drawbridge which had a spiked end. When the two enemy ships came close, the drawbridge was lowered and its spike stuck in the Carthaginian's deck, allowing **Roman soldiers** to rush across to attack the Carthaginian sailors (picture 1).

The persistent Romans gradually wore down the more experienced Carthaginians. In **241 BC** Carthage made **peace**; Rome gained **Sicily, Corsica and Sardinia**.

In **218 BC** the Carthaginian general, **Hannibal** (picture 2) led his army from their winter quarters in New Carthage (picture 3) on his **historic march** (extract A and picture 3). He defeated the Romans **at Trasimene** (217 BC) and **Cannae** (216 BC) and forced them to appoint **Fabius as Dictator**. He spent five years avoiding battle: Hannibal had neither the machines to besiege Rome nor the reinforcement expected from Carthage. In **211 BC** he retreated to a base at **Tarentum**. Meanwhile a Roman general, **Scipio**, defeated Carthaginian armies in **Spain** (210 – 206 BC). He returned to Italy, ignored Hannibal at Tarentum but led an army to North Africa. Here he defeated one Carthaginian army (202 BC) and drew Hannibal from Italy where they fought **the decisive battle of Zama** (extracts B and C). Over the next sixty years Rome turned on the **Macedonians, Syrians and Spaniards** (page 152, picture 1) who had helped Hannibal and these came under Roman control.

However, there was always a fear that Carthage would rise again. In a **third war (149 – 146 BC)** the Romans captured Carthage, set fire to its buildings, killed or enslaved its people and ploughed over the land on which the city had stood. Rome now had no rival to fear.

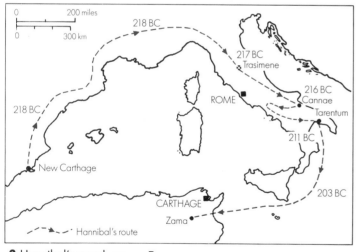

3 Hannibal's march across Europe

Extract A Hannibal's invading army, 218 BC

He crossed the Pyrenees with 37 elephants and about 40 000 men recruited from different parts of Africa and Spain, and added to on his way to Italy with Gauls. They were mostly mercenaries held together by his leadership and promises of plunder. Most of them were in the light infantry, each one armed with a short sword, spear, shield, and a little body armour. The best troops were the Numidian mounted javelin-men. The army was not so much numerous as highly efficient, and fit. The Carthaginians were outnumbered by the Romans who, in the year of the invasion of Italy, had raised their legions from five to eleven and, later, to over twenty – or 100 000 men.

Hannibal claimed that he did not want to destroy Rome, but to break her hold over Italy and force her to coexist with Carthage. 'I am not come to fight against Italians, but on behalf of Italians against Rome.'

(Adapted from *History*, Polybius, 204 – 122 BC)

4 Roman mosaic

5 The cavalry played an important part in battles

Extract B On the morn of the Battle of Zama, 202 BC

Both sides knew how important the battle would be. Before nightfall they would know whether Rome or Carthage should give laws to the nations. For it was not Africa, or Italy, but the whole world that would be the reward of victory.

(***History of Rome***, Livy, 59 BC – AD 17)

Extract C The final stage of the Battle of Zama, 202 BC

The Romans had routed two lines of the enemy. However, their first two lines had exerted themselves heavily and now had to face Hannibal's veterans, in perfect order and still fresh. At this point Scipio had the wounded carried to the rear, ordered the exhausted first line (hastati) to the flanks, and reformed the second (principes) and third (triarii) lines to come together in one extended line which overlapped the enemy's line of advance. Then the two lines charged each other with the greatest fire and fury. Being nearly equal in numbers, spirit, courage and arms, the battle was undecided for a long time, the men in their obstinate valour falling dead without giving way a step. Then the Roman cavalry struck Hannibal's infantry in the rear. The greater part of his men were cut down in their ranks; of those who tried to fly, very few escaped with their life. The battle was over.

(***History***, Polybius, 204 – 122 BC)

THE YOUNG HISTORIAN AT WORK

Knowledge and understanding

1 Make a list of the reasons why **(i)** the Romans were jealous of the Empire of Carthage and **(ii)** why the Romans were able to defeat Carthage by 241 BC.

2 (a) Make a list of **(i)** successes and **(ii)** failures in Hannibal's career as a general.
(b) What reasons for Hannibal's final defeat are shown in the text and in *extract C*?
(c) What were the effects of the Romans' victory over Hannibal **(i)** immediately after 202 BC and **(ii)** in the long term?

Interpretation

1 Do *extracts A and C* give a similar view of the character and abilities of Hannibal and his armies? Give reasons for your answer.

2 Do you think that you have enough evidence to show that Hannibal was a great general? Give reasons for your answer.

Use of sources

1 Is *extract C* a useful and reliable source for historians wishing to write an accurate account of the Battle of Zama?

2 Is *extract B* valuable to historians writing about how the effects of the Roman victory have been seen?

Project

1 You are one of Hannibal's surviving soldiers in 202 BC. Describe, in diary form, your journeys, victories and defeats, and your Roman enemies. Use *pictures 1–5* to help you make some illustrations for your diary.

2 Make a time line to show the story of the Roman–Carthaginian Wars: 261, 241, 218, 217, 211, 210, 206, 202, 149 and 146 BC.

151

A SICKLY REPUBLIC, 146 – 70 BC

Rome forced its conquered people to pay **tribute**, in money or in kind, so that **Roman citizens did not have to pay direct taxes**. The Empire also provided Rome with **slaves**: many rich Romans had as many as a thousand.
Cincinattus (page 147, extract B), a patrician, had been his own ploughman. Now slaves did the work. **Horatius** (page 146) defended Rome: now patricians tried to get as much out of the Republic as they could.

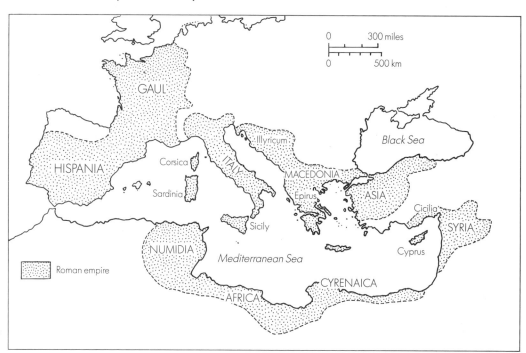

1 The extent of Roman domination in Caesar's time

Tiberius Gracchus (168 – 133 BC) feared the growing gulf between rich and poor. He proposed **to limit the size of anyone's estate**, the surplus to be divided among the poor. Senators murdered him. His brother, **Gaius** (158 – 122 BC) proposed similar laws: he was driven to suicide by senate-inspired riots. Their failures help to explain **the bitter Social Wars** (188 – 136 BC) in which armies of the poor fought for a better life, only to be crushed by patrician-led armies.

Generals made their reputations in various parts of the Empire *(picture 1)*. One such was **Marius** (186 – 157 BC). He was of plebian origin and had risen through the ranks on merit. He made **the army a professional one** *(extract B)*; now the legion standard *(picture 4)* was a symbol of greed as much as of patriotism. **In 73 BC the slaves rose in rebellion**. Thousands joined the gladiator-slave, **Spartacus**, and for two years

2 Roman soldiers cutting corn for the army

4 The standard was the rallying point for a legion during battle

152

Rome was in great danger. However, the slave army was pushed back to Vesuvius by **Crassus** and then annihilated by **Pompey** (106 – 48 BC). **He crucified 6000 slaves** along the Appian Way (page 154, picture 1) which ran south from Rome for 132 miles. These victims were symbols of Roman cruelty and dependence on ambitious generals.

Extract A Our slaves – friends or enemies?

I'm pleased that you live on friendly terms with your slaves. It is what one expects from people like you. Some people say, 'They're slaves.' No: they're human beings. I mock people who think it is degrading for a man to eat with his slave. After all, it's only a custom that the master should be surrounded at dinner by a crowd of slaves, who have to stand around while he eats more than he can hold, loading up his belly until it cannot do its job any more. Then, he uses more force to vomit it up than he did to push it down. And all this time the unfortunate slaves are forbidden to speak. The slightest murmur brings the stick: even a cough gets a beating. The result is that slaves who cannot talk in front of him, talk about him behind his back. That is why people say 'You've as many enemies as you've slaves.' They are not our enemies when we get them: we make them so. (Seneca, 4 BC – AD 65)

3 Forts were constructed along the frontiers of the Empire

Extract B Greedy generals, 1st century BC

Marius widened the basis of recruitment to the army. Instead of it being drawn from the land-owning class, he threw it open to volunteers. Because the state did not pay them, their loyalty was to the General who recruited them: they followed him while he was successful in the hope of loot. This change made possible the careers of the soldier-politicians: Marius, Sulla (138 – 78 BC), Pompey (106 – 48 BC) and Caesar (102 – 44 BC). It was the main cause of the struggle which, Sallust wrote, 'threw everything, human and divine into confusion, and rose to such a pitch of frenzy that civil disorder ended in war and the devastation of Italy.' Internal politics became a matter of naked force. (Adapted from *Warfare*, Field Marshal Montgomery, 1968)

THE YOUNG HISTORIAN AT WORK

Knowledge and understanding

1 (a) Make a list of reasons for **(i)** the Social Wars (173 BC) and **(ii)** the Slave rebellion (73 BC). **(b)** How were the effects of these Wars **(i)** similar but **(ii)** different?

2 How did the changes to the Roman Republic bring **(i)** benefits to some groups but **(ii)** sufferings for others?

Interpretation

1 (a) What differing interpretations of slavery are shown in *extract A*? **(b)** Do we have enough evidence to judge whether slaves were normally well treated in Rome?

2 (a) Do you think that *extract B* contains more opinion than fact? Give reasons for your answer. **(b)** Do you think the author of *extract B* approved or disapproved of Marius and the soldier-politicians? Give reasons for your answer.

Use of sources

1 (a) How can the map *(picture 1)* be used to show the changes in fortune of Rome between 202 BC and 49 BC? (You might find the map on page 146 useful.) **(b)** Do you agree that this source *(picture 1)* is not valuable in explaining why the Roman Empire grew?

2 What is the value of *picture 2* to historians wishing to reconstruct how Roman soldiers fought and fed themselves and their dependants?

Project

1 Write the speeches made in a Senate debate **(i)** attacking and **(ii)** defending Pompey.

2 How were the causes of the poor and the slaves similar to **(i)** the Peasants' Revolt in England (page 26) and **(ii)** the Civil Wars in England (page 66)?

ROMAN ROADS AND BRIDGES

The Romans built roads throughout the Empire, including Britain *(picture 5)*, and twenty major roads linked the Empire with Rome itself: the first major road was built by Appius Claudius *(picture 1)*. Goods roads were needed by:

1 The army so that men could march 48 km a day (page 148, extract D).

2 Traders so that goods could be taken in huge four-wheeled waggons to and from ports *(picture 2)*: roads were wide enough to allow two waggons to pass.

1 The Appian Way was the first major Roman road

2 Troops loading ships

3 Government which got most of its income from taxes on goods and wanted them carried quickly so that taxes would be collected regularly.

4 Government officials who drove light **chariots** as they took messages to parts of the Empire, **changing horses** every 16 km, and **eating at inns**, built about 50 km apart. On a good day an official could go 160 km.

5 Farmers who used them to take animals and produce to market.

Picture 3 is an artist's impression of road building. In the foreground a group of engineers watch **a surveyor** using a **groma** (a pair of crossed sticks with weights at each corner) getting a straight line (to his assistant at the top), by looking through the lines. Sometimes surveyors stood on the top of a hill and had their assistants on the tops of the next two hills.

3 Road building—slaves are laying flint on the prepared surface

4 Roman road at Blackstone Edge, Lancashire

5 Many, but not all, Roman roads were straight

6 This Roman bridge, in Spain, is still in use after 1800 years

Fires lit by the assistants were moved until they were in a straight line from where the surveyor stood.

Once a line had been fixed, **wooden posts** were hammered in to mark it out. **Ditches** (for drains) were dug on either side, and the earth piled on to the roadway to make it **higher** than the surrounding ground. **Slaves** cleared forests, dug and levelled the base, filled it with **large stones**, added a layer of **smaller stones**, and a third layer of even **smaller stones or flints**. Sometimes large paving stones were added to the surface *(pictures 1 and 4)* and a central channel made to help drain the surface *(picture 4)*.

Not all roads were straight *(picture 5)*: some had to double back along river banks to find a good crossing point. Roman engineers built over 2000 bridges in Italy alone, ten of them in Rome itself, two of which are still in use, as are bridges elsewhere in what was the Empire *(picture 6)*.

THE YOUNG HISTORIAN AT WORK

Knowledge and understanding

1 (a) Write down a list of the uses of roads to the Romans in the order of the importance of those uses. **(b)** Explain your answer.

2 (a) What difficulties had to be overcome in building roads? **(b)** What were the effects of the Roman roads on **(i)** the Empire; **(ii)** today's world *(pictures 5 and 6)*?

Interpretation

1 Why do you think that prisoners, slaves and Rome's enemies disapproved of the road-building?

2 Do you agree that historians do not have enough evidence to agree on where and how all the roads in the Empire were built? Explain your answer.

Use of sources

1 Explain how the pictures shown here are valuable to historians writing about **(i)** road design; **(ii)** road construction; **(ii)** military transport.

2 Why is an aerial photograph *(picture 5)* useful to historians writing about the building of Roman roads?

Project

1 Use the information in the text and also *picture 3* to help you make some sketches of how a road was built.

2 Write the diary of a government official describing his journeys by road in Britain.

TOWARDS THE END OF THE REPUBLIC, 70 – 44 BC

The city-state system of government was unable to control the world empire (page 152, picture 1). Men therefore fought for the supreme power which, they thought, would enable them to do so. The first was **Pompey** *(picture 1)*. He, along with **Crassus**, had put down Spartacus, and in **70 BC** they had been chosen consuls, giving Pompey a taste for political power. In **67 BC** he was sent to clear the **pirates** from the Mediterranean. With 200 ships (page 150, picture 1) he did so; he then took an army to the East and took lands in **Syria**, **Palestine and Asia Minor**. In **62 BC** he came home to a 'Triumph', a procession through Rome with him in a chariot *(picture 2)* heading his army. **Crassus**, Rome's wealthiest man, was jealous of Pompey's success. He supported the rise of another rich general, **Julius Caesar** *(picture 3)* and in **60 BC** they, with Pompey, formed the first **Triumvirate**: to confirm this political alliance, Pompey married **Caesar's** daughter, Julia.

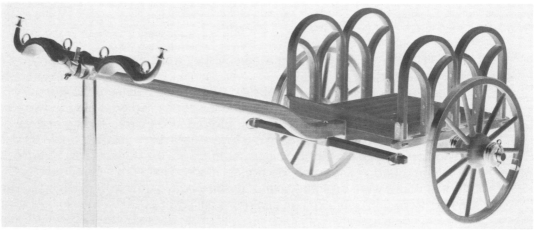

2 Model of a Celtic war chariot

Caesar was sent to **Northern Gaul** which he conquered in eight years of campaigning, during which he also invaded **Britain** *(extracts A–D)*. Meanwhile **Pompey** was strengthening Rome's control of **Spain** and **Crassus** was fighting in **Syria**. Pompey's wife died in **54 BC** which loosened his ties with Caesar: Crassus was killed while fighting the Parthians (**53 BC**) and Pompey decided to try to become 'sole consul' in **60 BC**. This brought Caesar back from Gaul. When he led his legion across the boundary between Cisalpine Gaul and Rome proper, he broke the law. But this '**crossing the Rubicon**' frightened Pompey, who fled to Greece, where he was defeated by Caesar at **Pharsala** (**48 BC**) after which he escaped to Egypt where he was assassinated.

Caesar then **marched to Rome** (48 BC). He defied the Senate's orders that he should return to Gaul and was warmly welcomed by the people. In **48 BC** he was made consul for five years; this was extended to ten years in **45 BC**, and in **44 BC** a Senate, composed mainly of his rich friends, made him Dictator for life. He had already shown that he was a

1 Pompey The Great

3 Julius Caesar

good ruler: he imposed a fairer system of taxes, built many new roads, planned the development of the centre of the city and helped poor people to settle on lands in outlying provinces. But his success led a democratic group led by **Brutus** to fear that he might try to become King. They murdered Caesar on **15 March 44 BC**.

Extract A A historian's praise of Caesar

The divine Julius was the first man ever to cross to Britain with an army. He scared the inhabitants by beating them in battle and he captured the coastal area. We must look upon Julius Caesar as the man who showed the island to future generations, rather than bequested it. (Tacitus, AD 55 – 120)

Extract B The Britons and the Gauls, by Caesar

It was now near the end of summer, and winter sets in early in those parts, because all that coast of Gaul faces north. Nevertheless, Caesar made active preparations for an expedition to Britain, because he knew that in almost all the Gallic campaigns the Gauls had received reinforcements from the Britons.
(*Gallic Wars*, Julius Caesar, 102 – 44 BC)

Extract C One Field Commander on another: Montgomery on Caesar

As a strategist Caesar was erratic. He systematically overran Gaul, but then spent a summer on an island which was remote and unimportant economically, politically and strategically, while a massive revolt was brewing up behind him. Caesar's own accounts of the invasions of Britain should be read with some suspicion; they give the impression of trying to cover up failure.
(*Warfare*, Field Marshal Montgomery, 1968)

Extract D Romans in difficulties

The barbarians realised what the Romans intended and had sent ahead their horsemen and charioteers. The rest of their forces had followed and were now in position to prevent our troops from disembarking. It therefore proved difficult for our men to get out of their ships. The ships were so large that they had to heave to a good distance from the shore. The men were in a strange land, their hands were not free because they were loaded with the great weight of their weapons and armour, yet they had to jump down from their ships, keep their balance in the cross-currents and fight the enemy all at the same time. By contrast the enemy had none of these problems and they knew the lie of the land very well. They stood either on dry land or moved forward a short way into the water and brazenly hurled missiles or whipped on their horses which were trained in such tactics. Our men were inexperienced in this kind of fighting and greatly alarmed. As a result they failed to push forward with the same alertness and vigour that they had always shown when fighting on dry land.
 (*Gallic Wars*)

THE YOUNG HISTORIAN AT WORK

Knowledge and understanding

1 (a) List the reasons why **(i)** the Triumvirate was formed in 60 BC; **(ii)** Caesar and Pompey were rivals. **(b)** What were the effects of the Battle of Pharsala on **(i)** Pompey; **(ii)** Caesar; **(iii)** Rome? (See pages 158–9 also.)

2 (a) Why was Caesar murdered on 15 March, 44 BC? **(b)** What were the effects of his death on Rome? (See pages 158–9 also.)

Interpretation

1 (a) How do historians differ in their views about Caesar's campaigns in Britain? **(b)** Do you think that *extract D* supports the views of **(i)** *extract A* or **(ii)** *extract C*? Explain your answer.

2 Do we have enough evidence to judge the greatness of Julius Caesar?

Use of sources

1 (a) Which TWO extracts are **(i)** primary; **(ii)** secondary sources? **(b)** Why might we question the reliability of all four extracts given here?

2 (a) Do the extracts offer valuable information about **(i)** why the Romans invaded Britain and **(ii)** the difficulties they encountered in Britain? **(b)** What sources would we use to check the information in *extract D*?

Project

1 Write the accounts of **(i)** a Roman and **(ii)** a Briton about Caesar's invasion.

2 Think of the headlines which might have appeared above reports of Caesar's death at the hands of Brutus.

THE END OF THE REPUBLIC, 44 – 29 BC

Caesar's murderers had feared that he meant to become King. He was already **Dictator for life**, and in control of the Republic's finances; **pontifex maximus**, in control of the armed forces and the state religion; **princeps**, or leader of the Senate. He chose its topics for debate and could suspend or nominate Senators.

The **imperium** given him for his lifetime was to be inherited by his children, or, because they had died, by his great-nephew and adopted son, Octavius. Perhaps people were right to fear that he meant to follow in the steps of the tyrant, **Tarquin, the last King of Rome** (page 146).

However, after his murder, there was a period of **anarchy** as leading men fought for power. The Senate blocked an attempt by **Mark Anthony** *(picture 1)* to assume control. He then formed a **second Triumvirate** with **Marcus Lepidus**, Governor of Transalpine Gaul, and **Octavius**, the eighteen-year-old heir to Caesar's wealth and name who had been in Greece at the time of the murder. The three joint rulers hunted down **potential enemies**. In the west, some were **executed**, including the orator **Cicero** who had spoken out against Caesar and Mark Anthony. Others, such as **Pompey's son**, were defeated in battle.

1 Mark Anthony

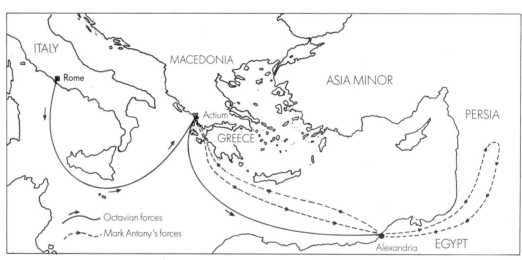

2 Mark Anthony and Octavius met in battle near Actium

Mark Anthony led an army to the **east** where at **Philippi** *(picture 2)* he defeated an army led by Caesar's murderers, **Cassius and Brutus**, who committed suicide rather than face capture (42 BC).

The young **Octavius** now turned on **Lepidus**, imprisoned him and took command of his twenty-two legions. He agreed with **Mark Anthony** that they would share power, with **Octavius** having Rome's **western provinces** and **Anthony the eastern ones**. Octavius stayed in Rome and governed sensibly and wisely.

3 Relief of a galley ship

4 Emperor Augustus

In the east **Mark Anthony** fought an unsuccessful campaign against the **Parthians**, the rulers of Persia *(picture 2)*. During this war he went to **Alexandria** where he fell in love with **Cleopatra**, Queen of Egypt. This was fatal on three counts:

1 He was married to **Octavius' sister**: his announcement that, in spite of that, he proposed to marry Cleopatra was an insult to Octavius.

2 Cleopatra had had an affair with **Julius Caesar** by whom she had a son. She had been living **in Rome with Caesar** at the time of his murder when she had fled to Egypt, naming Caesar's infant as joint-ruler with herself. When Anthony confirmed her position as **Queen**, many Romans thought this was **treachery**.

3 By staying in Alexandria, Anthony **neglected his work** and ignored letters in which **Octavius** pleaded with him to govern the eastern provinces. Octavius got the consent of the Senate to take a **fleet** to fight Anthony and Cleopatra. Anthony took command of **Cleopatra's navy** and the two fleets of galleys *(picture 3)* met in battle near **Actium** *(picture 2)*. Octavius' galleys rammed the Egyptian ships (page 150, picture 1) and either captured them or set them on fire (31 BC). **Anthony** fled to Egypt where he committed **suicide** rather than face the shame of capture. **Cleopatra** tried to charm Octavius as she had Caesar and Anthony. When that failed she, too, committed **suicide** rather than face being taken as a prisoner to Rome.

Octavius added **Egypt to the Empire** and returned in triumph to Rome (**29 BC**) where he took the title of '**Augustus**' or 'worthy of worship'. Like Caesar he was **pontifex maximus**, **princeps**, and **consul for life**. But he lived, and, like modern autocrats, had his special troop of bodyguards *(picture 5)*.

5 The Praetorian Guard—the Emperor's personal bodyguard

THE YOUNG HISTORIAN AT WORK

Knowledge and understanding

1 (a) What do you think were the reasons why some men wanted to succeed Julius Caesar? **(b)** What were the effects of the formation of the second Triumvirate on **(i)** the west and **(ii)** the east?

2 (a) List the reasons for the outbreak of war between Octavius and Anthony. **(b)** What were the reasons for Octavius' victory over Anthony? **(c)** What were the effects of Octavius' victory for **(i)** Rome; **(ii)** Egypt? **(d)** Why did these developments show that Brutus had failed (see pages 156–7)?

Interpretation

1 Do you think that you have enough evidence to decide whether Octavius was a greater success than Julius Caesar?

2 How do you think Mark Anthony would have justified his actions to Octavius and his followers?

Use of sources

1 What does the map *(picture 2)* tell you about the intensity of the battles between Octavius and Anthony?

2 Why are *pictures 1, 4 and 5* valuable to historians writing about the power of Octavius from the point of view of **(i)** control of money; **(ii)** military might; **(iii)** his claims to rule?

Project

1 Write the letters which might have been written by **(i)** Octavius and **(ii)** Anthony before their final battle.

2 Using the pictures, make a frieze illustrating the events that led to the crowning of Augustus as Emperor.

ROMAN BUILDINGS AND ART

Augustus said that he found Rome '**a city of brick**' which he left '**a city of marble**'. He did **restore many buildings** and **built many new ones**, including the **Forum of Augustus** *(picture 1)*. Later Emperors followed his examples as the **State became a major patron of the arts**: the **Colosseum** *(picture 2)* which was used for gladiatorial and other shows, sat 45 000 people and is a fine example of the use of **arches and vaults to support a large building**. Many forums were built to help administer the Empire: so too were **temples**, **basilicas**, and **baths**, of which Rome had over a thousand, and every town at least one *(extract)*.

1 The Forum of Augustus

2 The Colosseum

The Maison Carée *(picture 3)* was built in Augustus' reign – a reminder that the Romans built fine **towns throughout their Empire**. The roof is supported on **highly decorated columns** *(picture 5)* which the Romans developed from the simpler and less decorated ones built by the Greeks.

But the new work done by the artists of Augustus' reign was more a stage in an **evolutionary process** than something revolutionary in itself, as Augustus claimed. When Rome gained control of Italy (page 146) the people **learned about Greek art**, first from **the Etruscans** (page 144, pictures 2–4) and then from **the Greeks** of southern Italy. Later, with the **triumphs in the east** (page 152, picture 1) generals brought back loot, including statues, mosaics and paintings. In the last years of the Republic and the first years of the Empire, **Greek artists** came to work for Roman patrons. They built and decorated **great houses** using **mosaic tiles**, **statues** (pages 144–5 and 168) and **paintings** showing scenes from **Roman history** (pages 151, and 162–64). They helped their patrons **commemorate** either their **families** or **themselves** in various ways (pages 148, 156 and 162) on **tombs**, **memorials and monuments**, **both private and public**.

3 The Maison Carée at Nimes, France

4 Roman theatre at Orange, France

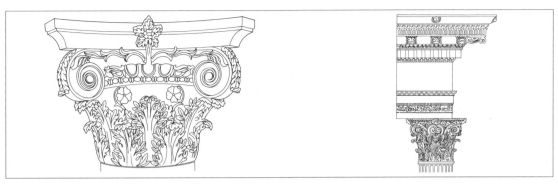

5 Intricate Roman column work

The most important period of development was during the last Republican years. New **methods of building**, using **new materials** such as concrete, allowed **Roman theatres** *(picture 4)* (unlike the Greek ones, which used the slope of the hill) to provide seating space. They were now built with tiered seating.

Extract The noisy baths

> I actually live over a bath-house. Imagine all the sorts of uproar. The muscle-men throw their hands about laden with leaden weights, and I hear their grunts and heavy breathing. When some lazy fellow comes to my notice, the smack of the masseur's hand on his shoulder resounds in my ear. Then there are those who jump in the bath with a tremendous splash, the cries of the pastry-cook, sausage-seller and sellers of refreshments, each with his own sing-song. And the yelling of the spectators at the wrestling and the quiet encouragement to the players at other games.
>
> (Seneca, 4 BC – AD 65)

THE YOUNG HISTORIAN AT WORK

Knowledge and understanding

1 Use the text and the sources listed in brackets below to help you answer the question. 'Explain how, by AD 14, the following people contributed to the creation of Rome as a beautiful city':

(a) *Long-term developments* **(i)** Etruscans (pages 144–5, pictures 2–4); **(ii)** Greeks in southern Italy (pages 146–8); **(iii)** Greek artists (pages 144, 162 and 168); **(iv)** Roman generals (pages 154–6 and 162).

(b) *Short-term developments:* Emperor Augustus (pages 158–59).

2 (a) How did the work of Roman craftsmen affect the people of Rome in these years? **(b)** Using pages 154–5 as a help, explain why you think there was enough money in Rome to pay for these huge building projects.

Interpretation

1 Read the *extract*. Does this document express **(i)** fact; **(ii)** opinion; **(iii)** both? Explain your answer.

2 Explain why slaves (pages 152–3) would have viewed the 'glory of Rome' in a different way to that of the patrons and Emperors.

Use of sources

1 What does the evidence in *pictures 1, 2, 3 and 4* tell you about how the effects of the work of Roman builders have lasted until today?

2 Do you think that visiting the sites shown in *pictures 1–4* can enable historians to reconstruct what life in Ancient Rome was like? Explain your answer.

Project

1 Draw or paint the pictures shown here for a frieze on Roman architecture.

2 Write the letter which a Greek artist might have written home as he worked in one of Rome's great houses.

FROM AUGUSTUS TO HADRIAN
31 BC – AD 138

1 Execution of German prisoners

Augustus (31 BC – AD 14) 'most successful of Rome's rulers' learned from Caesar's fall and Anthony's fate: **'treat the people carefully'**. His power seemed to be limited: **the Senate** met (but he always spoke first): the Assembly passed laws (but only ones he submitted). **Romans approved** of his **rebuilding** work (page 160), gifts of **free bread and money** for the poor, **land** for soldiers, and **games and circuses** for the people's entertainment. He built forts (page 153, picture 3) on the Empire's frontiers and tried, but failed, to subdue **the Germans** *(picture 1 and extract A)*.

None of the four Emperors from his 'house' were worthy of him:

Tiberius (AD 14 – 37), his stepson, was a drunkard who enjoyed seeing his enemies being thrown live over the cliffs into the sea at **Capri**.

Caligula (AD 37 – 41) Augustus' grandson, had prisoners tortured in front of him as he dined and set prisoners to fight animals in the arenas. He was murdered by his own Praetorian Guard (page 159, picture 5).

Claudius (AD 41 – 54), Tiberius's nephew, conquered **Britain**. He was poisoned by his fourth wife who wanted her son Nero to be Emperor.

Nero (AD 54 – 59) murdered his wife and mother, crucified thousands of Christians and had others thrown to feed wild animals in the arena. He committed suicide when the army marched on Rome to depose him *(extract B)*. In spite of the stupidities of these 'Augustans', **trade** developed and Rome got **richer**. Everywhere there were **new roads** and **bridges**, **aqueducts** *(picture 2)* and **great buildings**, both public and private. After Nero came a succession of **soldier-emperors**:

Vespasion (AD 69 – 79) built the **Colosseum** (page 160, picture 2) and suppressed the Jews in **Palestine** *(picture 4)*. His son, **Titus** (AD 79 – 81) completed the destruction of **Jerusalem** and had the **Arch of Titus** erected in his honour. **Domitian** (AD 81 – 96) was a cruel ruler who was murdered by his first wife.

2 Roman aqueduct at Segovia, Spain

3 Detail from the Arch of Titus, Rome, c AD 80, showing Titus in triumphal procession

The last two soldier-emperors were more successful:

Trajan (AD 98 – 117) conquered the regions now known as **Romania and Iraq**. His column *(pictures 1 and 4)* shows scenes from some of his battles and is **good source material** (page 152, pictures 2 and 3 and page 154, picture 2).

Hadrian (AD 117 – 138) is remembered for **Hadrian's Wall** (page 164) and the great fortresses at **York and Chester**. But he pulled back troops from Armenia and Iraq to shelter behind fortified walls. **The age of expansion was over**.

4 Trajan's column, Rome, c AD 113. The column is 38 metres high

Extract A Stubborn German armies

Few have swords or lances; they carry short spears that they use in close fighting and at a distance. Cavalry have only a shield and a short spear. Infantry wear at most a light cloak; few have breastplates and only one or two any helmet. They fight in wedges; to retreat, provided you advance again, they treat as tactics not cowardice. To abandon the fight is a disgrace; many survivors end their infamy with a noose; the great incentive to courage lies in family and kinship.

(*Germania*, Tacitus, AD 55 – 121)

Extract B Nero's clownish behaviour

He had long wanted to be a charioteer and to race with a curricle and four horses. He had another frivolous talent; he could play the harp and sing; he was often the minstrel at lively parties. Seneca and others tried to prevent the ridicule to which a prince might be exposed if he showed his talents to the masses. A wide space, at the foot of the Vatican, was enclosed so that the emperor could race his chariot in private. But he would not be thus confined; he invited in the masses. The general corruption encouraged Nero to throw off all restraint. He went on stage, and became a public performer, playing his harp and singing.

(*Annals*, Tacitus, AD 55 – 121)

THE YOUNG HISTORIAN AT WORK

Knowledge and understanding

1 Make a list of **(i)** who gained and **(ii)** who lost as a result of the rule of the Roman Emperors.

2 (a) Choose the TWO emperors who you think were **(i)** the most successful and **(ii)** the least successful. Explain your answers. **(b)** In what ways were the rule of Augustus and the rule of Hadrian similar?

Interpretation

1 Read *extract B*. **(a)** Does the account of Nero's reign by Tacitus give the historian a complete picture of Roman Emperors' rule? Give reasons for your answer. **(b)** How should we check the statements made in *extract B*?

2 (a) How do you explain the bias of Tacitus against Nero?

Use of sources

1 (a) What does *picture 1* tell us about **(i)** Roman cruelty; **(ii)** German bravery? **(b)** Why do you think this engraving was made? **(c)** How are *pictures 3 and 4* similar to *picture 1*?

2 (a) Why is *picture 1* valuable to historians writing about the impact made by the Roman Empire in **(i)** the short term; **(ii)** the long term? **(b)** Using all the written and visual sources shown here describe the Roman Empire's **(i)** cruelty; **(ii)** skills; **(iii)** wealth; **(iv)** vision.

Project

1 Make an illustrated time line of the story of the Roman Emperors.

2 Write speeches made by two senators **(i)** praising Augustus; **(ii)** criticising Nero.

MAKING A PROVINCE OF BRITAIN

The Romans had **traded** with the Celts of southern England for a long time (*extracts A and B*). In AD 43 the Emperor **Claudius** gave Aulus Plautius four legions and orders to conquer Britain. The legions landed at **Richborough** and fanned out to defeat the Celtic tribes. Within four years they controlled **the south**. Old soldiers were given **land** to help them settle and strengthen Rome's hold over the new Province. The Celts became either **slaves**, or, if they were lucky, **tenants** paying rent to their **new Roman lord** (*picture 1*).

1 Stone relief of farmers paying rent

The legions built their **roads** between their **fortress towns** (*picture 2*), from which they controlled surrounding areas. Tribes in the **north** and **Wales** fought the Romans for many years, and there were also many risings against Rome in areas previously conquered. In **AD 78 Agricola** was made Governor of Britain. He beat the **Welsh** tribes and crushed the **north**. He set up **a frontier** running from the **Solway Firth to the mouth of the River Tyne**. From here he marched against the tribes in the **Scottish lowlands and, later, the highlands**.

In **AD 84**, a legion was beaten by the Celts at **Mons Grapius**. Agricola may have meant to avenge that defeat by later victories, but a jealous **Emperor Domitian** recalled him to Rome and that was the end of attempts to conquer Scotland.

In **AD 118 the Emperor Hadrian** ordered the building of **the Great Wall** which still has his name (*picture 3*). Thousands worked for ten years on this project.

It was built of stone and concrete and ran for **seventy three miles** (117.48 km). Every four miles was **a major fort** (*picture 4*) and at each milestone **a smaller one** (*picture 5*) housing patrols guarding a length of wall.

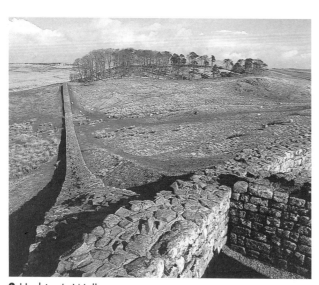

2 An artist's reconstruction of the forum at Caerwent, South Wales

3 Hadrian's Wall

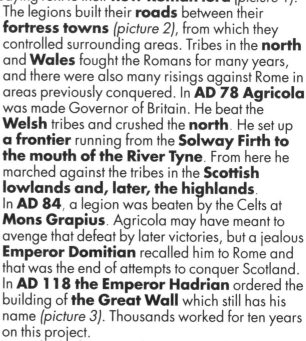

4 A major fort on the Wall.

Extract A A geographer's view of Britain's resources
Grain, cattle, gold, silver and iron are found on the island. They are exported along with hides, slaves and hunting dogs.
(*Geography*, Strato, 63 BC – AD 22)

5 Remains of Chesters, one of the smaller forts

Extract B A Greek historian on Britain's craftsmen

They have become civilised because of their contact with traders and other people. They work the tin, treating the ground which contains it in a clever way: it is like rock, but it has earthy seams from which the workers quarry the ore which they melt down to remove impurities.

(Diodorus, late first century BC)

Extract C Emperor Claudius needs a conquest

The Senate had decreed him the ornaments of a triumph, but he thought this was beneath his dignity as emperor. He sought the honour of a real triumph, and chose Britain as the best field in which to seek it because the island was in a turmoil because certain refugees had not been returned to the island.

(*The Lives of the Caesars*, 12 Biographies, Suetonius, AD 70 – 140)

Exract D A report of Emperor Hadrian's speech at a wall, AD 128

You built the defences in a single day, while others would have spread the work over several days. It took you as long to build a wall out of heavy stones as most troops would take to build one of light, easy-to-handle turf. You dug a trench in a straight line through hard gravel and trimmed it smooth. When this was done, you went into the camp, collected your food and weapons and then followed the cavalry out of the camp, ready for battle.

(Suetonius)

THE YOUNG HISTORIAN AT WORK

Knowledge and understanding

1 (a) Make a list of the reasons given in the text and in *extracts A–C* why the Romans wanted to conquer Britain.
(b) Was the conquest of Britain a rapid or a gradual process? Explain your answer.

2 (a) What changes did the Romans bring to Britain? **(b)** How did the impact of the Romans vary across the country?

Interpretation

1 (a) Read *extract D*. What does this tell you about Hadrian's opinion of the soldiers to whom he was talking? **(b)** What do you think **(i)** slaves and **(ii)** Britons (or Celts) thought about Roman soldiers?

2 (a) How does *extract C* differ in its view of the Britons (or Celts) from that given in *extract B*? **(b)** Does *extract A* support the interpretation given in **(i)** *extract C* OR **(ii)** *extract B*?

Use of sources

1 What is the value of *picture 1* to historians writing about the impact of the Romans on the Celts?

2 (a) How can historians use *pictures 2–5* to describe military life in Roman Britain?
(b) Do you think that models of reconstructed Roman forts are as reliable pieces of evidence, to historians, as excavated remains? Explain your answer.

Project

1 Write a play about the invasion ordered by Claudius. You might use scenes based on the following: sending the fleet; landing at Richborough; building roads and fortresses; putting down rebellion; defeats by the Scots.

2 Write an account of the building of Hadrian's Wall.

ROMAN TOWNS IN BRITAIN

By about AD 50, around 50 000 Romans lived in Britain along with another 50 000 soldiers, many of whom would settle in Britain on retirement. These Romans needed towns in which to live. They also hoped that these towns would attract the conquered peoples to the Roman way of life *(extract A)*.

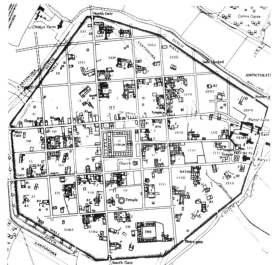

1 A plan of the City of Silchester

2 The market place (or Forum) at Wroxeter

The towns were **designed by legion engineers** and built by slaves. Like the forts and fortresses (page 164, pictures 3 and 4), the towns were built so that they looked like a **chessboard** *(picture 1)*. They were quite small. **Colchester**, Rome's first capital, had about 15 000 inhabitants. **Silchester** *(picture 1)* had only about eighty private houses, but at the centre of these and all Roman towns were the important buildings. You can see **the forum**, or meeting place, at the centre of Caerwent (page 164, picture 2). Along one side was **the basilica**, the equivalent of a town hall, where **officials and tax collectors** *(picture 3)* carried out the work of running the town for the benefit of Rome. The other three sides of the Forum were occupied by **craftsmen's shops** *(picture 4)* and shops selling the **goods imported** from other parts of the Empire. In the forum itself were stalls put up by travelling traders *(picture 2)*.

Each town had **temples** to various gods, and **a public baths** (page 170, picture 4) which was a kind of community centre (page 161, extract). There was also a **theatre** in larger towns and an **amphitheatre** (page 160, picture 2) where the public were entertained by **gladiators** (page 171, extract B) and by **chariot racing** (*extract C* and page 170, picture 1).

3 Paying taxes

4 A Roman draper showing cloth to customers

Extract A Why did the Romans build towns in their Provinces?

The people (of Britain) used to be scattered and uncivilised and therefore ready for war. In order that a race of primitive men might be made peaceful and calm through the delights of luxurious living, Agricola encouraged and helped people to build temples, market-places and houses. The sons of British chiefs were trained in the Roman way of life. And, little by little, the Celts came to like the Roman way of life, with its porticos, baths and luxurious feasts. In this way a simple people was persuaded into thinking that the path to slavery (under the Romans) was really the main road to culture.

(Tacitus, AD 55 – 120)

Extract B Busy, noisy and dangerous streets

One man jostles me with his elbow, another with a wooden beam he is carrying; a third bangs my head with a wine cask. A mighty boot tramps on my foot, a military hob-nail embeds itself in my toe and my newly mended tunic is torn. A waggon appears with a huge log swaying on top of it, another follows loaded with a whole tree, a third carries a load of marble. If the axle breaks and pours its contents on the crowd, what will be left of their bodies?

(Quoted in *Roman Britain*, P. Lane, 1980)

Extract C A dislike for chariot races

The races were on, a sight which has no attraction for me. I can find nothing new or different in them; once seen is enough, so it surprises me that so many thousands of adult men should have such a childish passion for watching galloping horses and drivers standing in chariots, over and over again. If they were attracted by the speed of the horses or the drivers' skill one could account for this, but in fact it is the racing colours they really support and care about. Such is the importance of a useless sport - I don't mean with the crowd, which is worthless anyhow, but with serious men.

(Pliny, AD 23 - 79)

5 Rome's biggest sewer emptied into the river Tiber

THE YOUNG HISTORIAN AT WORK

Knowledge and understanding
1 (a) From the text and *extract A*, explain why the Romans built towns in Britain. **(b)** Who enabled the towns to be built?

2 How were townspeople **(i)** entertained; **(ii)** fed and clothed; **(iii)** informed; **(iv)** governed?

Interpretation
1 (a) What opinions of Roman towns did the authors of *extracts B and C* have? **(b)** What statements of fact are contained in *extracts B and C*?

2 (a) Does *extract A* give **(i)** a similar OR **(ii)** a contrasting interpretation of town life to that given in *extracts B and C*? **(b)** Why do you think that we have these different interpretations of life in Roman towns?

Use of sources
1 (a) How can *pictures 2–4* be used by historians to describe life in Roman towns? **(b)** Do you think that the artist's drawing *(picture 2)* is more or less reliable for use by historians than *pictures 3 and 4*? Why?
2 What do *pictures 1 and 5* tell you about Roman design and technology?

Project
1 Make a model of the design of Silchester using modelling clay. Use picture 2 on page 164 to help you.

2 Paint or draw a frieze on the theme of town life.

VILLAS AND HOUSES

1 Remains of the Roman villa at Chedworth in Gloucestershire

Rich people built **large town houses** around courtyards, the rooms facing inwards, away from the noisy streets (page 166, picture 2). At the centre was a large room (**atrium**) around which were the bedrooms, kitchen and other rooms. **The tiled roof** sloped inwards towards the atrium, letting in air and light.

Wealthier Romans also built **country houses or villas**, as centres for their country estates. **Archaeologists** have found the remains of over 600 villas in Britain and these show us **(i) the size** of a villa (picture 1); **(ii) the tiles** which decorated floors and walls (picture 2); **(iii) the central heating system** (picture 3 and extract C); **(iv) the oil-burning lamps** which provided artificial light (picture 4); **(v) dishes** used in these homes (picture 5).

With this material, **artists** can show what a villa probably looked like (picture 6). From **carvings** made to decorate these homes, tombstones and other memorials, we have evidence of **life inside the home** (pictures 7 and 8) where **slaves** did all the work (page 172, picture 4).

4 Roman lamps. Oil was poured through the hole in the top

3 Remains of the hypocaust at Chedworth

5 An example of Roman silverware

2 Roman mosaic showing game birds from Hammaret, Tunisia

Extract A Finding a water supply for the country estate

If there is no nearby stream to provide running water, let a search be made for well-water close by. Make sure that the well is not too deep for raising the water, and that the water is neither bitter nor brackish in taste. If no well-water can be found, then have large reservoirs built for water for human consumption and tanks built to hold water for the animals. This last may be rainwater and it may also be suitable, if it is taken by earthenware pipes into a covered cistern, for human consumption.

(Quoted in *Roman Britain*, P. Lane, 1980)

7 Carving showing four stages in a boy's early education

Extract B Stages in a boy's education

The father should buy a young boy a chariot and either a pony or a donkey so that, from an early age, he will learn how to control a steed and a chariot. Then the father should help in ensuring that his son speaks properly, helping him also to know how to argue, to debate and to make a speech. Sometimes this may be left to Greek slaves, who, once the boy has learned to read and write without difficulty, should introduce the child to poetry and every kind of literature. The skilful teacher will make it his first task to find out how able the pupil is and what his character is like. He must also decide how to deal with the pupil. Some boys are lazy, unless forced to work; others do not like being controlled; some will respond to fear. Give me a boy who is delighted by success and ready to weep over failure. Such a boy must be encouraged by appeals to his ambition.

(Quintilian, AD 35 – 100)

6 Lullingstone villa in Kent, with temple in background

Extract C How to build a heated and waterproof granary

The best storage place for grain is a granary with a vaulted roof, the earth of which, before you pave it, has been dug over and soaked with fresh unsalted oil-lees and beaten down with rammers. Then, after it has dried off thoroughly, the surface is overlaid with a pavement of broken tiles mixed with lime and sand. This is then beaten down by rammers and smoothed off. And be careful to put the floor on piles so that your whole building may be heated by a supply of air from the furnace.

(Quoted in *Roman Britain*, P. Lane, 1980)

8 A young man reading a scroll

THE YOUNG HISTORIAN AT WORK

Knowledge and understanding
1 Make a list of **(i)** the similarities and **(ii)** the differences in the housing of wealthy Romans in Britain and of wealthy Normans in Britain (pages 36–9).
2 (a) Use pages 154–5 and 160–1 to help you explain why the Romans were able to build town houses and country villas. **(b)** In what ways were town houses and country villas **(i)** similar; **(ii)** different?

Interpretation
1 Read *extract B*. Make a list of the statements of **(i)** opinion; **(ii)** fact made in this source.
2 (a) Do you think that the evidence in *picture 6* gives a different impression of life in Roman villas to that given in *extracts A and C*? **(b)** Why is it difficult for historians to be certain of what life was like in Roman villas?

Use of sources
1 Use *pictures 7 and 8* to describe how boys in Ancient Roman towns were educated.

2 (a) Are *pictures 1–4* useful to historians wishing to understand what life was like in town houses and country villas? **(b)** Which picture do you think is the most useful to historians? Why?

Project
1 Arrange, label and display in a frieze **(i)** pictures and **(ii)** diagrams of life in either a villa OR a town house.
2 How does Roman housing compare with your own housing?

A TROUBLED EMPIRE, AD 138 – 275

Hadrian named **Antoninus** as his successor. Under his rule and that of his 'Antonine' successors, Rome had its **greatest prosperity**. **Cities** were rebuilt, great **monuments** erected, **larger ships** carried more goods *(extract A)*. However, the Empire was decaying. Most of Rome's two million inhabitants were **poor**. Emperors followed Caesar's example by giving them **free oil, corn and wine**, and putting on **expensive shows** in the amphitheatres *(pictures 1 and 2, extract B)*. Trajan had one show which lasted for 117 days – at great cost.

1 A chariot race

2 The Roman Theatre at St. Albans

4 The Roman baths in Bath are extremely well-preserved

3 Roman pot, made at Colchester, showing a gladiators' contest

This policy of '**bread and circuses**' destroyed the spirit which had inspired earlier Romans like Cincinnatus and Horatius. These later Romans wanted to '**take from the city**' rather than '**give to the nation**'. So did the generals who fought for the throne: between the years AD 210 and 294 there were 23 Emperors, 20 of whom were murdered by rivals, the rest dying in **civil wars**: laws were not obeyed, taxes not collected and legions encouraged to rebel.

The Empire also faced **attacks from outside**. **Germanic tribes** wanted to settle in the warmer south. The Romans managed to fight them off – but only for a time.

Extract A Private enterprise and Roman success

I built five ships, loaded them with a cargo of wine and sent it to Rome. But my luck couldn't have been worse. Every ship was wrecked. Neptune drank all my cargo in one day. Do you think that stopped me? Not a bit. I built more ships, larger, better, luckier ones. I loaded them with wine, bacon, fat, beans, perfume and slaves. I later built a mansion, bought young slaves and baggage animals.

(Quoted in *The Romans*, J.M. Jameson, 1981)

170

5 Hunting scene from a mosaic found in Sicily

Extract B Gladiators: fighters or murderers?

I happened to go to one of these shows at the lunch hour interval, expecting to find an amusing entertainment as a rest from seeing human blood. What I saw is murder, pure and simple. The fighters have nothing to protect them: their whole bodies are exposed and every thrust gets home. A great many spectators prefer this to the ordinary matches. And quite naturally. There are no helmets or shields. What is the point of armour? It just makes death slower in coming. In the morning men are thrown to the lions and bears. But in the lunch hour they are thrown to the spectators. These insist that, as soon as one has killed a man, he fights someone else so that, in turn, he too is killed. The final winner will be reserved for other forms of death.

The only exit is death. When there is an interval in the show someone shouts, 'Let's have some throats cut in the meantime so that there's something happening.' (Seneca, 4 BC – AD 65)

THE YOUNG HISTORIAN AT WORK

Knowledge and understanding

1 How did the 'Antonine' Emperors both **(i)** continue Augustus' policies BUT
(ii) fail to be as efficient as he had been as a ruler?
2 (a) Make a list of the reasons why German tribes wanted to attack the Roman Empire. **(b)** What dangers did the Emperors face from within the Empire?

Interpretation

1 Read *extract B*. **(a)** Write down the statements of **(i)** fact and **(ii)** opinion made by Seneca. **(b)** How would the Emperors and the wealthy have replied to Seneca's view of gladiatorial contests?
(c) Look at *picture 3*. What are **(i)** the similarities and **(ii)** the differences between the impression of gladiatorial contests given in this *picture* and those given in *extract B*?
2 Why is it to be expected that there would be different views about such things as the gladiatorial contests?

Use of sources

1 How can *extract A* and *pictures 1–4* be used to illustrate the Roman Empire's prosperity?

2 (a) *Extract B* is biased against gladiatorial contests. Does this mean that it is not valuable for historians writing about Roman entertainments? **(b)** How do *pictures 1 and 2* add to the information contained in *picture 3 and extract B*?

Project

1 Write an eyewitness account of a day at the St Alban's amphitheatre.
2 Draw or paint a frieze describing aspects of social life in the towns in the Roman Empire.

THE FINAL FALL

By the start of the 4th century there were **500 000** men guarding the Empire's frontiers. The **cost** of this huge army drained Rome of much of its wealth. Nor could Rome provide so many men from within the Empire. It **allowed some Germanic tribes** to settle inside the frontiers and to **join the army**. By about **AD 400** over **half the soldiers were** 'barbarians' – a possible 'enemy within'. And still the pressure grew from **migrating tribes** (picture 1).

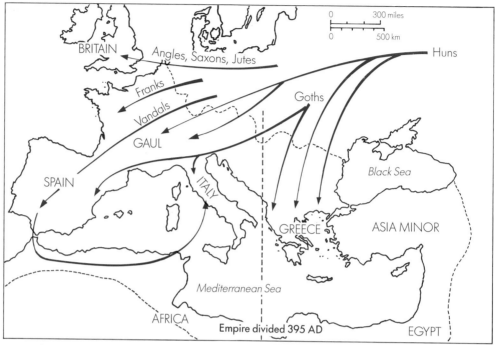

1 Invading tribes, AD 395

Diocletian (AD 284 – 305) blamed Rome's troubles on the growth of **Christianity** which he savagely persecuted. But he decided that the Empire could not be governed by one man. So he left **a general to govern from Rome** while he went to **Asia Minor to govern the eastern Empire**.

Constantine (AD 306 – 336) went a stage further. He **made the Empire's capital at Byzantium**, which he named **Constantinople**. When he became a Christian, he made Christianity the official religion of the Empire.

2 Part of a 4th century mosaic from Dorset. The picture is probably of Christ

4 A Roman having a meal – note how insignificantly small the slave is!

172

Theodosius (AD 379 – 395) went further still. He **divided the Empire** between his two sons. One, the **Western Emperor**, made **Ravenna** and not Rome his capital. The other, the **Eastern Emperor**, ruled in **Constantinople (Byzantium)**. It was these Byzantine Emperors who first fought the new enemy, **the Huns**. These were fierce tribes who surged from Siberia into Eastern and northern Europe *(picture 1)*, attacking the **Goths**, who were driven westwards to make further inroads into the Empire. The Western Emperor **brought back legions** from the frontiers and distant Provinces, such as Britain, to defend Italy. **Barbarian tribes** then poured into **Gaul and Britain** *(picture 1)*. **The Vandals** crossed Gaul into **Spain** and the **African portion** of the Empire. In **AD 410** the Gothic chief, **Alaric**, **captured Rome**. Because he was a Christian he was advised by the Pope and so did not destroy as much of Rome as might have been expected. It was **the Vandals** with their invasion of **AD 455** who sacked Rome, looting the great houses and **ending the Western Empire**.

3 Depiction of a marriage ceremony

Extract A Soldier's impression of the Huns

The nation of the Huns . . . surpasses all other barbarians in wildness of life . . . They all . . . have strong and well-knit limbs and fine necks. Yet they are of portentous ugliness and so crook-backed that you would take them for some sort of two-footed beasts.

Wandering at large . . . they are trained to bear from their infancy all the extremes of cold, of hunger, and of thirst . . .

(*Warfare*, Field Marshal Montgomery, 1968)

THE YOUNG HISTORIAN AT WORK

Knowledge and understanding
1 (a) Explain how the following factors led to the fall of the Roman Empire in the west: **(i)** taxation; **(ii)** non-Roman tribes; **(iii)** military weakness. **(b)** Look back at pages 170–1. What do you learn there about long-term causes for the fall of the Empire?

2 How did Diocletian and Constantine **(i)** differ from but **(ii)** resemble each other in their reactions to Rome's decline?

Interpretation
1 (a) Compare the opinions in the *extract* with that of Tacitus (page 163 extract A). Explain the similarity of views.
(b) Why do we not have much written evidence of the Huns' opinion of the Romans?

2 Do you think that Rome's fall was bound to occur? Why?

Use of sources
1 (a) What does the map *(picture 1)* tell you about **(i)** tribes invading the Empire and **(ii)** the division of the Empire? **(b)** How does this map help to explain long-term effects of the fall of the Roman Empire?
2 (a) Do *pictures 3 and 4* help to explain changes that took place in the lives of people in the Roman Empire? **(b)** Does the bias in the *extract* make it a valueless source? Explain your answer.

Project
1 Write a play describing how Britain was invaded by conquering tribes.
2 (a) Copy and label the map *(picture 1)*. **(b)** Find out how the names of modern counties of England owe their names to these tribes.

THE PROJECT (OR DOING-IT-YOURSELF)

WHY AND WHAT?

It is **not essential** that you write your own project for Key Stage 3 history. However, you **might well want to** tackle one. The pages that follow suggest **why** you should think about doing so; on the way there is advice on **what topics** might be suitable for project work. On pages 177–8 you will find some hints on **how** you might go about the work.

Firstly, why? **What are the benefits of making your own investigations?**

1 It will **increase your enjoyment of history** as a whole if you learn how to work independently of your teachers. You will, for example, be more able to **understand** the problems facing historians when they write books on much larger topics than the one you have chosen.

2 You will, it is hoped, **become excited** as, first, you try to find out more about the past, and then succeed in doing so. You will see that being an historian is really like being a **good detective** at some stages and being a **good author** at others.

3 You will learn **to use a variety of historical sources** as you ask, and then try to answer, questions about the past.

4 It will help you **to become more confident** as you work on your own, and learn how to deal with the problems of being an historian.

5 As you make your investigations, and deal with the various sources, you will find that you will be better able **to take part** in class **discussions,** school **debates** and in **conversations** at home about historical and current issues. Your work on the project will help you to present your own side of an argument, and will also help you to spot weaknesses in other people's arguments.

6 You will become **more expert** in at least one topic, and you will find great pleasure in being able **to help other people** when they need assistance with that or a similar topic.

7 You will be more ready and able to do well in **years 10 and 11** if you have already learned how to work on your own. Remember that individual projects and investigations are **very important in the courses you will follow at Key Stage 4 and in 'A' and 'AS' level courses.**

8 Finally, you will certainly develop many **different skills** (see below).

SKILLS DEVELOPED BY WORKING ON YOUR OWN PROJECT

1 **Sources** – you will learn to identify the **primary and secondary sources** needed for your investigation. You will be able to **(i)** distinguish between primary and secondary sources; **(ii)** realise that some primary sources may give a different interpretation of an event or person to the view given by other primary sources; **(iii)** find out which sources are reliable and which are not (and why they are not); **(iv)** see that very few sources provide enough evidence on their own, so that you have to refer to other sources to complete the picture you are trying to build up. And after all that, you will have some sympathy with the problems of authors as they tackle much larger issues than the one you have chosen!

2 **Questions and answers** – you will find out that **you have to ask certain questions** if you want to get on with your project. You will also discover that, having found the answer to one question, you probably now have further questions which need answering. This will help you to understand that, in history at least, **very few things are as simple** as you might hope! Then, as you find the answers to your questions, you will develop the skill of **writing down the answers** in a way which helps you to develop your work.

3 **Contents and indexes** – as you proceed with your investigation, you will find out how to use the contents and index pages of many books. While this will help you to get the information you need for a particular project, you will also find that this skill will be **very useful in every other subject** you study.

4 People and places – during your investigation you will have to talk to a number of people whose help you need. This will help you to become **more confident** in both asking for help and in talking to adults. You may also have to visit some places connected with your work, and then learn how to **(i) describe** a place (building, ruin, battlefield, etc.); **(ii)** perhaps **draw** or **present a photograph** of the place or object so that you learn how to label and explain its importance.

5 Maps and pictures – you may need to learn how to **use one or more maps** as part of your work, which is itself a useful skill. You may need to **re-draw** part of a map, or present an existing map in a way that is relevant to your work.

6 Telling the story – when you have done your investigation and collected the evidence, you then have to write the narrative account in as interesting a way as possible. This ability to write an account, in which you analyse events and present the evidence, will be a most useful skill – not only for schoolwork, but for many things you might do after you leave school.

7 Word processing – you will find that the ability **to use a word processor** will be almost invaluable as you come to make the first draft, and then correct, amend and add to your narrative.

WHAT TOPIC TO CHOOSE

1 Biographies of important people

(about whom you may have read earlier in this book).

In compiling a project about important individuals you might like to find out about:

(i) What influenced them and their life? Perhaps it was parents, friends, religion or simply accident. Would Henry VIII have quarrelled with the Pope if he had had a son and heir (pages 50–1)?

(ii) What drove them on, or motivated them? Was it personal ambition, fear, love of other people, hatred of other people or, perhaps, greed?

(iii) Their successes and failures and why they succeeded at one time but failed at others.

(iv) How later historians, as well as their contemporaries, have left us **different ideas** about the individuals you are studying, and why this us so.

(v) Whether the individual you have chosen to study has left any **lasting impression** on the world as we know it.

People about whom you might write:

One suggestion is that you write a biography of one important person found in each of the five Core Study Units contained in this book, e.g.:

Core Unit ONE	Choose one from: Augustus; Julius Caesar; Constantine.
Core Unit TWO	Choose one from: William I; King John; Simon de Montfort.
Core Unit THREE	Choose one from: Elizabeth I; Mary Queen of Scots; Oliver Cromwell.
Core Unit FOUR	Choose one from: Florence Nightingale; Feargus O'Connor; Elizabeth Fry.
Core Unit FIVE	Choose one from: Neville Chamberlain; Winston Churchill; Leonard Cheshire.

2 A project on your family history

You might very well enjoy researching and writing the history of your own family, using the following ideas as guidelines:

(i) A family tree in which you trace the history of your family. You should be able to find some information about some of the branches of that tree from your parents, grandparents and older relatives. You might find it interesting to notice how the use of first names (William, Mary and so on) have either changed or remained the same over the generations. It would also be interesting to find out how the number of children born in different generations has changed, or the rôle of women, in particular, or young people as a whole.

(ii) The country and area of origin of your family. From which part of Ireland or Wales, Scotland or England, India or Africa, the Caribbean or Pakistan did your family come to live where you are now? And why? And how did they get 'here'? You could collect pictures, maps, written accounts, taped conversations and general artefacts relating to different members of your family tree.

(iii) The religious faith or faiths that your family and ancestors have held and still hold. **The local library** (page 177) will have good books on all the **world's religions**, and the **histories of any country** which you may wish to write about. The authors of this book, for example, would look up the histories of Ireland and of Wales to find out more about the lives which their ancestors led before they came to live in different parts of England.

Taped conversations with **members of your family and their friends** will help you as you investigate the lives led by older generations.

Leaders of your religious community may also be invaluable sources, if you are investigating the religious faith of your ancestors.

3 Local historical investigations

A study of your **local area** (town, city, village or county) might be an enjoyable theme for a project. Many public libraries, museums, and historical societies run **competitions** for young people of your age group, with prizes for the best projects. Here are some suggested activities for your local history project, which should combine writing, sketches, maps, photographs and local newspaper cuttings:

(i) comparing maps of your locality, drawn, for example in 1850 and 1900, to show how your area has grown or decreased in size, and when streets, shops, and houses were built;

(ii) looking at the **trade directories** for your area in different years, to find out the types of work, businesses, and families that expanded and declined during your period of study;

(iii) local census returns, which you should also be able to find in the library on computer discs, will help you to find out about changes in the population numbers, birth and death rates, and immigration patterns. You might like to draw a **series of graphs** to demonstrate the evidence that you have discovered;

(iv) looking at buildings of houses and work places in your area will give you evidence of how buildings were added to, how architecture has changed through history, and how the lifestyles of the inhabitants of your home town have changed. For example, the building and extensions of hotels, guest houses and railway stations indicate a **growth in people's leisure time** over a period. In the years **after 1945**, you may find evidence of how aspects of your home area declined or grew; for example in the case of hotels and railways. Find out if they are closed, run down or extended;

(iv) most areas have **historic sites of special interest**; e.g. a castle, an archaeological dig, a Roman or Tudor house. Officers at these sites will provide you with free information sheets about the history of these sites. Your local museum or library will also give you additional information about historic sites. You might like to visit these places with your friends or family.

4 An extended study of a major topic. We suggest, as an example, the **Spanish Armada**. Useful books for this topic are:

Past Into Present, Book 2, published by Collins.

Involvement in History, Acland and Birt.

These will help you with the sources you will need to answer the following questions while you are studying this topic.

(i) What were the factors that led to the outbreak of war between England and Spain – religious, economic, political, the role of individuals (e.g. Francis Drake, Mary Queen of Scots)?

(ii) What were the **long-term** and the **short-term causes** for the sending of the Armada? Which of these causes were the most important?

(iii) What were the **motives** of Elizabeth I and Philip II of Spain in their relations with one another?

(iv) How was the Armada **prepared** in Spain?

(v) What preparations were made by the **English** against the Armada?

(vi) What factors led to the **defeat** of the Armada? Which of these factors were the **most important?**

(vii) Was the defeat of the Armada **inevitable?** Can you explain why?

(viii) What **propaganda** was put out by the English and the Spanish leaders?

(ix) What were the **consequences of the defeat** of the Armada for **(a)** England; **(b)** Europe?

HELPFUL PLACES AND PEOPLE

1 Using local libraries and, especially, the advice of the library staff are vital to the success of project work. You will find that the libraries will be able to offer you:

(i) A catalogue of books, magazines and published material related to your chosen topic.

(ii) Help in getting **any book** you may need to read. If it is not in your own library the librarian will use the Inter-Library Lending system, which makes it possible for you to borrow books from libraries elsewhere in the country.

(iii) Help in finding out the **addresses** of: **(a) places of interest** you may need to visit or to get in touch with; **(b) local Records Offices** where you may want to go to see materials in archives; **(c) local branches of the Historical Association**, whose members may well be able to help you with your work; **(d)** sources from which you can get photographs, maps and other material you may need to illustrate your project.

(iv) Details of talks to be given in your area by people who are expert in the topic you are investigating. Some local libraries organise such talks especially for young people.

2 Using the staff at your school will also be an essential part of your project work. **Your history teacher**, for example, will know whether the topic you are thinking of tackling is perhaps too big OR too small for you.

For example, you ought not to try to investigate a topic as large as The USA, 1777 – 1877. Equally, the topic 'My friends' would not be big enough for a good project. Your teacher will know your capabilities as a history student and so will be able to suggest how you, with your particular abilities, might tackle a subject. He/she will also be able to help you with reading lists, sources for material, suggestions of places to visit and so on.

You may well wish to ask the help of **other members of staff**. **The English teacher** may know of novels which you might read with profit to your work, of plays or films you might see, of videos you might try to borrow. Your topic may need the help of **an economics teacher** (if ,for example, you are doing anything about trade/tariffs/ industry). **Your maths teacher** will be able to help you if you need assistance with graphs – either in understanding the ones you come across, or in making your own for illustrations as part of your work. **Your music teacher** may have some useful suggestions to make if your topic deals with Church music or, say, 18th century Hanoverian Kings who patronised Handel. If you are doing work on the Renaissance then you will certainly need the help of **the art teacher**, who may also be the one who will help you learn how to present your work really well (see below).

ORGANISING AND LAYOUT

1 Organising your work

(i) Keeping the work together – you will find it useful to keep your notes, drawings, etc. in a loose-leaf A4 ring binder. This method will help you avoid the terrible fate that befalls some students – losing valuable notes which have been haphazardly 'shoved' into a file. It also allows you to divide your work into sections, using file-dividers for that purpose. Then – a very important point – you will be able to add to your work as you go along, without having to do a lot of crossing out, and you can add diagrams, slides, maps and other illustrations to your narrative. You might want to use see-through sleeves for the illustrations, to save them being damaged.

(ii) Keep a careful record of any tape-recordings you make so that you know which tape refers to which part of your narrative.

(iii) Visits to sites or museums – keep a diary and record of every such visit so that you can show, in note form:

when you decided to make the visit;

whether you wrote to anyone beforehand to apply for help;

what you hoped to get out of the visit;

what you saw and did during the visit;

how helpful it was to you in your work;

whether you wrote afterwards to thank people, if necessary.

You will find that many places of historical interest, and most museums, have ready-prepared worksheets to help students to get the most from their visits.

2 Laying out the work

(i) Different aspects of the topic should have **individual headings** which you could illustrate (like a medieval manuscript) or pick out in coloured capital letters.

(ii) Remember to write your narrative in **a series of paragraphs**, each dealing with one item only: you need more than one paragraph for an important item.

(iii) Pick out the important points by underlining some words or phrases: in a printed book this may be done by changing the size of the typeface, or by putting a word or phrase in *italics* or CAPITALS. In a handwritten text, underlining improves the appearance of the work.

(iv) Make **a summary at the end** of the **conclusions** you have reached and the **skills** you have used and developed during the investigation.

(v) Make **a contents list** to go at the start of your work.

(vi) Take care with **the presentation and appearance** of any illustrations you use: use a rule when drawing diagrams; if you have to shade something, do it neatly; add a line or two of explanation about a photograph or map – you may know what it's about, but other people may not.

GLOSSARY

Alliance   A treaty of friendship joining countries together.

Altar   A flat-topped table used during religious ceremonies.

Amphitheatre   An oval-shaped or circular building with seats rising behind and above each other around a central open space.

Ancestor   Someone from whom you are descended.

Apprentice   A young person learning a trade or a craft.

Arable   Land which is being used to grow crops.

Archaeologist   Someone studying the past, usually by digging for remains of buildings, pottery or other finds.

Archbishop   'A chief bishop': a very important post in the *Church*.

Arena   The open space in the *amphitheatre* where various races and contests take place, as in a Spanish bullring.

Aristocracy   People with special titles, such as Duke, Earl, Count: usually very important landowners and *nobles*.

Auxiliary soldier   A soldier recruited from a place conquered by Rome.

Bailey   The courtyard, or walled enclosure, of a castle.

Baptism   A religious service and *sacrament* in which someone becomes a Christian, when water is used as a sign of new life and to symbolise the washing away of sins.

Barbarian   Roman (and Chinese) description of any foreigner: a savage.

Baron   An important nobleman (see *aristocracy*).

Besiege   To surround a town or castle in an attempt to capture it.

Bias   Having and presenting a one-sided view about a person or event, sometimes without knowing it, but often deliberately.

Bishop   The person in charge of a large area of the *Church* (see *diocese*).

Black Death   The bubonic *plague* which killed one-third of the population in the 14th century.

Borough   A town which received a royal *charter*, allowing it to have an elected council (corporation) and certain other privileges: these included, later, the right to send two MPs to parliament.

Burgess   A citizen of a *borough* who had all the rights listed in its *charter*.

Calvinist   An extreme *Puritan* who accepted the ideas of the Swiss Protestant reformer, John Calvin (1509 – 64).

Cannon   A large gun usually mounted on wheels.

Cavalry   Soldiers on horseback (see *knights*).

Centurion   A man in the Roman army in charge of 80 legionaries.

Ceremony   A special occasion, often religious.

Chancellor   (Medieval) An important adviser to the King: (modern) German and Austrian name for Prime Minister.

Chariot   A two-wheeled (sometimes four-wheeled) car pulled by horses.

Charter   A list of rights for a borough, or, as in 1215, for the people as a whole.

Chastity   To abstain from sexual relations.

Chronicle   A history of events.

Church   **(i)** A building where Christians worship; **(i)** the organisation of the people who belong to a certain faith.

Christianity   The religion of those who believe that Jesus Christ is the son of God.

City-state   The independent territory based on a city and its neighbouring countryside.

Civil Service   The paid officials who administer the government's laws.

Classical period   This describes the period of Greek civilisation (from around 800 BC) and of Roman (from about 100 BC to about AD 350).

Colony	The territory taken by, and used by, a foreign power.
Compensation	A payment made to make up for something else.
Concentric	A castle with more than one set of walls, one inside the other, the outer walls being lower than the inner so that archers from both walls could fire out their missiles.
Congregation	People at a Church service, or who belong to a certain *Church*.
Coronation	The crowning and anointing of a *monarch*.
Court	**(i)** The place where the *monarch* lives; **(ii)** the people among whom the monarch lives and who advise him/her.
Cruck house	The medieval peasant's cottage; the crossed timbers (crucks) at either end held up the roof.
Crusade	One of the Holy Wars in which Christians went off to fight the Turkish invaders of Palestine.
Diocese	An area of a country where a *bishop* controls the *Church*.
Dissolution	**(i)** The ending of a meeting of *Parliament*; **(ii)** the shutting down of *monasteries* (so ending monks' meetings).
Dynasty	The *succeeding* leaders of the same family (e.g. the Tudors).
Emperor	The ruler of an *empire*.
Empire	Countries belonging to a ruling state (see *colony*).
Enclosure	The use of walls, fences or hedges to make separate fields or farms from former open land and commons.
Epidemic	The rapid spread of a disease affecting many people.
Estate	**(i)** Originally the land owned by a person; **(ii)** nowadays the value of one's belongings (or assets).
Evidence	What we get from a historical source (books, letters, photographs, paintings, houses, objects) when we examine it and ask the right questions. Some sources will have a *bias* and our questions, too, may be biased.
Excavate	To dig out so that we find what lies beneath ground level.
Excommunicated	To be forbidden to be a practising member of a *Church*.
Faith	A set of religious beliefs (Christian, Islamic, Jewish, Hindu, etc).
Fallow	Land on which no crops are being grown.
Fertiliser	Something put on the land to make it more productive.
Flint	Hard stone(s).
Forum	The market and central area in a Roman town.
Freedman	A person who had been a slave in Rome, but had been freed.
Freeman	Someone who has political and civil liberties, and, in medieval times, was free from most (or all) duties to a lord.
Frontier	The border between two countries.
Governor	Someone who rules a country (e.g. Roman Britain) or a state (e.g. in Britain's American colonies) on behalf of a *mother-country*.
Guild	An organisation or society to which medieval merchants and crafts-men belonged.
Heaven	The home of God to which, believe Christians and members of other faiths, good people will go after death.
Hell	The home of Satan (the Devil), to which, believe Christians and members of other faiths, evil people will go after death.
Heretics	People who believe (or teach) something opposed to the teachings of the religious belief of the *Church*.
Hypocaust	The Roman underfloor central heating system: the floor of the house stood on small columns and a furnace at the side of the house pushed hot air into the hollow space.

Infantry	Foot soldiers.
Javelin	A spear used as a weapon thrown by infantry.
Journeyman	A craftsman who worked for a master and was paid a daily wage.
Joust	A medieval sport in which two mounted *knights* fought each other.
Jury	A group, originally of men only, who decided if a prisoner was telling the truth.
Justices of the Peace	People appointed to deal with law and order in a particular area: for many centuries they were also the only form of local government in many areas.
Knights	**(i)** Soldiers on horseback; **(ii)** men who, in return for a grant of land (a *manor*), promised to serve their lord in war.
Lawyer	Someone who advises people about the law.
Legend	An ancient story, usually passed down by word of mouth. It often contains a mixture of fact and exaggeration, and is believed by many people to be true.
Legion	The important unit of the Roman Army.
Long-term results	When the effects of an event develop, or take place, a long time after the event: e.g. *the short-term result* of the Black Death was a fall in population: one long-term effect was a speeding up of the switch away from feudal service to a system of giving workers money wages.
Mail	Armoured clothing made by linking metal rings together.
Manor	The estate owned by a medieval lord, who lived in a manor house.
Manuscript	Something written by hand (Latin 'manus'= hand).
Martyr	A person who is killed for his or her beliefs (usually religious).
Mass	The main religious ceremony of the Catholic Church.
Masterpiece	A piece of work done by a journeyman which the officers of his *guild* thought good enough to allow him to become a master crafts man and employ his own workmen.
Medieval	Means Middle Ages. Some people say that it refers to the period from the end of the Roman Empire (5th century) to the *Renaissance* (around 1400): others think the starting date may be as much as 400 years later.
Merchant	A person who buys and sells things made or grown by others.
Monarchy	Rule by a King or Queen.
Monastery	A place where men (monks) live to give their lives to religion.
Monument	A building to remind people of some historic person or event.
Mosaic	A pattern made from small pieces of coloured tiles.
Mother-country	One which uses the *colonies* in its *empire* for its own benefit.
Motte-and-bailey	A castle on a mound (motte) with a courtyard *(bailey)*.
Myth	A made-up and traditional story, often involving supernatural beings (e.g. Greek and Roman gods), heroes and heroines.
Noble	A lord or lady of the *aristocracy*.
Nunnery	A place where women (nuns) live to give their lives to religion.
Oath	A very serious promise, usually calling on God as a witness, to tell the truth or to honour an obligation (e.g. to a lord).
Pagan	One who does not believe in the God of the Jews, Muslims or Christians.
Parish	A small area (once the *manor*) which has its own church and ministers.

Parliament	Originally the people called to advise the monarch and give him the right to collect taxes. The House of Lords was once more powerful than the House of Commons which, at first, was made up of two *knights* from every shire and two *burgesses* from each chartered *borough*. The relative power of both Houses began to change in the 17h century and the Commons is now the more powerful House.
Penance	**(i)** A *sacrament* in the Catholic Church where one expresses sorrow for *sin* and is asked to perform some act of self-denial by way of showing that sorrow; **(ii)** punishment for sins.
Pilgrim	A person making a special journey to a holy place.
Plague	A disease spread by fleas living on black rats.
Pope	The head of the Catholic Church.
Priest	**(i)** A man who leads people in religious worship; **(ii)** a man who organises and controls the Church in a *parish*; **(iii)** a Catholic clergyman.
Primary sources	Ones which give us *evidence* from the period being studied; e.g. eye-witness accounts, pictures made at the time, objects such as *mosaics* coming from the period, letters or diaries. Historians use this raw material to present students with *secondary sources* in the form of books or articles.
Propaganda	**(i)** Information, which may be true or false, given to try to get people to think in a certain way; **(ii)** the method of spreading an opinion (true or false) in an effort to get it accepted by others.
Protestant	**(i)** Any of the Churches which broke off from the Catholic Church during the *Reformation*; **(ii)** a member of such a Church.
Puritans	People who thought that the Elizabethan Church of England was too much like the Catholic Church and wanted to 'purify' it.
Rebellion	An organised armed resistance to the government of a country, as in Britain, 1642 – 60. It may lead to a *revolution*.
Reformation	The religious movement of the early 16th century which began in an attempt to reform abuses in the Catholic Church, but which led to the formation of break-away *Protestant* Churches.
Relics	Parts of a holy person's body, or belongings which are kept, after his or her death, as objects of reverence.
Renaissance	The period (14th – 16th centuries) of the re-birth of interest in classical Roman and Greek art, literature and ideas.
Reservoir	A place where water is stored for later use.
Revolution	A complete change of methods of production (industrial/ agricultural) or of rulers (American, French, English, Russian).
Sacrament	A religious *ceremony* or act which believers see as an outward sign of God's gift of a particular grace. The Eastern and the Catholic Churches name seven sacraments: *Baptism*; *Penance*; Confirmation; Holy Communion, or the Eucharist; Matrimony; Orders (given to *priests*); Extreme Unction (or the last rites). Most *Protestants* name only two: *Baptism* and the Eucharist, or the Lord's Supper.
Sacred	Holy – of places, people or things especially devoted to God.
Sacrifice	Something offered to a god, or the act of making such an offering. For Catholics, the *Mass* is a sacrifice.
Saint	Someone who, after death, is seen by the Church as having been unusually holy: their *relics* will be highly regarded.
Secondary sources	These provide us with *evidence,* as they give accounts of events written by later historians. All biographies are secondary sources (although their writers may have used *primary sources*) as are, for example, books written today about the Norman Conquest.

Senator	**(i)** A member of the Roman Senate; **(ii)** a member of the Upper House (Senate) of the US Congress.
Sewer	A drain to carry away waste water and refuse.
Sheriff	A royal official who kept law in a particular *shire* (county) in medieval times, before *Justices of the Peace* were named.
Shire Court	The law court of a particular shire or county.
Short-term results	The immediate effects of an event (see *long-term results*).
Sickle	A wooden-handled tool with a short, curved metal blade, used for cutting grass and grain.
Sin	The breaking of God's law; anything which offends God.
Slave trade	The business of capturing, transporting and buying/selling slaves.
Stadium	An open space, surrounded by seats, used for sporting events – see also *arena*.
Standard-bearer	The man who carried the banner of a *legion* (Roman), King, *knight* or regiment.
Stirrup	The support for a horse-rider's foot: usually an iron loop with a flattened base which hangs by a leather strap linked to the saddle.
Succeed	To follow on in someone's place – e.g. Henry VIII succeeded Henry VII, John Major succeeded Mrs Thatcher as Prime Minister.
Surveyor	A person who measures and plans roads (Roman), boundaries or estates (at the time of the Enclosure Movement in the 18th century).
Synod	An Assembly representing the whole Church.
Tapestry	Cloth with a picture woven into it (e.g. the Bayeux Tapestry, which shows the Norman version of the Conquest).
Tax	Money paid by people to their rulers.
Temple	A building (usually large) specially built for religious *ceremonies* by Greeks and Romans, and by the Jews who had their own Temple in Jerusalem.
Tithe	The tenth part of a person's produce (in agricultural times) or income, given for the support of the Church.
Tournament	An organised mock battle between two groups of *knights*.
Treason	A crime against King or country.
Treaty	A signed agreement, usually between countries and often marking the final end of a state of war.
Tribute	Money or goods paid as a *tax*, usually by people of a *colony* to representatives of the *mother-country*.
Triumph	A special procession held in Rome to mark an important victory.
Vatican	**(i)** The place in Rome where the *Pope* lives; **(ii)** sometimes used to describe the government of the Catholic Church.
Veterans	(Roman) soldiers who had completed their military service.
Villein	A *medieval* peasant who was obliged to perform certain work for, and make certain payments in kind to, the lord of the *manor*.
Wattle-and-daub	Rods and twigs woven together with mud and straw to make walls, fences and roofs, particularly in medieval times.
Week-work	Work which had to be done every week by medieval people on a *manor* as part of their feudal payment for their land.
Witan	The Council of important *nobles* who advised Anglo-Saxon Kings. The word 'witan' is an old English word for 'men of knowledge'.
Yeoman	An owner of free land valued (for taxation) as being worth a rate of £2 a year, who had the privilege of serving on a jury and of voting to choose the *knights* of his shire who were sent to *Parliament*.

Index